CONTEMPORARY
SUBURBAN
AMERICA

Prentice-Hall, Inc., Englewood Cliffs, New Jersey 07632

CONTEMPORARY SUBURBAN AMERICA

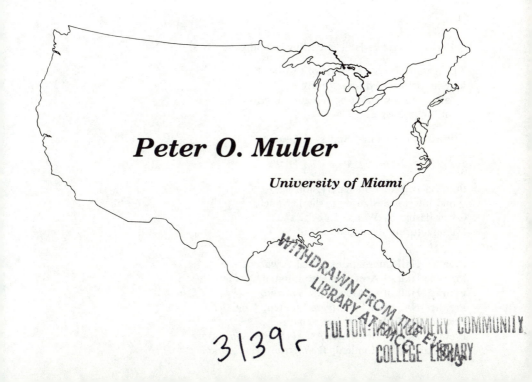

Peter O. Muller

University of Miami

Library of Congress Cataloging in Publication Data

Muller, Peter O.
   Contemporary suburban America.

   Based on the author's The outer city.
   Bibliography: p.
   Includes index.
   1. Suburbs—United States—History. 2. Metro-
politan areas—United States—History. 3. Sub-
urban life—History. 4. Suburbs—Economic aspects—
United States. I. Title.
HT351.M84   307.7′4′0973   80-25653
ISBN 0-13-170647-0

Credits for quotations are as follows:

Page ix. From Samuel Kaplan, *The Dream Deferred: People, Politics, and Planning in Suburbia* (New York: The Seabury Press, 1976), p. 1.

Page 1. From Louis Masotti, "Urbanization of Suburbia," *Real Estate Today*, 5 (National Association of Realtors, September, 1972), p. 26.

Page 1. Reprinted from *The Changing Face of the Suburbs* by Barry Schwartz, Editor, p. vii. By permission of The University of Chicago Press. Copyright 1976 by the University of Chicago.

Page 19. From "Suburbia: The New American Plurality," *Time*, March 15, 1971, p. 14. Reprinted by permission from *Time*, The Weekly Newsmagazine. Copyright Time Inc., 1971.

Page 61. From George Sternlieb, "The City as Sandbox," *The Public Interest*, No. 25 (Fall, 1971), p. 21. Copyright 1971 by National Affairs, Inc.

Page 119. From Gurney Breckenfeld, "'Downtown' Has Fled to the Suburbs," *Fortune*, October, 1972, p. 82.

Printed in the United States of America

10 9 8 7 6 5 4 3 2 1

Editorial/production supervision
  and interior design by Leslie I. Nadell
Cover design by Wanda Lubelska
Manufacturing buyer: John Hall

Prentice-Hall International, Inc., *London*
Prentice-Hall of Australia Pty. Limited, *Sydney*
Prentice-Hall of Canada, Ltd., *Toronto*
Prentice-Hall of India Private Limited, *New Delhi*
Prentice-Hall of Japan, Inc., *Tokyo*
Prentice-Hall of Southeast Asia Pte. Ltd., *Singapore*
Whitehall Books Limited, *Wellington, New Zealand*

For
Nancy and Betsy

Contents

Preface

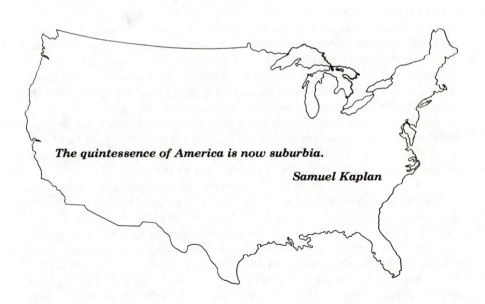

The quintessence of America is now suburbia.

Samuel Kaplan

When future urban historians look back upon the 1970s, they will very likely view those years as an evolutionary milestone because it was a period during which the traditional metropolis—composed of a dominant central city and a subservient ring of suburbs—was both turned inside-out and split asunder. This transformation represents the climaxing of the postwar exodus from the nation's older large cities, and with the opening of the 1980s a wholly new metropolitan reality has emerged. Today's suburbia has all but eliminated the regional economic dominance of the central city by attracting a critical mass of leading urban activities to relocate to the outer ring. The new suburbanization is exquisitely symbolized by the photograph on the front cover, which shows the corporate headquarters facility of the Burroughs Wellcome Company within the Research Triangle Park that is located in the suburbs of Raleigh and Durham in North Carolina. The mere thought that one of the country's most prestigious research and scientific development complexes could locate in suburbia, let alone contain the home office of one of the biggest corporations, would have been unthinkable twenty years ago when the suburban image was one of cookie-cutter residential developments full of the "little boxes" that Pete Seeger immortalized in the ballad written by Malvina Reynolds. Yet, beginning in the middle 1960s and with accelerating speed ever since, the suburbs have not only fully come of age but have acquired a remarkable degree of sophistication. In a surprisingly short span of years, suburbia has become the essence of the contemporary American city. And that is what this book is all about, as it explores why this momentous transformation came about so suddenly and what it portends for our way of urban life.

This book is an elaboration of an earlier 54-page monograph that was published in 1976 as Resource Paper No. 75-2 by the Association of American Geographers under the title *The Outer City: Geographical Consequences of the Urbanization of the Suburbs*. It was written to introduce undergraduate college students to the evolution and contemporary functioning of America's suburbs, an intention that remains unchanged in this expanded version. Its preface also noted that the vitally important topic of suburbanization was woefully under-represented in the urban studies text-

books of the mid 1970s, a situation that persists with a few notable exceptions at the start of the eighties. The topic of suburban America has now
grown so large that even this expansion of *The Outer City* cannot presume
to be anything but a highly generalized survey—at best it barely keeps pace
with the original in.interpreting the general dimensions of a rapidly burgeoning subject that urgently requires far wider scholarly attention. By the
end of the seventies that badly-needed growth in the academic literature was
beginning to materialize as perusal of the References will demonstrate.
One can only hope that the heightened curiosity about what makes today's
suburbs tick, which is certain to occur as the findings of the 1980 census are
published, will unleash a research effort commensurate with the increasingly
prominent place that suburbia has now come to occupy in our national life.

The approach used here is a broad examination of the historical, social,
and economic forces that shape suburban patterns, and their consequences
for the current and future course of urbanization in the United States. The
subtitle of the original work and the author's disciplinary affiliation do
not, however, herald a particularly geographical treatment of the subject
matter. Whereas the geographical perspective is often a useful integrating
framework for handling a topic as vast and diverse as suburbia, human
geographers have been just as stingy as urbanists in the other social sciences
in applying their talents to the suburban research arena; therefore, apart
from an occasional "spatial" and a heavier-than-usual use of map figures,
this book is decidedly aimed at a general urban studies audience.

To avoid cluttering the opening paragraphs of Chapter 1 with definitions, six constantly used terms are defined here for those readers uninitiated
in the language of academic urbanology. The word *urban* applies to the
entire built environment of the metropolis that includes both the central
city and its surrounding band of suburbs; thus, the term *metropolitan* has
the same meaning as *urban*. Intraurban or intrametropolitan *deconcentration* refers to the general increase of people and activities in the suburbs
vis-à-vis the central city; *decentralization* refers to the specific relocation
of people and activities from city to suburb. The term *city* when used by
itself, unless otherwise indicated, means the political entity of the central
city. The terms *suburb(s)*, *suburbia*, and *suburbanization* refer to the ring-
shaped territory that remains when the central city is subtracted from the
metropolis; the finer distinctions of that definition and its basis in census
aggregations are discussed in Chapter 1.

As this book evolved between 1974 and 1980, I have received valuable
support from a number of quarters that I wish to acknowledge here.

In the preparation of the original Resource Paper, Salvatore J. Natoli,
Educational Affairs Director of the Association of American Geographers,
provided constant encouragement and superb editorial guidance. Dennis J.

Dingemans of the University of California at Davis, Arthur Getis of the University of Illinois, and Truman A. Hartshorn of Georgia State University supplied most insightful reviews of the final draft. Through a variety of subsequent professional experiences, Dennis and Truman have continued to enhance my understanding of the changing suburban scene of the late 1970s. Where that process has not advanced sufficiently, the errors that remain are, of course, mine alone.

This book was prepared during the final three years of my affiliation with Temple University, on whose faculty I served from 1970 to 1980. I am especially grateful to that institution for granting me study leaves in 1975 and 1979 as well as a summer research fellowship in 1977, all of which were devoted to new data analyses and writings on numerous suburban topics. Unless otherwise indicated, design and production of illustrations were undertaken by Cartografik of Philadelphia (my former colleague David J. Cuff, and Mark T. Mattson). Several other individuals at Temple were extremely helpful too. Gloria Basmajian of the Word Processing Center cheerfully typed the manuscript as rapidly as possible. Betty Hansen of the Ambler Campus Library was indispensable from 1973 to 1980 in the swift acquisition of new literature on suburbia. Linda Gelfin, Tish Ulmer and another departmental colleague now retired, Henry N. Michael, gave unselfishly of their time and energy in preparing a number of photographic figures. The final stages of this book were completed at the University of Miami with the kind assistance of Sally Kiernan and Yolanda Cabrera. I would also like to give credit to the many students in my various urban geography and urban studies courses who greatly helped me to sharpen my perception of the transforming metropolis.

Three publishers were most generous in allowing me to reuse and expand materials that were originally prepared for them: the Center for Information on America, the University of Wisconsin-Milwaukee (sponsor of the journal *Urbanism Past and Present*), and, above all, the Association of American Geographers (Muller, 1978; 1977; 1976). I am also grateful to all the others who kindly permitted me to reproduce portions of their work herein. Among the staff at Prentice-Hall, Logan Campbell, Sally Schwertman, David Stirling, and Ivy Ponton were most supportive; I particularly want to express my appreciation to my production editor, Leslie Nadell, for her enthusiasm, diligence and special care in putting together this handsome volume while its author was in the process of transferring halfway across the continent.

Finally, I offer thanks to my wife Nancy for her continually perceptive suggestions, 24-hour editorial service, and inspirational support that qualify her as a silent collaborator.

Peter O. Muller

Coral Gables, Florida

CONTEMPORARY SUBURBAN AMERICA

chapter 1

An Introduction to the Outer Suburban City

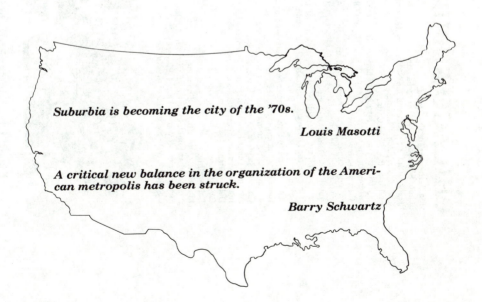

Suburbia is becoming the city of the '70s.

Louis Masotti

A critical new balance in the organization of the American metropolis has been struck.

Barry Schwartz

CHICAGO SUBURB

by Carl Sandbag

Hog Barbecuer for the World,
School Segregator, Mower of Lawns,
Player with Golf Clubs and the Nation's Wife Swapper;
Bigoted, snobbish, flaunting.
Suburb of the White Collars.

They tell me you are lazy, and I believe them; for I have seen your
women in the super-market parking lots, tipping box boys to load
their station wagons.

And they tell me you are brutal, and my reply is: At the stations of
your commuter trains, I have seen old ladies trampled by men in
quest of seats on the shady side.

And they tell me your soil is rotten and vengeful, and I answer: Yes,
it is true, for I have seen crab grass killed and rise up to grow
again.

But still, I turn to those who sneer at this, my suburb, and I give
them back the sneer and say to them:

Come and show me another town with eight drive-in mortuaries and a
Colonel Sanders on every block;

Show me a suburb with mortgage payments so high that men worry
themselves into heart attacks at forty,
    Debt-ridden,
        Overdrawn,
            Embezzling,
Financing, defaulting, re-financing,

But pleased as punch to be Hog Barbecuers for the World, School
Segregators, Mowers of Lawns, Players with Golf Clubs and
Champion Wife Swappers of the Nation.

Figure 1.1 (Source: Reproduced by permission of *MAD*, copyright © 1974,
E.C. Publications, Inc.)

Although enlivened by *MAD*'s sense of satiric humor, "Chicago Suburb" (Figure 1.1) depicts a false image of suburbia that is still accepted by far too many Americans. This perception derives in large part from the antisuburban biases that marked the writing of many social critics, novelists, and journalists in the 1950s and 1960s. Intellectuals, particularly, have singled out the suburb as a target for elitist attacks on what they see to be the mediocre level of national tastes. Many urban planners, because they do not understand that contemporary suburbia is a major mutation of the traditional American city, reject it on the grounds that any new dispersed metropolitan development is aesthetically undesirable (Hall, 1968). Until recently, a similar outlook pervaded the work of social scientists, whose main pre-1965 "contribution" was the creation of the *suburban myth*, a misconception based on faulty generalizing from a handful of shallow and poorly chosen sociological case studies that proclaimed the emergence of a uniquely suburban way of life (see Donaldson, 1969; Berger, 1971). This postulation of a monolithic lifestyle, all too readily adopted as a stereotype of suburban society, was characterized by a complex of purportedly universal attributes: suburbanites comprised a homogeneous middle-class population of white-collar central city commuters residing in split-level "little boxes" with cracked picture windows surrounded by lawns full of crabgrass, and living a gregarious, highly conformist, and superficial existence.

Myths, once ingrained, are not easily dispelled. It is only in the last few years that a critical mass of new research has permitted an accurate picture of current suburban patterns to be assembled, but the dynamics and diversity revealed in these findings so thoroughly contradict the earlier image that they demand a complete reassessment of the much-maligned American suburb. Perhaps most significant of all is the realization that the postwar suburbanization of people and activities does not represent a repudiation of the aging central city and its problems, but active participation in the creation of a totally new kind of metropolitan settlement pattern that owes almost nothing to urban forms of the recent past.* Put simply, "bedroom"

*Readers who have overlooked the Preface are reminded that "city," "metropolitan," and other frequently used terms are defined there.

suburbia of the early postwar period has now evolved into a self-sufficient urban entity, containing its own major economic and cultural activities, that is no longer an appendage to the central city. Before examining this fundamental restructuring of the metropolis, we begin our survey of contemporary suburbia with a brief portrait of its vital statistics.

STATISTICAL DIMENSIONS
AND DEFINITIONS OF SUBURBIA

The 1970 decennial census confirmed that the United States had become a decidedly suburban nation during the 1960s. More recent data clearly document that the trend toward the growing dominance of suburbia has continued unabated into the late seventies:

- 39.1 percent (83.1 million) of the U.S. population resided in the suburbs in 1977, with 28.2 percent (60.0 million) living in central cities and 32.7 percent (69.5 million) in nonmetropolitan rural areas; in 1970, these proportions were 37.1 percent suburban, 31.5 percent central city, and 31.4 percent rural.

- 58.1 percent of the nation's 1977 metropolitan population lived in suburban rings, up from 54.1 percent in 1970; in the largest metropolises containing more than 1 million residents, 61.3 percent of the population lived outside the central city in 1977 vs. 56.8 percent in 1970.

- despite the attention focused on nonmetropolitan gains since 1970, suburbia continues to be the mainstay of national population growth: during the 1970–1977 period the suburbs grew by 12.0 percent while rural areas advanced 10.7 percent (but only 9.4 percent when counties designated metropolitan since 1970 are deducted); central cities lost 4.6 percent of their population from 1970 to 1977.

- in the 1960s the suburban share of metropolitan employment in the largest urban areas grew by 44 percent compared to a 7 percent decrease for the central cities; latest available data show an enormous suburban job increase of more than 3 million in the 1965–1974 period, and that in 1973 suburban employment nationwide surpassed the cities' job total for the first time.

- suburban political power by 1975 had expanded to the point where it accounted for the largest bloc of seats in the U.S. House of Representatives (131 suburban, 130 rural, 102 central city, and 72 mixed districts with many partially suburban), giving rise in 1977 to an emerging Suburban Caucus of more than 50 Congress members; the 1981 reapportionment is certain to enhance suburban political clout both in the federal Congress and in several key state legislatures.

One must temper the interpretation of these data by the continuing difficulty of defining exactly what constitutes "suburbia" (for a recent attempt, see Lineberry, 1975). The *Urbanized Area*, as defined by the census, includes what is today only a portion of the urban fringe; at any rate, the rapid expansion of the outer suburbs in the last few years almost certainly renders most 1970 Urbanized Areas obsolete. Most researchers utilize the "outside central cities" portion of the *Standard Metropolitan Statistical Area* (henceforth *SMSA*), itself rendered conservative by omitting suburbs added in the 1970s.* Although in the past some have criticized this use of outer ring counties on the grounds that such areas may include nonmetropolitan population, the recent work of geographers has shown that metropolitan dispersal has been so extensive since the mid-1960s that, if anything, SMSAs now tend to undercount the outlying urban population (see Berry, 1973b, pp. 38–43). These studies indicate that a vast *exurbia* now extends outward from the built-up suburban frontier in most large urban areas, which is a semirural home for millions who daily travel 50 miles or more to maintain a full range of economic and social contacts within the metropolis. Exurban growth has proceeded most swiftly in countrysides endowed with superior natural amenities (which often originated as resort areas), such as Cape Cod's new commuting ties to the Boston SMSA, the New Jersey shore to Philadelphia and New York City, the Front Range of the Rockies to Denver, and the central California coast to the San Francisco Bay Area metropolis.

Thus, the outer metropolitan rings of the 243 1970 SMSAs will constitute our data base and definition of suburban America, unless otherwise indicated. Even by utilizing this definition, several million suburban residents of smaller metropolitan areas containing central cities of fewer than 50,000 remain unaccounted for (as well as those in SMSAs designated since 1970—see the preceding footnote). Also excluded are *de facto* suburbanites by virtue of lifestyles and movement behavior who reside within the political limits of central cities either through recent annexation of former suburban territory, or retarded development of once remote fringes such as Los Angeles's San Fernando Valley (approximately 1 million in 1970) or Philadelphia's Northeast (ca. 500,000). From these observations any number of upwardly revised calculations of the total U.S. suburban population can be offered, and even estimates in the 100 million range should probably not be considered excessive. Although major census redefinitions of suburbia are not likely in the near future, the White House Office of Management and Budget—the Executive agency that confers SMSA status— did take a ground-breaking step in 1972 by designating Greater New York's

---

*All SMSA data used in this book are based upon the 243 Standard Metropolitan Statistical Areas that existed in 1970. If they had included the 33 SMSAs added between 1970 and 1979, suburban percentages would undoubtedly be higher.

Long Island salient (Nassau and Suffolk Counties) America's first all-suburban SMSA:

> If [Nassau–Suffolk] were a city, it would be the fourth largest city in the nation. . . . While these two counties have close economic and social ties to the City of New York, they also have an independent economic and social base which is larger than that of all but a handful of the nation's largest metropolitan areas (*Newsday*, 1973, pp. 28–29).

The true size and diversity of suburbanization in the 1980s, however, is not completely captured by sterile statistical measures. To provide a better feeling for the reality encountered by active workers in the field, Anthony Downs' (1973, pp. viii, 201) operational definition is offered as a complement:

> . . . *suburbs* refers to all parts of all metropolitan areas outside of central cities. It therefore includes unincorporated areas as well as [18,000] suburban municipalities. Communities that are considered *suburbs* by this definition range in population from a few hundred to over 80,000, in land-use composition from entirely residential to almost entirely industrial with nearly all possible mixtures in between, and in distance from the central city from immediate adjacency to over a hundred miles away.

CONTEMPORARY METROPOLITAN CHANGE AND THE URBANIZATION OF THE SUBURBS

However one regards these data, the urbanization trends they describe have made suburbia the essence of the late-twentieth-century American city. In the process, the term "suburbs" itself has been rendered obsolete because such settlements are simply no longer "sub" to the "urb" in the traditional sense. This is chiefly the result of the intensified intrametropolitan deconcentration of economic activity that has been under way since the mid-1960s, a movement following in the wake of the massive population exodus from the central cities during the two preceding decades:

> . . . the suburbs have emerged from an amorphous, bedroom community status to an organized economy clustered around recognizable employment centers drawing on fairly close commuting sheds . . . (Hamer, 1978, p. 6).

By the late 1970s a critical mass of metropolitan employment activity had irreversibly suburbanized to these burgeoning new centers, further transforming suburbia into an increasingly independent and dominant *outer city* vis-à-vis the older central city that spawned it.

As the functional city turns inside out, a fundamental reorganization in metropolitan structure has occurred. This metamorphosis is embodied

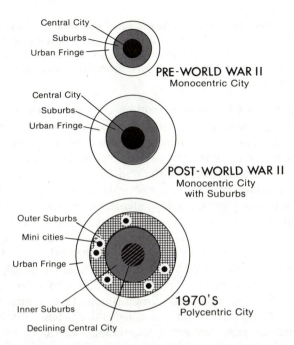

Figure 1.2 The changing form and structure of the twentieth-century American metropolis.

in the shift from the tightly focused single-core urban region of the past to the widely dispersed multicentered metropolis of the 1980s (Figure 1.2). Most prominent are the new multiple-purpose centers or *minicities* that have emerged in the suburban ring since 1970. These major outlying concentrations of retailing, employment, entertainment, and other activities, formerly found only downtown, increasingly rival the central city's central business district (henceforth CBD), and such suburban minicities as Houston's Galleria (Figure 4.2), Chicago's Schaumburg (Figure 4.3), Philadelphia's Cherry Hill (Figure 4.12), and Los Angeles's Newport Center (Figure 1.4) are already widely known beyond their local areas. Underlying this dispersal of highest-rank urban activities is a modern freeway network that promotes such efficient circulation among all metropolitan centers that the downtown CBD has lost its regional centrality advantage. This condition and its significance for metropolitan restructuring was first observed in Los Angeles more than a decade ago by the architectural historian Reyner Banham; with the subsequent completion of urban expressway systems in the 1970s that observation now holds true for the American metropolis in general:*

*Banham, 1971, p. 36. Copyright © Reyner Banham, 1971. Reprinted by permission of Penguin Books Ltd.

> . . . all [intrametropolitan] parts are equal and equally accessible from all other parts at once. Everyday commuting tends less and less to move by the classic systole and diastole in and out of downtown, more and more to move by an almost random or Brownian motion over the whole [urban] area.

With high-speed freeways permitting ever wider urban expansion and major activity deconcentration, the metropolis grew so dispersed in the 1970s that it has also split asunder. The urbanologists Louis Masotti and Jeffrey Hadden were among the first to report this monumental event to the social sciences community in the mid-1970s when they introduced the notion of the *urbanization of the suburbs*, defined as "the growing economic, cultural and political independence of suburbia" from the central city (Masotti, 1975, p. vii). However, earlier independent work by geographer James E. Vance, Jr., had recognized such intraurban spatial change in the San Francisco Bay Area as long ago as the early 1960s (Vance, 1964; 1977, pp. 353–354, 408–416). Vance observed that as people increasingly dispersed to the outer suburbs, daily interaction across the whole expanding metropolis became more and more difficult. This, in turn, strengthened economic and social forces to decentralize entire urban activity complexes, which themselves were becoming locationally footloose as expressways were eliminating the regionwide accessibility differential between the central city and suburban ring. The resulting suburbanization of retailing and employment not only enabled the outlying population to sever its constant direct ties to the city, but simultaneously gave rise to separate and self-sufficient suburban *realms*, which soon became self-acting urban systems independent of the parent central city and increasingly duplicate in function. Thus, today's metropolis is no longer a single evolving system but is composed of distinct parts that have their own character, attitudes, and functions:

> . . . in general the basis of [metropolitan form and structure] is no longer relative location with respect to, or distance from, the [central] city center. Instead we have today a world of *urban realms*, each of economic, social, and political significance and each contributing the main force in shaping itself (Vance, 1977, pp. 408–409).

The Urban Realms Model of Metropolitan Structure

The recent emergence of the multicentered metropolis of realms has ended the usefulness of conventional core-periphery models* for understanding

---

*Models, those indispensable tools that social scientists build to simplify a complex world, are defined by Haggett (1965, p. 19) as idealized representations of reality created in order to demonstrate certain of its important properties.

urban spatial organization (see Guest, 1975). Researchers, however, have still not widely recognized this methodological development, and a comprehensive structural model appropriate to the new metropolitan reality—let alone its theoretical underpinnings—has yet to be fashioned. Although some additions and refinements are suggested in Chapter 4, the best alternative model available at the outset of the 1980s is Vance's Urban Realms construct. We now examine this model in more detail and provide an example of its empirical application, so that the reader may obtain the clearest possible conception of the nature of the contemporary metropolis and the role of its increasingly dominant outer city.

The extent, character, and internal structure of the central and each suburban realm is shaped by four criteria (Vance, 1977, pp. 411–416). The first influence is terrain, especially topographical and water barriers. Second is the overall physical size of the metropolis. Third is the amount and type of economic activity contained inside a realm, whose internal coherence derives from its residents utilizing economically important places within that realm rather than metropolitan-level centers outside it. For a suburban realm, the number of minicities localized within it is of obvious significance. The final and most important criterion is the regional transportation network, because intrarealm ease of movement is essential, particularly toward its activity centers. Interaccessiblity among suburban realms is also vital, especially circumferential links and direct airport connectors that no longer require them to turn to the central realm in order to reach other outlying realms and distant metropolises. These notions may easily be applied to any major urban area; metropolitan Los Angeles is the case study chosen here, and its realm structure can readily be observed in Figure 1.3.

The vast overall size of the Los Angeles metropolis has enabled five sectoral realms to emerge around the central one and radiate across a suburban ring that extends outward for up to 50 miles. Topographical constraints have channeled that growth between the Pacific coast and the San Gabriel Mountain Range, with development emanating from the Los Angeles Basin along the shoreline and into major inland valleys. In fact, the northwestern San Fernando Valley and eastern San Gabriel Valley Realms (II and VI) are essentially defined by their surrounding mountain ridges. Each outer city realm is also anchored by radial transportation arteries that have shaped suburbanization for more than a century. These routes were initially forged by five railroads in the third quarter of the nineteenth century, which radiated outward from the central Los Angeles pueblo area (today's CBD) northwest to San Fernando, west to Santa Monica, southwest to Wilmington, southeast to Anaheim, and east to Pomona; the succeeding Pacific Electric trolley network duplicated that same corridor pattern at the beginning of this century, a five-fold axial thrust that was once again reinforced by building early postwar freeways (the Hollywood, Santa

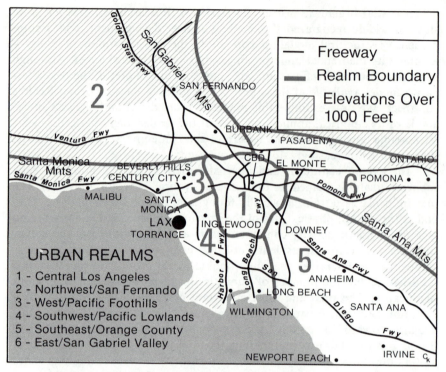

Figure 1.3 The Urban Realms of metropolitan Los Angeles.

Monica, Harbor, Santa Ana, and San Bernardino Freeways) parallel to the earlier rail lines (Banham, 1971, pp. 75–93). Subsequent expressway construction has emphasized circumferential movement, which assured the maturation of a system of internally unified urban realms after 1960.

Central Los Angeles (I), at the hub of the freeway matrix, serves more as a crossroads than a regional core, although this central city CBD-dominated realm does contain a diversified commercial economy as well as the area's leading cultural and sports facilities. The Northwest Realm (II), focused on the San Fernando Valley and its tributary freeway corridors leading west and north, is a typical self-sufficient suburban realm whose more than 1.5 million residents are served by large clusters of retailing and employment activities, which include much of the region's aerospace and motion picture industries around Burbank. The adjacent West Realm (III), organized along the Pacific foothills lying between the Santa Monica Mountains and the sea, contains both the wealthiest and most nonconformist residential areas, the lion's share of the media-entertainment industry, and the elegant Century City–Beverly Hills minicity. The Southwest Realm (IV), initially defined by the Harbor and Long Beach Freeways, which led from the CBD to the port and oil refining complex around Wilmington, has become reoriented to the circumferential San Diego Freeway corridor, minicities in Torrance and Inglewood, and particularly the Los Angeles International Airport (LAX); the realm's economy is dominated by the expanding airport commercial complex as well as the huge aerospace facilities located near Long Beach and LAX. Orange County, the Southeast Realm (V), has become one of the most spectacular suburban growth areas in the nation since 1970 and is profiled separately (see pages 11–13). The East Realm (VI), which follows the San Gabriel Valley beyond San Bernardino to the edge of the desert, contains many of the region's heavy manufacturing districts and its leading science complex focused on the California Institute of Technology in Pasadena.

The Growing Dominance of the Outer City in American Life

One of the most noteworthy aspects of the suburbanization trends discussed above is their universality. An analysis of mid-1970s population data indicated that every U.S. census region and every metropolitan size class experienced a suburban percentage gain (Muller, 1980). Some of the largest 1970–1975 increases were recorded in the metropolises of the Sunbelt: Atlanta's suburban percentage of the SMSA population advanced from 69 to 76 percent, New Orleans 43 to 49 percent, Dallas 48 to 53 percent, Denver 53 to 60 percent, and Phoenix 40 to 46 percent. Commensurate economic growth reinforced this rapid metropolitan transformation, with one of the most spectacular suburban gains occurring in Orange County, California (see pages 11–13). Although the younger central cities of the Sunbelt have enjoyed better economic health through the recent past, there were clear signs by the end of the 1970s that these urban centers were becoming more like their troubled northern counterparts while their suburbs increasingly thrived. A current study by Bourne (1978, pp. 23–24), for instance, has discovered widening city/suburb income disparities in Miami, San Antonio, and San Jose. Nowhere is the struggle better illustrated than in Houston, the self-appointed "Golden Buckle" of the Sunbelt, which became a highly prosperous metropolis by persistently annexing its suburbs during the postwar era but now faces mounting resistance to this method of political and economic growth.

Orange County: Quintessential Suburbia of the 1980s

Southern California's Orange County, located between the state's two largest cities of Los Angeles and San Diego, is a classical example of the vitality of the Sunbelt's and the nation's urbanizing suburbs

(*Business Week*, 1977a). This outer realm of metropolitan Los Angeles (V in Figure 1.3) is one of the fastest growing U.S. urban counties—more than 25 percent since 1970—and its population of just under 2 million ranks it second in California in size as well as density. Orange County also ranks among America's wealthiest counties: its 1978 median family income of $22,300 was 20 percent above the national median of $18,500, and its legendary housing prices (a $107,000 *average* for a new home in 1977) may well be the highest anywhere.

Orange County's boom began a quarter-century ago with the 1955 opening of Disneyland in Anaheim. That town is now the county's largest population center and best-known location, as the Disneyland and nearby Knott's Berry Farm theme parks rank as America's second and third most popular tourist attractions (after Disney World in Florida). Anaheim's national identity is further reinforced by its baseball Angels and football Rams, with the latter team relocating from Los Angeles in 1980 in response to Orange County's more glamorous image, higher-income population, and locational convenience for fans (Niedzielski, 1979). The real key to the county's rising stature, however, is the massive economic development that has radiated outward from Anaheim since the late 1960s, so that today this urban core is increasingly viewed as the center of gravity for the entire southern California region (Lindsey, 1979).

Originally spawned as a spinoff from the aerospace industry complex in nearby Los Angeles during the early-postwar period, the burgeoning economy of Orange County had achieved all but complete independence from that city by the end of the 1970s. Its economy today is best described as an intensely developed, diversified postindustrial business complex dominated by major office and scientific manufacturing activities. That complex has expanded so rapidly and attracted so many growth industries in recent years that Orange County is already regarded as one of the most important economic centers in the country. As the premier growth area of California and possibly the entire Sunbelt, the county between 1970 and 1977 experienced an annual doubling in demand for industrial space and a quintupling of office space that accommodated the opening of more than 4000 new office companies. Many of the latter were born right in Orange County—including a sizable segment of the minicomputer industry—but a large number also relocated from Los Angeles, attracted by a better-quality labor force as well as a business environment possessing greater amenities and a more prestigious identity.

Nowhere is the new locational prestige for business more evident than at Newport Center (Figure 1.4), a minicity in Newport Beach that became Orange County's newest economic focus in the

Figure 1.4 Newport Center, a classic 1970s-style suburban minicity located in Orange County's Newport Beach. (Courtesy The Irvine Company.)

seventies. Its core is the Fashion Island Regional Mall, a huge shopping facility anchored by six major department stores, including California's first Dallas-based Neiman-Marcus branch. This retail center is ringed by a complex of ultramodern high- and low-rise office facilities that employs over 9000 workers and contains half of the county's 7.5 million square feet of office space, which here achieves rental rate equivalency with prime locations elsewhere in the Los Angeles metropolis. Completing the multipurpose minicity is a myriad of medical buildings, restaurants, theaters, hotels, and luxury apartment towers.

The prospects for further growth in Orange County are excellent as enormous private landholdings in the southern half of the county begin to open for development at the end of the seventies. Best known is the Irvine Ranch, which occupies the central one-fifth of the county. Besides Newport Center and the new Irvine campus of the University of California, a series of additional well-planned activity cores and residential areas are scheduled to be built in the near future. These include the nation's largest industrial park and the new towns of Irvine, Mission Viejo, and Laguna Hills (Robertson, 1976). At the outset of the 1980s several other signs clearly point to the still increasing popularity of Orange County: its airport is now the second busiest in the United States in takeoffs and landings; demand for housing even at today's prices is so prodigious that new subdivisions sell out completely within hours; and there is unceasing talk about seeking statehood (O'Donnell and Gregory, 1979)!

Houston's rapid expansion, which saw more than one-third of its present land area added since 1960, was sanctioned by a Texas law that permitted any urban center containing a population exceeding 100,000 to unilaterally annex unincorporated territory lying up to 5 miles beyond its borders. The city's political and business leadership vigorously pursued a policy of such annexation as the best way to maintain low taxes and a growing tax base, cleverly establishing an at-large system of city council government that avoided having councilmen identify with local political turfs which they would be loath to having redistricted. For a while this strategy was quite successful, but as police, fire, water supply, sewer, garbage collection, and transit services were stretched even thinner in the seventies, Houstonians began to protest as their city was increasingly beset by violent crime and other northern-style urban problems (Stevens, 1979; Crewdson, 1979). This antigrowth rebellion coincided with a successful 1978 U.S. Justice Department effort to alter the at-large council government so as to provide greater representation for the large inner-city Hispanic and black populations of the East Side ghettos (now comprising almost half of Houston's population), who were constantly outvoted as all-white suburbs were continually annexed. Moreover, a new resistance movement among suburbanites surfaced in 1978 and may turn out to be the most formidable threat of all to the future of annexation. The conflict is centered in Clear Lake City on the southeastern edge of Houston, where the 25,000 residents of this affluent community adjacent to NASA's Lyndon B. Johnson Space Center are seeking to undo their 1977 annexation (Stevens, 1978). Propelled by their increasingly negative perception of Houston, resident groups were so fearful of property value declines and losing local political control that lawsuits were initiated in both state and federal courts to void annexation on the ground that due process had been denied in the city's unilateral action. The outcome of these legal challenges has yet to be determined, but U.S. Department of Justice support was expected as a further guarantee to prevent the dilution of the minority vote within the city. However the annexation issue is resolved, it appears likely that Houston and its suburbs will increasingly go their separate ways as new and more stable urban realms can emerge.

The growing dominance of the outer city in American urban life is also demonstrated by the changing attitudes of suburbanites. A particularly revealing survey was undertaken by *The New York Times* in the spring of 1978, based on 3500 telephone interviews throughout the Greater New York suburban ring, whose more than 10 million residents now constitute the nation's largest "city" (Feron et al., 1978). The most important findings of this poll involve residential satisfaction and suburban ties to the central city.

Several scholars have recently asserted that suburbia exhibits the most comfortable mass-living conditions ever achieved, and the *Times* poll concurs. The overwhelming response to the question "what do you dislike most about your community?" was "nothing." Ninety percent of the interviewees said they led happy lives, and 65 percent both happy and interesting lives; only 4 percent complained that they lived a boring existence. Although about half of those interviewed wanted to halt all local growth, 72 percent thought their community would be no worse a place to live in 1990 (a very optimistic outlook given the national "malaise" that prevailed in 1978). Asked what most attracted them to the suburban environment, residents cited quiet, clean air, and spaciousness, but did not list escape from the central city as a deciding factor. Contrary to the popular stereotype of hypermobility, half of those surveyed said they were residents of their local community for at least 11 years and an additional 18 percent for 6 to 10 years.

The most startling findings to the *Times* concerned suburbanite relationships to New York City. Only 20 percent of household heads said they worked in the city. Fifty-three percent visited New York fewer than five times a year—16 percent only once or twice—and an additional 25 percent never went there at all. Among trip categories, 58 percent said they would travel to the city to see a play or concert and 40 percent to attend a sporting event, but only 20 percent would go to visit a medical specialist and a mere 8 percent to consult an attorney or make a major retail purchase. Moreover, only 32 percent of those polled had ever lived in New York City; therefore, it is not surprising that 54 percent reported that they do not even feel they belong to the New York metropolitan area, and that 76 percent believed that events occurring in the city did not affect their lives. Overall, the *Times*'s conclusions strikingly support the Urban Realms model:

> . . . the residents of the [suburban] ring around New York City, once regarded simply as a bedroom for commuters, no longer feel themselves subordinate to New York. The suburbs have become a multicentered urban chain with surprisingly limited ties to the metropolitan core. . . . Suburban residents have established their own institutions and go about their lives in an increasingly separate world. They see their future even further from the [central] city, rather than closer to it (Feron et al., Nov. 14, 1978, p. B-3).

Suburban Socioeconomic Heterogeneity

The *Times* poll also concluded that today's suburban society is anything but uniform, and is best characterized as a kaleidoscope of diverse income, ethnic, and lifestyle groups. Moreover, the current trend is definitely away from a middle-class, nuclear-family-dominated suburbia: nearly one-third of those interviewed ranked themselves as working class or underclass; 21 percent reported they were single, and an additional 15 percent widowed, separated, or divorced. The increasing social heterogeneity of the outer

Table 1.1 Selected measures of suburban social
heterogeneity, 1970 and 1977

Measure	1970	1977
Percent families without children under 18	39.5	42.8
Percent families headed by women	8.4	10.9
Percent family heads over 65	11.1	11.8
Median age	27.4	29.1
Single persons over 21 (in millions)	12.7	16.9
Divorced persons (in millions)	1.5	2.9

SOURCE: U.S. Bureau of the Census, 1978.

city is further confirmed in national census data for the 1970–1977 period
(Table 1.1). Childless and fatherless families, the elderly, and single and
divorced persons have all substantially enlarged their presence in suburbia
in the 1970s, undoubtedly abetted by the recent rapid growth of apartment
housing. Economic diversification of the suburban population is also occurring. Although the effects of inflation must be taken into account, the
trend toward even higher affluence in suburbia stabilized since 1970: median family income actually *dropped* from $17,160 in 1969 to $17,101 in
1976 (reckoned in constant 1976 dollars).

As the deconcentration of leading urban activities is accompanied by
the intensifying heterogeneity of the outer city's population, it is widely asserted that differences between the central city and suburban ring are disappearing. Whereas compelling evidence for such convergence can be introduced in the case of economic activity (the theme of Chapter 4), the
argument that a parallel socioeconomic trend affects the two residential
populations is much weaker. In fact, the latest data indicate no change in
the continual widening of the central city/suburbia income disparity that
has persisted for the last half-century. While suburban income leveled off,
central-city median family income decreased from $14,566 in 1969 to $13,952
in 1976, a drop from 84.0 to 81.6 percent of the suburban median.

Most of the claims of socioeconomic convergence are based on the
broad observation that such serious central-city-type problems as violent
crime, poverty, and housing deterioration are "spilling across" the city line.
Although this phenomenon is undoubtedly widespread, the geographical
extent to which these problems have penetrated suburbia has not been
comprehensively studied. Yet many researchers readily make the generalization that the inner suburbs are most heavily affected, assuming a concentric zonation of suburban development over time in which distance from
the city line is the controlling force. As we shall see in Chapter 2, the spatial
evolution of suburbia involved a rather more complex form; certain rail
corridors gave rise to factory suburbs a dozen miles beyond the city line
decades before inner suburban growth began in other sectors. This does

not deny that the most serious problems are inordinately concentrated in older suburbs, but simply points out that their distribution does not coincide with the innermost suburban ring. The age of suburban settlement and susceptibility to central-city-type problems has yet to be determined. It is likely that high-density preautomobile suburbs built before 1920 are most affected; Vance (1977, pp. 406–407) also suggests that a major watershed may have been the arrival of government-guaranteed mortgage loans in the mid-1930s, which proved a decisive force in creating the modern low-density suburban housing pattern. Although the entire matter urgently needs investigation, high-problem suburban areas may not be multiplying: the *Times* poll revealed that even in the New York area, with its large number of industrial satellites and pre–World War I suburbs, 64 percent of the respondents said their communities were not becoming "more like a big city."

Summary

This introductory chapter has provided a brief overview of contemporary suburban America and has tried to capture some of the flavor of ongoing change as "bedroom" suburbia completes its transition to outer city in the late 1970s and early 1980s. The major dimensions and consequences of social and economic organization in that outer city are treated in Chapters 3 and 4. Our survey of contemporary suburbia is preceded by a cultural and historical overview of suburbanization in Chapter 2, which is needed to understand today's suburban scene. Although significant new forces have emerged in the last two decades, they were imposed on a suburbia that has been evolving in stages since the mid-nineteenth century and achieved major proportions by 1900; subsequent growth of the suburbs during the first two-thirds of this century produced social and economic patterns that still endure in their original or reshaped form. In fact, the modern history of suburbia is really all about the suburbanization of the American city itself: by ending the practice of having cities annex their suburbs in much of the United States early in the twentieth century, most metropolitan development occurring after 1920 thus took place beyond the interposed city boundary, which was no longer permitted to expand in order to enclose new urban growth.

SUGGESTED READINGS

DOLCE, PHILIP C., ED. *Suburbia: The American Dream and Dilemma* (Garden City, NY: Anchor Press/Doubleday, 1976).

DONALDSON, SCOTT. *The Suburban Myth* (New York: Columbia University Press, 1969).

HAWLEY, AMOS H., AND VINCENT P. ROCK, EDS. *Metropolitan America in Contemporary Perspective* (New York: Halsted Press for Sage Publications, 1975).

HUGHES, JAMES W., ED. *Suburbanization Dynamics and the Future of the City* (New Brunswick, NJ: Center for Urban Policy Research, Rutgers University, 1974).

JOHNSON, JAMES H., ED. *Suburban Growth: Geographical Processes at the Edge of the Western City* (London: John Wiley & Sons Ltd., 1974).

MASOTTI, LOUIS H., GUEST ED. "The Suburban Seventies," *The Annals of the American Academy of Political and Social Science*, 422 (1975), vii–151.

MASOTTI, LOUIS H., AND JEFFREY K. HADDEN, EDS. *Suburbia in Transition* (New York: New Viewpoints, for *The New York Times*, 1974).

MASOTTI, LOUIS H., AND JEFFREY K. HADDEN, EDS. *The Urbanization of the Suburbs* (Beverly Hills: Sage Publications, Urban Affairs Annual Reviews, Vol. 7, 1973).

MULLER, PETER O. "Suburbanization in the 1970s: Interpreting Population, Socioeconomic, and Employment Trends," in Stanley D. Brunn and James O. Wheeler, eds., *The American Metropolitan System: Present and Future* (Silver Spring, MD: Victor H. Winston & Sons, 1980), pp. 39–51.

SCHWARTZ, BARRY, ED. *The Changing Face of the Suburbs* (Chicago: University of Chicago Press, 1976).

VANCE, JAMES E., JR. *This Scene of Man: The Role and Structure of the City in the Geography of Western Civilization* (New York: Harper's College Press, 1977), Chap. 8.

ZIKMUND, JOSEPH, II, AND DEBORAH ELLIS DENNIS, EDS. *Suburbia: A Guide to Information Sources* (Detroit: Gale Research Company, 1979).

chapter **2**

The Historical Evolution of American Suburbs

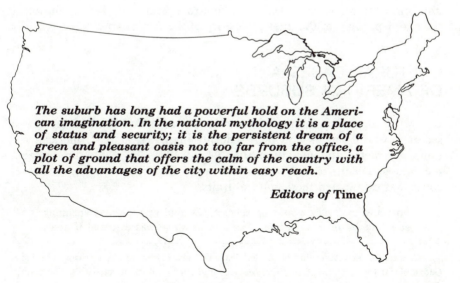

The suburb has long had a powerful hold on the American imagination. In the national mythology it is a place of status and security; it is the persistent dream of a green and pleasant oasis not too far from the office, a plot of ground that offers the calm of the country with all the advantages of the city within easy reach.

Editors of Time

Although the nation's suburbs have only recently emerged as a dominant metropolitan force, they are not a distinctively new type of urban settlement. Development of the city fringe extends back to the dawn of urbanization, and the modern American process of suburbanization—the sustained growth of city edges at a rate faster than that of central areas—has been in evidence for the last century and a half (Jackson, 1973). The U.S. Bureau of the Census first employed the concept of "suburb" in 1880 in its analysis of Greater New York, and the census of 1910 initiated the regular decennial reporting of non-central-city metropolitan data (Singleton, 1973, p. 30). The growth trajectory of America's suburbs in the twentieth century is displayed in Figure 2.1, Table 2.1, and Table 2.2. Our purpose in Chapter 2 is to explain the forces underlying this accelerating suburban trend. We shall see that since 1850 a series of new urban forms, built up in stages during eras marked by certain intrametropolitan transport innovations, have appeared in suburbia, and that their evolution is the major product of the modern history of the American city.

CULTURAL BASES AND THE RISE OF AMERICAN SUBURBS

Central to an understanding of the evolution of these suburban forms is a set of powerful values and beliefs deeply ingrained in the American national character and native culture. Berry (1975a, p. 175), summarizing the late-eighteenth-century observations of the French traveller Crèvecouer, has catalogued these cultural traits:

> Foremost . . . was a *love of newness*. Second was the overwhelming desire to be *near to nature*. *Freedom to move* was essential if goals

Chapter 2 is an elaboration of Muller, Peter O. "The Evolution of American Suburbs: A Geographical Interpretation." In *Urbanism Past and Present*, 4 (Summer, 1977). The permission of the editor and publisher to draw substantially from that article is gratefully acknowledged.

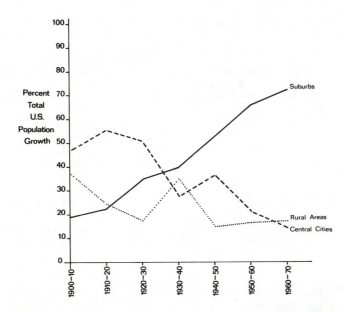

Figure 2.1 Percentage share of total U.S. population change, 1900–1970. (Source: Reproduced by permission of The Association of American Geographers.)

were to be realized, and *individualism* was basic to the self-made man's pursuit of his goals, yet *violence* was the accompaniment if not the condition of success—the competitive urge, the struggle to succeed, the fight to win. Finally, [there is] a great *melting pot* of peoples, and a manifest *sense of destiny.*

In the first half century of national life in preurban America, these traits were most strongly embodied in a prevailing *rural ideal* whose philosophical roots lay in the Jeffersonian perception of democracy, particularly its interpretation of the agrarian doctrine of the eighteenth-century Enlightenment (see Zelinsky, 1973, pp. 41–53, 61–64). This ideal rested on the fervent belief that the rural life is best for the soul, as it minimizes the opportunity for individual sin, and was expressed through the democratic structuring of the small agrarian community that allows for face-to-face interaction, equal participation, and control over the functions of local government. Moreover, compared to other modes of living, only the country was seen to truly stand for life "in the fruits of the soil, in green growing things, in the healthy human family, and in the freedom from arbitrary political and social constraints" (Tuan, 1974, p. 236).

Inherent in the Jeffersonian rural ethic is a powerful popular image against living in cities, which are viewed as symbols of corruption with

Table 2.1 Relative percentages of urban population growth, 1900–1970

Decade	Population growth rate of cities	Population growth rate of suburbs	Percent total SMSA growth in cities	Percent total SMSA growth in suburbs	Suburban growth per 100 increase in central city
1900–10	37.1	23.6	72.1	27.9	38.7
1910–20	27.7	20.0	71.6	28.4	39.6
1920–30	24.3	32.3	59.3	40.7	68.5
1930–40	5.6	14.6	41.0	59.0	144.0
1940–50	14.7	35.9	40.7	59.3	145.9
1950–60	10.7	48.5	23.8	76.2	320.3
1960–70	5.3	28.2	4.4	95.6	2153.1

SOURCE: U.S. Census of Population, 1960. Selected Area Reports: SMSAs, Social and Economic Data for Persons in SMSAs by Residence inside or outside Central City, Final Report PC (3)–1D, 1963. (1960–70 updated figures were computed from the 1970 census by the author.)

Table 2.2 Suburban percentage of total SMSA population for the 15 largest 1970 SMSAs, 1900–1975

Metropolis	1900	1910	1920	1930	1940	1950	1960	1970	1975ᵃ
New York[b]	*32.2	32.4	33.8	36.2	36.1	38.9	47.3	51.2	n.a.
Los Angeles	44.9	*37.4	*36.6	*40.7	42.8	46.5	53.2	54.9	56.2
Chicago	18.5	*19.1	20.4	*24.1	25.7	30.1	42.9	51.8	55.8
Philadelphia	31.6	31.7	32.8	37.8	39.6	43.6	53.9	59.6	62.2
Detroit	*33.1	24.1	*23.9	*28.0	31.7	38.7	55.6	64.0	67.9
San Francisco	24.5	26.7	28.4	31.9	35.9	45.7	58.2	65.4	68.3
Washington	26.4	25.7	23.5	27.6	31.5	46.8	63.2	73.6	76.4
Boston	57.5	58.1	*60.0	64.0	65.1	66.8	73.1	76.7	77.2
Pittsburgh	*58.3	63.7	*66.6	66.9	67.7	69.4	74.9	78.3	80.2
St. Louis	30.4	33.4	33.7	40.7	44.3	51.2	64.4	73.7	77.8
Baltimore	26.2	27.5	*18.7	*22.4	24.6	34.8	47.9	56.3	60.3
Cleveland	17.2	*15.1	*18.0	*27.6	*30.7	40.3	54.1	63.6	67.5
Houston	*30.0	*31.9	*25.9	*18.6	*27.3	*36.3	*33.9	*38.0	42.0
Minneapolis–St. Paul	20.4	16.9	*15.5	16.6	19.4	27.6	46.3	59.0	64.2
Dallas	*79.8	*65.8	*54.7	*43.2	*44.1	*44.4	*39.3	*45.7	50.8
Mean	35.4	34.0	32.8	35.1	37.8	44.1	53.9	60.8	64.8
Mean for all SMSAs	37.9	35.4	34.0	35.4	37.3	41.4	48.6	54.2	n.a.

ᵃIntercensal estimate; not adjusted for annexations or SMSA definitional change.
ᵇStandard Consolidated Area data.
*First census following greater than 10 percent territorial annexation by the central city.
SOURCES: U.S. Census of Population, 1960 and 1970; Jackson, 1972, pp. 443, 445.

permitted maximum freedom to organize individual lives, reside among socially compatible neighbors, and swiftly put down (or take up) local roots, yet carefully served the child-raising needs and functions of the family. Unlike the central city, *violence* in suburban America is channeled into an aggressive striving to get ahead, by people of varying social background, in order to gain acceptance and increasing respectability within the mainstream *melting-pot* society. And, as we will also presently see, prestige suburbs in this century are imbued with a firm *sense of destiny* that they are the places where the American Dream has best been realized.

The full blossoming of the suburban ideal occurred after World War I as the arrival of the automobile allowed the suburbs to develop a completely independent landscape that was no longer an adjunct of the older central city (Meinig, 1979, p. 169). As we will see, this new automobile culture introduced a sharpened image of the arcadian ideal—the Southern California horticultural suburb—which swept across the nation by the end of the 1920s (pages 49–51). A half-century later the appeal of that image remains undiminished, although for many the quest now apparently involves looking beyond the frontier of today's increasingly urbanized suburbs. A recent Gallup poll reported that no less than 57 percent of the American population prefers the small towns and farms of nonmetropolitan areas, which lends credence to Vance's claim (1972, p. 186) that each succeeding generation "finds it necessary to recreate the pristine conditions its parents have looked for in residence." Yet the actual migration behavior of the 1970s, as has been shown, still favors suburbia over rural areas. However, while the residential choices of Americans in the postindustrial society of the 1980s may be variable, there can be no doubt about the growing response to the suburban ideal by now footloose metropolitan economic activities (as we will see in Chapter 4).

Apart from their cultural significance, suburbs throughout their long history have always performed important functions for the cities that spawned them. From the outset, a dual role has characterized the evolution of urban perimeter settlements (see Tuan, 1974, pp. 225–232; Schaeffer and Sclar, 1975, pp. 14–16). On one hand, the city fringes were perceived by the wealthy as desirable retreats for country living in ancient Mesopotamia, classical Athens and Rome, renaissance Florence, and eighteenth-century London; on the other, they were regarded as the domain of society's misfits, illicit activities, its poor, and its less than fully civilized elements (hence "*sub*-urb"). By the late Middle Ages, these fringe settlements had acquired an additional function as sites for warehousing and manufacturing operations. Soon thereafter, many were directly absorbed into the expanding urban economy as city walls were torn down. By the seventeenth and eighteenth centuries, most European cities were actively spawning new peripheral *faubourg* or *vorstadt* ("fore-settlement") districts of factories, inns, and houses of entertainment. With the opening of the New World, these poly-glot functions were transplanted to the suburbs that had arisen alongside the colonial American city, and French-settled New Orleans even had proper faubourgs on its perimeter (Wirt et al., 1972, pp. 5–10). In the succeeding post-Revolutionary period, as the relentless pace toward industrialization intensified during the early nineteenth century, fringe settlements that had sprouted around such larger centers as Boston and Philadelphia came to perform increasingly vital commercial and commodity-production functions for the central town. This geographical interdependency proved to be highly significant, as these urban centers soon expanded, by incorporating the new suburbs and their activities, to form the complete city.

INTRAURBAN TRANSPORTATION AND THE STAGES OF SUBURBAN GROWTH

Modern suburbanization developed early in the second half of the nine-teenth century as urban residents were increasingly able to live on the fringes of the American city. Two new factors brought about the transformation of earlier peripheral settlements: more efficient means of intraurban transport and the beginnings of residential sorting by economic class in city society. Since transportation technology has been a significant force in shaping the geographical structure of suburbia for well over a century (see Holt, 1972; Tarr, 1973), it is profitable to trace the growth of modern suburbs within a framework of urban transport eras. Adams (1970) has suggested a four-stage evolutionary model which coincides with major innovations affecting move-ment and spatial organization in the metropolis. Although these stages did not occur everywhere at once, because of different timings in the introduc-tion and replacement of various technologies, they accord reasonably well with the general sequence of suburban development:

1. Walking-Horsecar Era (pre-1850 to late 1880s)
2. Electric Streetcar Era (late 1880s to 1920)
3. Recreational Automobile Era (1920 to 1945)
4. Freeway Era (1945 to the present)

Within this scheme two broad forms of urban growth can be observed: uni-form transport surface conditions (Eras 1 and 3), allowing directional free-dom of movement and a circular development pattern, and movement network biases (Eras 2 and 4), producing an irregularly shaped metropolis in which axial growth along radial transportation arteries outruns that of the less accessible interstices. Figure 2.2 shows the cumulative impact of

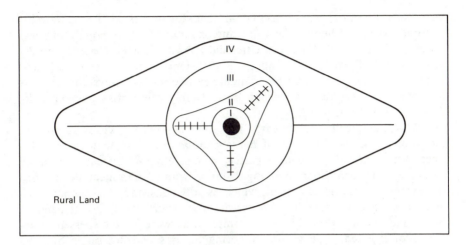

Figure 2.2 Intraurban transport eras and metropolitan growth patterns. (Source: Adapted from Adams, 1970, p. 56. Reproduced by permission of the Association of American Geographers.)

the four transport eras on the overall geographical pattern of urban spread. In turn, each era made several distinctive contributions to the evolving structures and functions of the suburban landscape.

Walking-Horsecar Era

Prior to 1850, the American city was a small tightly compact urban settlement (Figure 2.2, Era 1) in which walking was the dominant mode of movement. With people and activities forced to concentrate within walking distance, the pedestrian city's internal spatial arrangement was not a mosaic of specialized land-use districts but a nearly random intermingling of homes, shops, and workplaces. The population was fairly homogeneous, with few social cleavages, although prosperous merchants and the wealthy maintained their distance by residing in prestigious walled-off areas that dotted the city center. The latter also had relative freedom of movement in horse-drawn carriages and, after the mid-1830s, on newly built railroads that gave them the option of living entirely outside the early industrial city.

The Growth of Early Rail Suburbs

By the middle of the nineteenth century most large cities possessed rail suburbs, but the high cost of outlying housing and train fares, together with the extra commuting time, meant that only the affluent had access to them. In general, the only people who accompanied the wealthy to the suburbs were their servants, who clustered in shacktowns beside the undesirable railroad tracks. Whereas the total antebellum suburban population was quite small, some northeastern cities did spawn considerable outlying development. In Boston, for instance, successful merchants, professionals, and other *nouveaux riche* came to dominate rail commuter flows, and in 1848 no fewer than 118 daily suburban trains were serving brisk passenger demand (Ward, 1971, p. 130).

Morphologically, these early rail suburbs—really exurbs in today's terminology—took the form of narrow radial corridors that contained a linear "rosary bead" settlement pattern of discrete nodes isolated from the city as well as each other. Walking distance from each railhead determined the extent of local development, which usually consisted of a compact residential center and a few shops; otherwise, the suburb was totally dependent on the city. Some of the wealthiest communities were more dispersed settlements of isolated large estates, favoring hilltops and accessible only by local carriage. These areas, such as Philadelphia's suburban Main Line, always possessed superior environmental amenities. In fact, most had originated as resorts and summer-home localities for affluent urbanites seeking escape from yellow fever and other diseases that regularly ravaged unsanitary cities during hot, humid weather. With improving commuter train service and the increasingly hectic pace of urban life, many by midcentury would choose to reside outside the maturing industrial city year-round.

Street Railways, Horsecars, and Their Impact

Except for these more fortunate segments of urban society, access to a less citified residential setting depended upon advances in transport technology. Horse-drawn omnibuses were introduced as the first mass transit innovation in the 1820s, but these small stagecoach-like vehicles were too slow and clumsy. Street railways offered the best hope, and numerous experiments were conducted in cities after 1830 (see Holt, 1972, pp. 324–333; Schaeffer and Sclar, 1975, pp. 19–24). Whereas the street steam engine was a failure and most later cable car systems proved impractical, horse-drawn streetcars were successful and became widespread after 1850. Although these light-rail horsecars were only slightly faster than people on foot (up to 5 mph), they permitted urban expansion to a distance of 3 miles from downtown and thereby opened up sizable new areas for home construction at the city's edge. Horsecar lines followed both radial and lateral crosstown routes. Because of superior accessibility, radials emanating from the city core encouraged both higher residential densities and the precursors of commercial strips. At the same time, however, crosstown lines enabled the development of interstitial space and the city maintained its more-or-less circular shape. This newly accessible outer ring that surrounded the pedestrian city became the *horsecar suburbs*, and its land was used nearly exclusively to build larger and better-quality housing (see Ward, 1971, pp. 128–134). The improved residential environment evidently attracted as many city dwellers as could afford relocation, judging from this 1859 description of Germantown (Figure 2.3) in northwest Philadelphia by the lawyer-historian Sydney Fisher:

> [Horse railroads are] dispersing the people of the city over the surrounding country, introducing thus among them, ventilation, cleanliness, space, healthful pursuits, and the influences of natural beauty, the want of which are the sources of so much evil, moral and physical, in large towns. . . . They are scarcely more than two years old, yet they . . . offer to those who live in the country a pleasant way of going to town at all hours and in any weather at trifling expense (Still, 1974, p. 160).

Horsecar suburbs became particularly important in the social geography of the city with the arrival of the industrial revolution after the Civil War. The massive labor demands of burgeoning industry in the 1870s and 1880s resulted in the rapid growth of the urban population in both size and density. Since factories were geographically bound to water and rail ter-

Figure 2.3 A mid-nineteenth-century view of the residential landscape of Germantown, an outer neighborhood (and former horsecar suburb) located 4 miles northwest of downtown Philadelphia. This picture originally appeared in the Rev. Samuel F. Hotchkin's 1889 history of the city's northwestern sector. (Courtesy Temple University's Paley Library Urban Archives, and Henry N. Michael.)

minals around the city core, homes had to be squeezed in nearby so that blue-collar workers could live within easy walking distance of their jobs. Modest wages and long factory working hours precluded commuting by horsecar, and the inner-city ring adjoining the emerging downtown central business district (CBD) soon became a jumble of high-density slums heavily populated by immigrant working-class families of heterogeneous national origin. Because it was not yet possible for these lower-income ethnic groups to sort themselves into distinct neighborhoods, unavoidable tensions and social friction created an increasingly stressful inner-city residential environment. Those of better means opted for the horsecar suburbs, and the relocation of these longer-term residents quickly began to erode the fairly uniform society of the pedestrian city. Thus, social and geographical stratification of economic classes within the expanding industrial metropolis had begun as growing numbers of middle-income families forsook the inner city for the urban perimeter. Soon thereafter, the American city was locked into a residential spatial structure dominated by closed social cells, wherein ability to pay and quality of one's lifespace went hand in hand.

The localization of middle-income groups at the edge of the industrial city, however, was a relatively short-lived phenomenon. A new technological breakthrough was about to throw open the countryside beyond the built-up city frontier, and the horsecar suburbs soon came to serve as staging areas in the rapid development of true outlying mass suburbs whose appearance "coincided with the beginning of the era of middle-class ascendancy, with the revolution in intraurban transportation, and with the new segregation by social class" (Goheen, 1974, p. 370). At the close of the horsecar era in the late 1880s these forces were set into motion, and during the century's final decade residential suburbia was swiftly transformed from small upper-class enclaves into a landscape dominated by middle-income housing tracts.

Electric Streetcar Era

One of the key turning points in the history of American suburbs occurred in 1888 with the invention and successful application of the electric traction motor to the streetcar. Although an electric trolley was first demonstrated in Cleveland in 1884, regular service was inaugurated in Richmond 4 years later when Frank Sprague, one of Edison's technicians, oversaw the completion of a 25-mile route that linked downtown to the outlying Virginia Exposition Grounds (Still, 1974, pp. 245–246). The innovation was adopted by more than 20 other cities within a year, and by the early 1890s electric streetcars became the dominant mode of intraurban transportation. Higher average trolley speeds of 15 to 18 mph—three times that of horsecars—immediately enabled the range of commuting to increase significantly, so that the urban development radius could now be feasibly extended outward for distances up to 10 miles from the city core. Thus, in one fell swoop, at least five times the surrounding area of the horsecar city now potentially came within 30 minutes' travel time of the CBD. This opportunity, abetted by the easy conversion of horsecars into self-propelled trolleys, launched a prodigious expansion of urban street-rail systems; the Boston area alone more than doubled the length of its network, from 212 to 445 track miles, between 1887 and 1904 (Ward, 1964, p. 385). Inside the city the existing web of radial and crosstown routes was intensified and improved the accessibility of areas lying outside the center. However, the greatest impact of the electric trolley was experienced beyond the city along the new light-rail traction lines that were quickly extended into the urban countryside. By the mid-1890s, supported by new electricity transmission, well-drilling, and septic tank technologies, this transit revolution had ushered in the era of middle-class streetcar suburbanization (Sternlieb and Hughes, 1975, p. 12).

The newly tapped areas beyond the city's horsecar suburbs were rapidly developed in a manner consistent with the American arcadian ideal. The absence of city economic pressures caused by the high cost of land allowed a more lavish use of space, characterized by the lower residential densities associated with the much desired detached single-family house in a garden. Although development soon stretched several miles out, the trolley lines permitted easy access to the CBD for the new suburbanites, who still depended on the central city for everything except locally supplied everyday goods and services. The same geographical separation shaped home-workplace linkages, which steadily lengthened for the middle- and upper-income residents of streetcar suburbs.

Urban morphology in the Electric Streetcar Era was dominated by the narrow fingerlike linear development of housing tracts, which thrust outward from the city line along traction routes and their parallel utility service lines. In other axial sectors electrification of railroads and interurbans now permitted frequent stopping, and the addition of more closely spaced stations saw the older discrete centers coalesce into a continuous built-up corridor. The total pattern was one of a distinctly star-shaped metropolis (Figure 2.2, Era 2) with elongated corridor development in sectors containing public transportation and empty interstices lying between these radial axes. Local suburban development within streetcar corridors was typified by a continuous strip of largely commercial uses which lined both sides of the tracks (trolleys commonly stopped at every corner). Behind them gridded residential streets, the easiest subdivision scheme for real estate developers who surveyed properties and recorded deeds, also paralleled the tracks to the usual depth of a few blocks on either side (Figure 2.4).

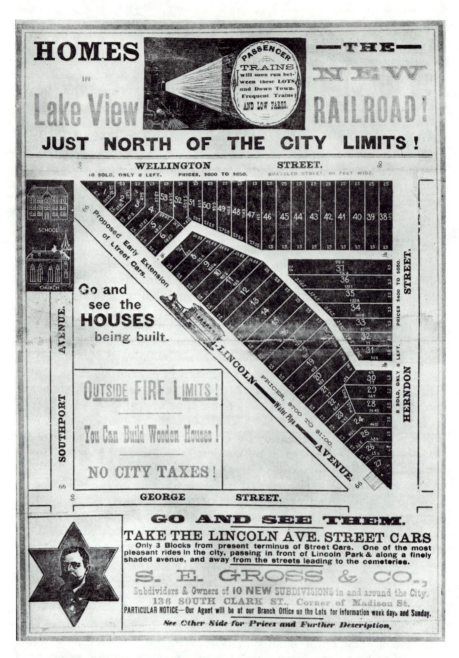

Figure 2.4 A late-nineteenth-century newspaper advertisement heralding a new suburban streetcar subdivision in Lake View just outside Chicago. Note the close orientation of housing lots to the Lincoln Avenue trolley corridor. (Source: S. E. Gross & Co., Chicago: M. B. Kenny, Printer, 1883. IChi-06578. Reproduced by permission of the Chicago Historical Society.)

Detached dwellings on rectangular plots lined these streets, with house facades often imitating those of the rich. Beyond the few-block-wide streetcar corridor lay open space, frequently dotted with small market gardening farms, that was available to all for recreation both on foot and atop newly popular bicycles.

Although the suburban streetcar corridors were overwhelmingly the domain of the new middle class, city dwellers did have access to the recreational facilities that often clustered around the outer end of the trolley line. This arrangement was promoted by traction companies because it attracted riders on otherwise dormant weekends and holidays, and by the end of the century these Sunday outings became the habit of millions. Picnic grounds, bathing beaches, and especially amusement parks such as New York's Coney Island, Philadelphia's Willow Grove, and Boston's Castle Garden were most popular (Hall, 1977). Other trolley corridors terminated at cemeteries, which at that time were designed to accommodate thousands of visitors in search of relaxing open spaces and the architectural wonders of tombstone paraphernalia; the remnants of this way of life may still be glimpsed at the edges of Boston (Forest Hills and Mount Auburn), New York (Woodlawn), and Philadelphia (Laurel Hill). Fairgrounds were also commonly situated at outlying streetcar terminals, some even large enough to host a World's Fair, as did St. Louis's Forest Park, the scene of the Louisiana Purchase Exposition in 1904.

Social Geography of the Streetcar Metropolis

In addition to opening up substantial new suburban territory, the streetcar helped revolutionize the social geography of the metropolis. The new overall pattern of intrametropolitan residential differentiation took the general form of concentric belts in which income rose with increasing distance from the city center. Before focusing on middle-class streetcar suburbia, we briefly review the class structure of the lower-income central city it enclosed and the more distant enlarging enclaves of the wealthy.

By eliminating the residual geographic necessity for maintaining the compact pedestrian city, the electric trolley enabled the residential sorting of the urban population into homogeneous neighborhoods to quickly proceed along social and economic class lines. Continuing inner-city social ferment in the last three decades of the nineteenth century had reinforced desires to live among one's "own kind," a sentiment shared by immigrant newcomers, who also preferred the security of congregating with fellow ethnics in uniform communities. Encircling these sharply defined inner ethnic neighborhoods were the former horsecar suburbs, whose fairly inexpensive housing was in the process of filtering down from the suburbanizing middle-class to moderate-income working-class groups. With the increased density and speed of the urban transit network and the beginnings of factory decentralization along rail axes toward the city's outskirts, blue-collar laborers, despite long working hours and little time for commuting, could now successfully occupy many peripheral neighborhoods.

The outermost suburbs—deliberately oriented to steam railroads and away from middle-class trolley sectors—were home to upper-income groups, with their elegant houses, estates, and newly formed country clubs (the last an innovation that first appeared in the Boston suburb of Brookline in 1882). Some of these residents were holdovers from the earlier period of rail exurb development during the horsecar era, but a new wave of prosperous migrants moved into the far suburbs in the final quarter of the century. The latter, although certainly attracted by superior residential amenities, also came in response to ongoing social change in the cities. With the removal of much of the emerging middle class from the inner city, which had formerly served as a buffer population between the rich and the poor, residents of wealthy center-city "silk stocking" districts were finding it increasingly difficult to maintain their traditional social distance in a more heterogeneous urban society that was becoming increasingly dominated by lower-income groups. Although many affluent families remained downtown by reinforcing other social barriers, a sizable number joined the exodus to such exclusive suburban extremities as New York's Tuxedo Park, Chicago's Lake Forest, and San Francisco's Hillsborough (see Burns, 1980). Their ranks were further swelled by the rich of closer-in suburbia, who sought to keep *their* distance from the newly arriving middle classes; and when the streetcar era came to its end, upper-class family life had become a decidedly suburban experience (Baltzell, 1958, p. 197).

The internal workings of middle-class streetcar suburbs are worth examining at greater length because these settlements gave rise to a social organization that has persisted almost intact to present-day suburbia. The astonishing growth of these suburbs after 1890 was fueled by the steady expansion of the middle-income urban population, which was at least able to realize its dream of homeownership in a garden setting. A strong class consciousness and matching set of widely shared values were immediately acquired, and these became the hallmarks of the new suburban society. Status awareness was now paramount in the choice of residence, and the urge to foster social distance from the status-challenging working class, combined with an even stronger desire to be as near the wealthy as possible, made the streetcar suburb an ideal solution. At the same time, the new freedom of the middle-class nuclear family to pursue its own socioeconomic objectives became a pervasive force; however, such a way of life, focused on the narrow upwardly mobile social interests of the individual family unit, was hardly conducive to the formation of cohesive communities (Yeates and Garner, 1976, p. 191). Residents of middle-income suburbs soon became acutely aware of fine social distinctions among themselves, and an intricate sifting and sorting occurred as its increasingly mobile population was willingly stratified according to a plethora of minor income and status differences. Frequent upward movement within this society became the norm. Any major salary increase or promotion was immediately signified by a move to a "better" neighborhood, as families always searched for means of demonstrating improved social standing. Berry (1973b, pp. 50–51) attributes this growing link between social and spatial mobility to the *drive for achievement* (see page 65), an adaptation of several American cultural dynamics to the new middle-class suburbia.

The residential location decision, therefore, was now and hereafter governed by aggressive achievement-oriented behavior, and once made was constantly reaffirmed in the active defense of one's home territory to avoid its downgrading through the admission of lower-status groups. Understandably, such efforts frequently unleashed "definitional struggles" to exclude working-class families from streetcar corridors (J. Schwartz, 1976, pp. 13–18). Conflict typically centered around the entry of saloons, with most middle-class areas voting to remain "dry" while the blue-collar mill towns of suburban intercity freight-rail corridors chose to go "wet." Intra-middle-class exclusion was also widely practiced: for example, Warner (1962) reports that several public and private suburban institutions kept lower-middle-income groups bottled up in cramped streets and "three-decker" attached housing at the inner, Boston end of new trolley corridors. Yet, because of the overriding emphasis on the family's income level and its aspirations of gaining acceptance within the nativist culture, we should not be surprised that he also reports that few durable ethnic congregations developed in streetcar suburbia.

Each streetcar suburb, besides offering class identity and security, possessed its own blend of uniformly supported social values, which invariably glorified the family as a means for its perpetuation, a creed solidly expressed on the cultural landscape by such "icons" as schools, churches, and recreation centers (Tuan, 1974, p. 237). Numerous group organizations thrived, yet their residentially dispersed memberships, specialized interests, and parochial outlooks tended to keep the local population fragmented, and true community development ultimately became an elusive goal. Warner (1962, p. 158) attributes much of the blame to settlement morphology:

> [The] physical arrangement, however—the endless street grids and the dependence upon the downtown for work and shopping—failed to provide local centers where all the residents of a given area might, through frequent contact, come to know each other and thereby be encouraged to share in community-wide activities. Aside from class segregation there was nothing in the process of late nineteenth century suburban construction that built communities or neighborhoods: it built streets. [The grid plan] was an economically efficient geometry [for the developer] which divided large parcels of land as they came on the market. . . . The result was not integrated communities arranged about common centers, but a historical and accidental traffic pattern.

Annexation and Its Aftermath

Similar problems arose in the effort to maintain a level of suburban public services commensurate with a good-quality residential environment, especially after 1900, when hopes of metropolitan political unification ended with the demise of the city annexation movement in the industrialized Northeast and Midwest. During the late nineteenth century, annexation of surrounding suburban territory, including absorption of already incorporated satellite municipalities, was the predominant method of city growth. The peak enlargement period among large cities was the eighties and nineties, led by Chicago's annexation of most of the South Side in 1889 and New York's political consolidation of its four outer boroughs with Manhattan in 1898. The leading motives for such expansion were boosterism to inspire confidence in the city's future among investors (yes, cities actually promoted their suburbs at this time, and quite vigorously, too!); lobbying by suburban real estate interests to reassure prospective home buyers that suitable public services would be available; and various political strategies involving the conflict between big-city machines and state legislatures (Jackson, 1972). Suburbanites were often sharply divided on the annexation issue. While longer-term residents remained bitterly opposed, the majority of newcomers, at least initially, wanted such unification because they viewed the suburb not as a symbol of separation but an extension of the city which possessed many admirable characteristics (Still, 1974, p. 259). Not that it really mattered, because annexation in most states was involuntary and accomplished by legislative edict, which simply extended the territorial limits of the central city's corporate charter.

After the turn of the century, however, the annexation movement noticeably subsided as the changing social geography of the big city and fear of its expansion made political union far less attractive for the increasingly powerful suburbs. To offset the lack of a complete range of local public services, many incorporating suburban municipalities pooled resources to form *special service districts* that handled schools, hospitals, police and fire protection, water supply, and sewage disposal.* Nonetheless, these attempts only temporarily solved the problem of providing a level of suburban public services adequate for a rapidly growing population. The central difficulty, then as now, was the failure to develop a viable set of cooperative suburban governments that could effectively plan for, and respond more broadly to, the changing needs of their residents.

---

*Despite the growing suburban resolve to go it alone, a number of central cities continued to supply them with municipal services. Detroit, for instance, contributed to rapid suburbanization in its region by selling water supplies cheaply, and saw nothing amiss in contracting to deliver other services for prices well below the level that new suburbs would have paid had they been required to provide their own (Reynolds, 1976, p. 484).

The Beginnings of Suburban Industrialization and Metropolitanization

Important suburban economic development also occurred during the trolley era, particularly in intercity rail corridors, where the onset of urban manufacturing decentralization was giving rise to both "reverse" (city-to-suburb) commuting and a growing number of satellite industrial mill towns (Taylor, 1915). Factories had continued following the railroads outward as they discovered that profitable sites for assembling raw materials and distributing manufactures were not limited to the metropolitan core. The centripetal force once exerted by downtown rail-terminal locations had been superseded for certain industries by centrifugal factors at the close of the last century. Among the latter were the growing shortage of adequate space as the CBD expanded, the subsequent land value spiral that drove up site costs enormously, increasing traffic congestion, escalating taxes, nuisance legislation, and the like. Chicago's experience was typical (Cutler, 1973, pp. 52–57). At first, short-distance moves were undertaken as in the case of the Union Stockyards, which was relocated to the city fringe in the mid-1860s. In the following decade improved transit allowed workers to reach more distant locations, and manufacturing nodes arose at the intersections of the city's radial trunk railroads with the circumferential belt line. By the early 1880s plant sites several miles from the downtown Loop were being developed, most notably Pullman, next to Lake Calumet on the Far South Side. Because of its 10-mile distance from the city frontier, Pullman had to supply residential facilities for its workers. It soon became the prototype and most famous example of the "company town," with its meticulously planned housing and living environment (see Buder, 1967).

By 1920, the intraurban dispersal of industry was becoming even more widespread. Mass-scale assembly-line producers requiring huge outlying railside plants quickly came to dominate the suburban economic landscape; around Detroit, for instance, in the years following 1910 the automobile manufacturing complex shifted completely from small central city facilities to the gigantic factories of such satellites as Dearborn, Highland Park, and Hamtramck. In other cities, public transportation improvements—especially the arrival of rapid transit elevated and subway systems—gave manufacturers an even wider choice of outlying railroad locations. Thus, by the eve of World War I it was possible to differentiate between sectors of "bedroom" suburbs that housed middle- and upper-income city commuters, and industrial suburbs employing local working-class populations. Invariably, the latter adhered to the flat river valleys, whereas the affluent lived an entirely separate existence (including their own central-city-linked rail corridors) in surrounding uplands, with elevation most often a function of income and social rank. Although Pullman-type company towns were founded with noble intentions, their "model" features soon deteriorated into drab high-pollution environments that increasingly attracted saloons, commercial strips, and the servant population for wealthier suburbs (J. Schwartz, 1976, p. 9).

The latter half of the Electric Streetcar Era, in the first two decades of the twentieth century, was marked by a slackening in the growth of urban traction-line networks, as sharp increases in construction costs would often necessitate intolerably high fares. At the same time, many existing streetcar systems encountered trouble in sustaining profitable operations because of unexpectedly high maintenance and new-equipment costs, the withdrawal of builder subsidies as trolley corridors filled up, and the rising competition from commuter railroads, buses, and automobiles. Social factors also contributed to the modest pace of post-1900 streetcar suburbanization. Unlike the more affluent English and Canadian migrants of the preceding decade, who often settled directly in the suburbs, the new wave of poor southern and eastern European immigrants arriving after the turn of the century stuck to the ethnic enclaves of the inner central city (Ward, 1964). Nevertheless, as the trolley era closed around 1920, the suburbs housed more than 25 percent of the nation's nonrural population, and it became clear that the burgeoning rail-produced metropolis of the World War I years embodied the geographical metamorphosis of the American city "from the stage of simple urbanism to complex metropolitanism" (Vance, 1964, p. 50).

Recreational Automobile Era

The metropolitan trend slowly turning the city inside out heightened after 1920 as the widespread adoption of the private automobile helped launch the age of mass-scale suburbanization which persists to the present day. The rate of suburban population expansion, once and for all, surpassed that of the central city in the twenties.* By the following decade, the suburbs began their domination of metropolitan and national population growth trends (Figure 2.1; Table 2.1).

An extraordinary burst of economic growth, led by the rapid expansion of the white-collar services sector needed to manage the booming industrial economy, fueled the momentum of suburbanization in the 1920s as the national wealth came to be shared by an ever-increasing number of

*When adjusted for annexation, however, faster rates of population growth in the suburbs have occurred in every decade since 1900 (Kasarda and Redfearn, 1975, p. 53). Indeed, Jackson (1973, p. 206) stresses that nineteenth-century suburbanization trends on the whole went largely unrecognized precisely because suburbs were constantly being absorbed by expanding cities, which could not have achieved great size without this leading source of new urban population.

middle-class Americans. With much apparent satisfaction, these prosperous residents of interwar suburbia embraced and augmented those improvements in streetcar-era urban life that promoted solid social identity, family-centered activities, and recreation in the surrounding countryside. Although the Great Depression of the early and middle 1930s did slow down metropolitan expansion, its overall impact in the suburbs was much less disastrous than in the cities (which grew only a third as much as suburbia from 1930 to 1940), and by late in the decade recovery was all but complete. The automobile was the major new force that influenced the physical extent of interwar suburban growth, not only by greatly widening the area of intrametropolitan accessibility but also by providing increased flexibility and range in locational choices and movement patterns. While motoring for pleasure generally characterized this early "recreational" auto era between 1920 and 1940, the constant proliferation of modern intraurban highways was simultaneously spawning vast new outlying residential development and radial traffic flows increasingly dominated by suburban drivers commuting to work. Thus, quietly but steadily, by the eve of World War II the automobile had become an integral component of the urban environment and was well on its way to further transforming the geography of the American metropolis.

The Automobile and Interwar Metropolitan Form

The initial appearance of the auto in the 1890s marked the culmination of a long period of experimentation by European and American inventors aimed at perfecting a practical means of personal transport. A leading motivation was the desire of the wealthy to replace their slow and burdensome horse-drawn carriages, and they quickly took to the new innovation. After 1905, however, following further technological refinement and Henry Ford's successful introduction of the mass-produced Model T (which reduced the unit selling price to $825 in 1908 and then below $350 after 1915), the automobile began to make the transition from a rich man's toy to an efficient mass transportation mode available to a majority of Americans. By the time the electric starter was universally adopted in 1916, more than 2 million automobiles were registered nationwide and, despite World War I, more than 8 million only 4 years later. The number of such vehicles grew very rapidly thereafter, nearly tripling in the twenties to 23 million and increasing yet another 10 million during the thirties; by 1940, the U.S. auto registration rate exceeded 200 per 1000 population and the average number of cars per capita (which was 13 in 1920) had fallen to less than 5.

The mass adoption of cars after 1910 occurred first outside the metropolis, where movement needs were far more critical given the generally poor condition of local rural transportation. Whereas the auto penetrated the central city only gradually before the late 1930s, its presence was increasingly felt in the suburbs throughout the interwar period. As early as 1922, 135,000 suburban homes in 60 urban areas were already fully dependent on motor vehicles (Flink, 1975, p. 164). Rapid subsequent expansion of automobile suburbia in the twenties, however, so adversely affected the metropolitan public transportation system that, through the resulting diversion of streetcar and even commuter rail passengers, the big city began to experience the negative effects of the auto several years before accommodating to its actual arrival.

By opening up the unbuilt areas lying between suburban rail axes, the auto quickly lured real estate developers away from the densely settled streetcar corridors to the more profitable and newly accessible interstices. Thus, land speculators and the home building industry no longer needed to privately subsidize traction companies to provide cheap access to their housing tracts. With the removal of this financial support, the modern urban transit crisis began to emerge. Public transport companies were obliged on the one hand to offer a decent level of service, yet, on the other, the boosting of fares in order to earn profits large enough to attract new capital on the open money market would have been prohibitive and caused massive rider desertion (Schaeffer and Sclar, 1975, pp. 38–44). Other factors also contributed to the decline of city–suburb transit in the early automobile age. These included: the shifting of population away from high-density corridors that generated passenger volumes sufficient to support fixed-route transit; the dispersion of employment within large cities, which served to diffuse commuter destinations in addition to origins; reduction of the workweek from 6 to 5 days; increasing congestion where trolley and auto traffic mixed; and the general dislike of riding in more flexible-routed buses that were better able to follow residential development but rarely capture significant numbers of new passengers. Although government subsidies eventually mitigated the crisis somewhat, the quality of transit service steadily deteriorated so that by World War II the American metropolis had all but lost its efficient trolley-era regional public transportation network.

As the interwar transition from rail to auto metropolis proceeded, the shape of urban development, although radially more extensive, reverted to the circular uniform transport surface pattern (Figure 2.2, Era 3). New suburban growth assumed far lower densities as built-up residential areas expanded laterally beyond the older transit lines. At first, these new automobile-inspired developments functioned as appendages to existing suburban corridors. Economic dependence on the central city continued unabated, as did the geographical differentiation between the now more dispersed middle-class residential areas and the linearly clustered working-class industrial suburbs located within intercity railroad corridors. Further diversifying the overall pattern was the addition of high-density spillover residential development in the innermost suburbs, as the annexation movement came to an end in the now politically underbounded but still expanding older central cities of the Northeast and Midwest. By the close of the interwar period the suburbs as a whole were characterized by a diffuse settlement fabric increasingly dependent on near-total automobility.

Highway Building and the Growth of Residential Suburbia

The emergence of this residential pattern was accelerated by the rapid growth of the intrametropolitan highway network. Pre-1920 urban thoroughfares were designed for horses, but considerable pressure from bicyclists and early auto owners had prompted many cities to begin replacing gravel and cobblestone with smooth, hard-surfaced asphalt and concrete roads (Schaeffer and Sclar, 1975, pp. 47–48). Foremost in this effort was Greater New York, which not only improved its roads but embarked on an ambitious modern highway building program before the start of World War I. Central to those plans was a network of lavishly landscaped *parkways*. These scenic greenery-lined routes for pleasure driving, which banned truck and bus traffic, were intended to give city motorists direct access to the recreational opportunities available in the open suburban countryside (Figure 2.5). The first of these was the Bronx River Parkway, conceived as early as 1906 and opened in 1921. By the end of the decade, largely through the political efforts of regional planner Robert Moses, nearly 100 miles of four-lane limited-access parkways stretched deep into Westchester County on the north and Nassau County on Long Island to the east. Many of the

Figure 2.5   A view of the Bronx River Parkway near Scarsdale in Westchester County north of New York City. This mid-1920s photograph originally appeared in the 1929 multi-volume *Regional Plan of New York and its Environs* (reprinted in 1974 by Arno Press, Inc.) and clearly reveals the aesthetic values that governed highway building in suburban America during the Recreational Automobile Era.

weekend motorists must have been pleased with what they saw because significant numbers of them began to move into the many new tract housing subdivisions which soon sprang up alongside of these suburban parkways.

Other metropolises quickly followed suit, and after the mid-twenties recreational highways were actively shaping the course of automobile suburbanization across the nation. Also facilitating city/suburb auto access at this time was the widespread construction of major bridges and tunnels across urban waterways, which served to open for development every possible metropolitan sector. Among the more noteworthy of these catalytic facilities were Philadelphia's Benjamin Franklin Bridge spanning the Delaware River (1926), New York's Holland Tunnel (1927) and George Washington Bridge (1931) across the Hudson, and San Francisco's Bay (1936) and Golden Gate (1937) Bridges. By the end of the 1930s urban highway plans became even more grandiose, especially in Greater Los Angeles, where the newly opened Arroyo Seco (Pasadena) Freeway (1940) had become the first link in the prototype high-speed expressway network that would initiate the postwar transformation of the American city from single-core to multicentered metropolis.*

The suburban land development process itself (see Clawson, 1971; Sargent, 1976) was controlled by the myriad and uncoordinated decisions of thousands of speculator-developers. Profit from the fast turnover of land was the motivation. Subdividing a large parcel into lots and then auctioning them off was the chosen method, although property improvements were necessary when sales slackened. Thus, developers preferred open areas at the metropolitan fringe where large packages of land could be easily and cheaply assembled. Quietly subsidizing this kind of low-density suburban spread were federal and state public policies that included financing highway construction, insuring private mortgages, obligating lending institutions to invest heavily in new home building, and later granting low-interest loans to special groups such as war veterans.

Although this system was popularly hailed as a great success and resulted in widespread economic growth and homeownership, it was not without its detractors. The most outspoken critic was the historian-planner Lewis Mumford, who incessantly castigated suburbia as a bastion of ungovernable growth that was incapable of relieving the intensifying evils of the central city (Still, 1974, pp. 367–370). As the fledgling urban planning profession emerged in the interwar years, conflicts frequently arose with housing subdivision developers, who were judged responsible for piece-

---

*Although new radial highways were often constructed into interstitial suburban sectors, a good number of them also closely paralleled older transit corridors. Again, the outstanding example is metropolitan Los Angeles (Figure 1.3), where the dispersed settlement pattern was initiated in the late nineteenth century by five radial rail lines that were almost exactly duplicated by the major postwar freeways (Banham, 1971, pp. 75–78).

meal disorderly growth, unimaginative community design, and the declining level of amenities in the suburban living environment. The critics pointed with pride to what they considered to be a better answer, embodied in the fruits of a short-lived but noteworthy movement of suburban community planning that created several alternative settlement types during the first four decades of this century (reviewed in detail by Gallion and Eisner, 1975, pp. 127–160).

The Planned Suburb Movement

The formal planning of suburban communities had begun in the third quarter of the nineteenth century with such "Romantic" garden villages as Llewellyn Park near Newark, New Jersey (1853), Riverside southwest of Chicago (1868), and Garden City on New York's Long Island (early 1870s). They were followed by several streetcar-era garden suburbs, the most notable being Baltimore's Roland Park (1891) and New York's Forest Hills (1909), which attempted to integrate housing, shopping, and other local facilities. All were independent compact settlements, planned according to high standards, and limited to upper middle-class and wealthy buyers. After 1920, planned communities quickly adapted to the automobile age by using space far more lavishly. Residential densities were no higher than a few dwellings per acre, and large open spaces for recreation—especially golf courses—characterized such famous mid-twenties developments as Palos Verdes Estates (outside Los Angeles), Shaker Heights (Cleveland), River Oaks (Houston), and the Country Club District (Kansas City). These planned suburbs were still affordable only by the affluent, but they offered a fuller range of community services and a higher-quality living environment than did the neighboring unplanned housing tracts.

Planning efforts peaked in the late 1920s, and involved experimentation with many new residential designs. One innovation, the garden apartment complex (introduced in 1926 at Sunnyside Gardens in New York City), was destined to become an important feature of today's suburban landscape. Another promising planning idea was the brief flirtation with *greenbelt towns;* these were modifications of British planner Ebenezer Howard's "garden cities," the forerunners of modern Europe's new towns, which were themselves inspired by Chicago's city-in-a-garden rebuilding motif following the 1871 fire. The prototype development was Radburn in Fair Lawn, New Jersey, a few miles northwest of Manhattan, where two residential superblocks separating auto and pedestrian traffic were completed in 1928. The Depression wrote a sudden end to this planning episode, however, and a similar fate befell the federal government–backed greenbelt town program of the early 1930s, although three of these aborted settlements survive as ordinary suburbs outside Washington, Milwaukee, and Cincinnati (for the full story, see Arnold, 1971).

The Partitioning of Suburban Social Space

The sorting of residents according to economic status became even more sharply etched in suburban social space after World War I. With the price of housing the filtering mechanism and builders now favoring larger-scale uniform developments, the new mobility via automobile produced bigger, more separate and dispersed congregations of similar-income groups. Thus, the opportunity to reside among compatibly perceived neighbors and maintain social distance from others, a choice hitherto exercised largely by the wealthy, now extended fully to the urban middle class. The nearly complete suburbanization of the latter by the end of the interwar era was greatly accelerated by government policies that aided millions of families to become houseowners, the most important being the home loan insurance programs launched by the Federal Housing Administration in 1934.

The social complexion of many central cities changed significantly during the Recreational Auto Era as the suburban exodus of the middle class was accompanied by the arrival of large numbers of black migrants. Rural southern blacks were increasingly attracted to northern cities as unskilled industrial workers to replace the supply of cheap foreign labor that was abruptly cut off by the national origins quota system established in the immigration legislation of the middle 1920s. Whites, however, immediately signaled their refusal to share urban residential space with the black newcomers. The resulting accommodation of the central-city real estate industry was to steer the expanding black population into segregated inner-city enclaves, which quickly became walled-off ghettos whose externally maintained social barriers prevented the wider dispersal of this racial minority group (see Rose, 1969).

The social geography of interwar suburbia was characterized by an increasingly fragmented residential mosaic composed of locally homogeneous populations congregated by income level. The most insulated communities were peopled by groups belonging to the opposite ends of the socioeconomic spectrum. The lower-income working class and the poor were confined to industrial towns within intercity rail corridors that had been scrupulously avoided in the development of automobile suburbs. The wealthy also remained withdrawn inside their tightly-knit enclaves, commonly wielding their political clout to deflect new suburban growth away from their turf. The numerically dominant middle-income suburbs, as in the Streetcar Era, were marked by a finely grained sociospatial stratification that produced a kaleidoscope of local residential congregations distinguished by a plethora of minor status-related differences. Builders, of course, catered most efficiently to this balkanized settlement fabric by repeatedly constructing the most expensive houses that could be sold in each residential area; their buyers, in turn, carefully sought homes in appropriate price ranges, "consistently electing to remain in neighborhoods where they [felt] socially at home" (Dingemans, 1975, p. 27).

Any residue of the relatively heterogeneous society of the streetcar suburb, with its tradespeople and local service workers, was therefore eliminated by the capability of the automobile to support a geographically-extensive highly differentiated mosaic of socially uniform suburban localities. Moreover, to ensure the stability of this system, the residential partitioning of suburbia was codified in two ways. Most municipalities were quick to adopt *zoning ordinances* (legitimized by the courts in 1916) to preserve their existing character through control of residential lot and building standards, so as to command housing prices consistent with the income and status levels of its current population. Besides these exclusionary economic practices, the widespread utilization of *racial and ethnic covenants* or deed restrictions sought to enforce the social status quo of local congregations. These clauses in contracts between developer and home buyer attempted to prevent resale of the property to Jews, blacks, and other minorities, and were highly effective in perpetuating the white Christian makeup of nonindustrial interwar suburbs; although a 1948 Supreme Court ruling declared restrictive covenants unenforceable by the courts—but not illegal—the convention is still widely adhered to, as we shall see in Chapter 3.

Activity Suburbanization in the Interwar Period

Led by industrial producers, the intraurban deconcentration of economic activity became a clearly recognizable trend during the Recreational Auto Era (Figure 2.6). The locus of much large-scale manufacturing had already shifted to railroad-oriented complexes on the outskirts of large cities, and the continuing dispersal of factories within the interwar metropolis was aided by the arrival of the motor truck. In the trolley era, before the advent of trucking, urban people could circulate far more easily than could freight (except for mail and newspapers, streetcars failed as freight carriers); the only alternative mode of intraurban goods movement was the slow and expensive horse-drawn wagon, and manufacturing remained tightly bound to railside locations. Although trucks—whose registrations increased from 1 to 3½ million during the 1920s—helped to lessen this transport deficiency, their overall impact on the intrametropolitan distribution of industry was quite modest before 1945. Few urban areas possessed efficient regionwide highway networks before the 1950s, and new interwar suburban factories were usually limited to sites where major roads and radial rail lines intersected. Moreover, trucking technology was not well adapted to the economies of large-sized goods hauling, and it would be two decades into the postwar era before central city/suburban plant location cost differentials

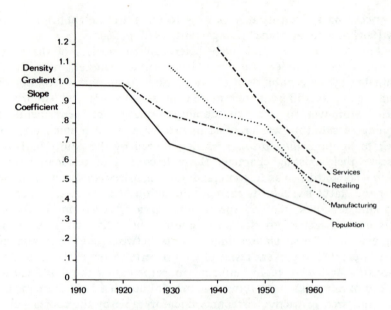

Figure 2.6 Intrametropolitan population and activity density gradients, 1910–1963. (Source: Adapted from Mills, 1970, p. 14. Reproduced by permission of *Urban Studies*.)

could be eliminated. Nonetheless, other developments between the world wars combined to produce a considerable degree of industrial decentralization within the range of suburban locations that were attainable. These included the extension of public utility networks (especially high-voltage power lines) into the newer suburbs, the steady shift from vertical to horizontal fabrication methods, which required larger manufacturing sites, and the accumulation of congestion, taxation, zoning, and disamenity problems that were gradually undermining the central city as an attractive location for industry (see Colby, 1933).

As Figure 2.6 indicates, the suburbanization of retailing also became noticeable during the interwar period. Although the first auto-oriented stores appeared at the edge of Baltimore in 1907 and the highway shopping strip had become a common sight in southern California suburbs by the early twenties, suburban America as a whole experienced only modest retailing activity before the middle of the twentieth century. Most of the roadside retail facilities built in the twenties and thirties were associated with planned suburban communities such as the Country Club District in outer Kansas City, whose builder, Jesse Clyde Nichols, opened the first complete shopping center in 1922 (Country Club Plaza, Figure 2.7). The innovation, however, did not spread; few additional centers were built, and the only notable

(a)

(b)

Figure 2.7 Two views of Country Club Plaza: (a) the original center as it appeared in the 1930s, and (b) a contemporary panorama of the Nichols Memorial Fountain, Giralda Tower, and other newer high-rise structures. This retail complex is still one of the high prestige shopping districts in the Kansas City metropolis, and its annual Christmas lighting display is perhaps the nation's most spectacular. (Courtesy of J. C. Nichols Company.)

refinement of the concept before 1945 was the surrounding of a cluster of stores by a large parking lot, which occurred at Highland Park Shopping Village near Dallas in 1931. Whereas diversified retail centers failed to catch on, the chain stores Sears Roebuck and Montgomery Ward discovered that they could very successfully operate at suburban highway locations. Also thriving were the occasional single branch stores of leading downtown retailers; Filene's of Boston, for example, has been in business in suburban Wellesley since 1923 (Still, 1974, p. 365).

The slow growth of suburban retailing before 1940 was due to the reluctance of both retailers and their customers to break long-established shopping habits. With the exception of food and convenience goods stores that followed people into the newly built auto suburbs, larger clothing, furniture, and department stores heavily preferred the core-city CBD; suburban consumers saw no reason to complain, especially since downtown automobile access was not yet beset by the congestion and parking crises that would surface in early postwar America. Despite the often substantial population growth of outlying sectors in the interwar years, probably nothing short of total suburban development would have transformed the met-

Figure 2.8 The 69th Street shopping district in Upper Darby, Pennsylvania on Philadelphia's western edge as photographed in 1937. This inner suburban transit hub located at the terminus of the city's Market Street subway line (right center) spawned a major retail center shortly after it opened in 1907, and continued to serve a wide area before it lost out to two new regional shopping centers in the early 1970s. In 1980, 45,000 daily commuters still passed through the terminal, using more than a dozen trolley and bus routes which fan out into the surrounding suburbs. (Photograph courtesy Ronald DeGraw, *The Red Arrow*, Haverford Press, Inc., 1972, p. 175. Courtesy of Eleutherian Mills Historical Library, Greenville, Delaware.)

ropolitan retail pattern. Furthermore, the continuing spatial gulf between middle/upper-income residential suburbs and largely autoless working-class industrial suburbs, tended to perpetuate a system of separate routes to downtown stores that made standardized mass selling in the suburbs an impossibility until the late 1940s (Vance, 1962, p. 496). Only a few inter-mediate-level suburban retail centers existed between the metropolis-serving CBD and small clusters of local shops. These were usually situated at strategic road and rail nodes in older streetcar corridors (Figure 2.8), and in addition to convenience goods contained a few limited-appeal spe-cialty stores which reflected the particular socioeconomic character of nearby neighborhoods.

The New Suburban Culture Complex and Its Environmental Problems

By the close of the interwar era, a distinctly new automobile culture had crystallized and was rapidly diffusing through metropolitan America (see Meinig, 1979, pp. 169–172; Flink, 1975, pp. 140–190). This new cul-ture complex was most visibly expressed in the suburban landscape, which was no longer a "mere adjunct of older urban areas, but a discrete and in-dependent landscape, detaching the term from its literal meaning . . . not *sub*-ordinate, but the dominant pattern" (Meinig, 1979, p. 169). The physi-cal elements of that car-produced landscape—widely dispersed housing tracts, curvilinear streets, residential driveways and garages, drive-in shop-ping and auto service strips, and high-speed highways—were first fully integrated in southern California during the 1920s. California had taken to the automobile more rapidly than any other region of the country, con-sistently exhibiting car ownership rates that were double the national average. A majority of its rather young population was comprised of trans-planted American heartlanders, who took pride in their belief that the low-density horticultural suburbs they were building represented the long-desired achievement of a truly humane and livable urban environment. And southern California was also spawning a new kind of affluent leisure society that broke with the older Puritan work ethic, stressing "a relaxed enjoyment of each day in casual indoor–outdoor living with an accent upon individual gratification and physical exercise . . ." (Meinig, 1979, p. 171).

That combined image of the southern California lifestyle and environ-ment was instantly broadcast across the nation by the Hollywood movie, which emerged there at the same time and repeatedly employed the local landscape as a motion-picture setting. Not surprisingly, millions of film-goers were captivated by what they saw on the screen, and the California suburb became the specific expression of the arcadian ideal that has shaped much of new residential America ever since. By the late twenties the southern California bungalow and Spanish architectural styles were being copied everywhere, even though stucco and related building materials were ill suited to the humid climates of the East. Entire communities were often built as replicas of the cinematic version. Florida's Coral Gables (incorporated in 1925), for example, was planned as Miami's "master suburb" and, with its Spanish-style villas and old world Mediterranean flavor, quickly became one of the Southeast's most prestigious communities (Longbrake and Nichols, 1976, p. 43). In other parts of the country, many such 1920s developments survive, although they have since been engulfed by newer suburban growth (Figure 2.9). And when the low-roof ranch house became the leading California dwelling type in the late 1930s and 1940s, it swiftly followed identical routes of diffusion across the United States.

Important technological advances allowed the suburbs to expand dramatically in the Recreational Auto Era. The automobile is usually credited as the primary new force, but we should remember that it was merely the most impressive machine and visible agent of change (Brownell, 1972). Other technologies also played major roles, especially electricity and telephones. Radio, the talking motion picture, and the phonograph enabled city-class entertainment media to follow people into suburbia (with the television revolution soon to come in the early postwar years). Finally, a powerful new culture complex took root and guaranteed the continued growth of automobile suburbs, reinforced not only by the cinema but also

Figure 2.9 Hollywood, Pennsylvania outside Philadelphia, vintage 1926, is a classic example of widespread attempts to authentically reproduce the Southern California suburb. Stucco walls, tile roofs, Mediterranean doorways, and West Coast street names all buttressed the fantasy. The original palm trees, however, couldn't survive the winter weather and had to be replaced with more appropriate vegetation. (Courtesy Linda Gelfin.)

by popular music, family-based radio shows, magazines, and best-selling books.

However high the general level of satisfaction, life in the early automobile suburb was not without its problems. Whereas access to the central city had been fairly well maintained, the other chief interwar physical planning goal—creating a level of public services consistent with a good-quality living environment—was beyond realization given the unrelenting pace of local suburban growth (Fagin, 1958). Although some attempts at reviving the earlier dream of metropolitan government had been made in the 1920s (most notably the New York Regional Plan effort), this movement came to naught in its crusade to organize the disorderly development of suburbia: the public at large was well enough satisfied with the uncoordinated developer-dominated suburbanization process; universal demand for local control created a fragmented system of small municipal governments that frequently duplicated expensive services and made broader planning controls a political impossibility; and the coming of the Depression quickly focused the energies of supralocal government agencies on more pressing economic problems.

Freeway Era

The scale of suburbanization was so greatly enlarged after 1945 that it quickly became the conventional wisdom that suburbia did not occupy a major position in national urban life until the opening of the postwar era. This view, however, was but one of the many 1950s-vintage myths that colored the perceptions of commentators and even social scientists vis-à-vis suburban America. Now that the rich social and economic history of the suburbs in the century preceding World War II is being rediscovered, the consensus today is that intrametropolitan deconcentration since the mid-1940s

> . . . cannot be considered a break in long-standing trends, but rather the later, perhaps more dynamic, evolutionary stages of a transformation which was based on a pyramiding of small scale innovations and underlying social desires (Sternlieb and Hughes, 1975, p. 12).

Because Chapters 3 and 4 survey in detail contemporary trends in suburban social and economic life, the rest of this chapter will concentrate on the earlier postwar emergence of suburbia as the dominant component of metropolitan America.

Suburban growth since World War II has indeed been monumental, even compared to earlier periods of mass suburbanization (see Figure 2.1, Table 2.1, and Table 2.2). Whereas the interwar population of suburbia expanded by only a modest 3 percent (17 to 20 percent) of the national total from 1920 to 1940, very rapid growth after 1945 produced a sharp increase of an additional 13 percent by 1960 and another 6 percent to just under 40 percent of the U.S. total by the late 1970s. There is little doubt that the start of this great suburban boom in the forties and fifties was the key to speedy postwar national economic recovery and reestablishment of 1920s-style prosperity. In fact, many economists believe that without the enormous wave of construction of new suburban homes, highways, and other public facilities after the war, the country would have returned to a depressed economy.

Urban geographical structure in the auto-dominated freeway era has largely been shaped by catalytic new expressways, and the accessibility differentials they produced among outlying sectors resulted in a return to the network-biased metropolis (Figure 2.2, Era 4). With the suburbs spreading in ever-widening arcs since the 1940s, high-speed freeways have created a new sense of almost total intrametropolitan flexibility and spatial freedom in the range of locational choices available to a majority of urban residents; the dramatic upsurge in the postwar deconcentration of nonresidential activities (Figure 2.6) reveals that producers and sellers also increasingly shared that perception.

High-Speed Urban Freeways and Their Impact

Intraurban road construction accelerated in the late forties, and by the end of that decade wide highways were commonplace in the metropolitan landscape. In the 1950s and 1960s roadbuilding continued steadily, with increasing emphasis on radial and circumferential limited-access super-highways. The main force behind the proliferation of urban freeways was the 1956 Interstate Highway Act, which created a trust fund through which the federal government paid 90 percent of local construction costs. Of some 42,000 miles in the national network, more than 5000 miles of new interstates were planned for metropolitan areas (nearly 1000 miles in the New York and Los Angeles suburbs alone). Although a large proportion of these expressways have been completed, the remaining unbuilt links inside central cities encountered rising opposition in the 1970s from neighborhood, ethnic community, environmentalist, and other special-interest-group coalitions; as a result, many freeway projects were scaled down (e.g., Denver, Atlanta, and Philadelphia) and some even canceled outright (most notably in Boston and San Francisco). Local resistance in the suburbs, although not unknown, has been minimal, owing to the antecedent nature of most of its new expressways: suburban penetration usually occurred in open sectors, with growth being shaped by the freeway first in the form of commercial and other nonresidential development clustered around interchanges, and then lower-density residential land uses spreading outward from these initial growth points.

The shift to intrametropolitan highway dominance quickly destroyed whatever remained of the tenuous prewar balance between public transportation and the private automobile. From 1945 to 1950 alone, annual transit ridership nationally fell by 30 percent (23 to 17 billion trips), and by the late 1970s the yearly passenger volume was less than 6 billion. As the early-twentieth-century CBD-focused transit network became increasingly irrelevant to travel demands in the postwar metropolis, deficits soared. Although basic operations are still maintained by government subsidy, the quality of service and equipment in many cities has badly deteriorated.

The postwar prevalence of freeways and widely dispersed intraurban development is the outcome of the full flowering of the automobile age. By the middle 1970s more than 100 million cars were annually being driven over 1 trillion miles, with about three-fourths of the total mileage accounted for by nonvacation trips. Whereas the man/auto ratio in the national population is now approaching 1:2, vast suburban areas of multicar-owning households frequently exhibit ratios of less than 1:1.5—the automobile "saturation level" (Horvath, 1974, p. 178). Constant auto use is, of course, practically a prerequisite for postwar suburban living. Except for the young, the elderly, and the poor, nearly everyone drives. With automatic transmissions commonplace since 1950, stop-and-go urban driving has become effortless, as manual-gear-shifting and foot-clutch skills are no longer necessary. Suburban residents therefore spend considerable amounts of leisure time in their increasingly comfortable cars, with work journeys now constituting only about one-third of all auto trips. Because suburban America is so heavily dependent on auto transportation, the gasoline shortages and price increases of the 1970s have raised questions as to whether suburbia can survive in its present form. Those doubts notwithstanding, suburban survival and even widened predominance are increasingly assured at the beginning of the 1980s, as we shall see in our discussion of the energy "crisis" in Chapter 4.

The Accelerated Suburbanization of People and Activities

Underlying the massive early-postwar migration to the outer city were all the prewar attractions of suburbia, greatly reinforced by the pull of new dispersive forces. Immediately following World War II the nationwide housing shortage, which had been intensifying for 15 years since the onset of the Depression, became exacerbated by an unprecedented increase in the need for new dwelling units. More than a decade's worth of pent-up demand was quickly unleashed: potential home buyers began to spend freely their considerable personal savings amassed during years of wartime prosperity, and returning servicemen had no trouble securing down payments and mortgages in a time of easy money and widespread availability of housing loans guaranteed by the Federal Housing and Veterans Administrations. The construction industry responded with a prodigious spurt of home building, further abetted by the rapid rate of postwar family formation as nearly 10 million new households were established in the decade following 1945. The resulting "baby boom" of the 1950s and early 1960s thus created a continuing need for not only more but larger-sized housing units than were required earlier. The fastest and most profitable way to supply these needed dwellings was to bypass central city neighborhoods for open land on the urban fringe, where it was much cheaper to build. With government-backed loan guarantees overwhelmingly favoring new housing, very little public or private money was invested in the renovation of older homes within the city limits. It is therefore not surprising to observe that fully 60 percent of suburbia's housing stock has been built since 1950, whereas only 37 percent of central city residential units—most of them high-rise inner-city public housing projects—are less than 30 years old.

Mass production of new houses, whose modest prices and easy financing enhanced the attractiveness of early postwar suburbs, became possible as developers and builders achieved new economies through larger-scale undertakings. This was accomplished by shifting from many small to fewer big operators, perfection of house prefabrication technology, repetition of large numbers of identically designed houses, and concentration on developing huge but relatively inexpensive outlying tracts. Hundreds of such residential developments, typified by the immense Lakewood Village complex south of Los Angeles, which accommodated a population exceeding 100,000 on 16 square miles, sprouted across the country. Perhaps most famous among them were the three northeastern Levittowns: the Long Island, New York (1947), and Bucks County, Pennsylvania (1952), tracts contained about 17,000 detached units on ¼-acre lots, and the later Burlington County, New Jersey (1958), community built 10,000 units at a similar residential density.*

As the price of entry declined—Levittown Cape Cods originally went for $100 down and $60 per month—postwar suburbs were settled by an increasingly heterogeneous white population. Many were earnest young war veterans possessing strong familistic values, who desired to educate themselves, work hard, and achieve the "good life." Working-class families, thanks to higher unionized wages and the ubiquitous low-interest FHA and VA loans, made the most of their first opportunity to reside outside central cities, and blue-collar suburbanization rates were as high as those for nonfactory workers. With lower-income groups now also able to own cars, the prewar schism between residential and industrial suburbia lessened, although sharp class distinctions between the two still remain. By the late 1950s, retailers had discovered that mass selling in suburban shopping centers was not only highly lucrative but necessary as old ties to

---

*The New Jersey development—focus of sociologist Herbert Gans' (1967) great classic study, *The Levittowners*—chose in the early 1960s to revert to the local township's original name of Willingboro.

the downtown CBD loosened. Ever-greater intraurban auto mobility also meant that workers were no longer constrained to live near their places of employment. Longer work journeys became the norm, and desire to reside in the highest-possible-status neighborhood gradually superseded workplace accessibility as the leading factor governing the choice of a suburban residential location.

City and Suburb in the Transformed Metropolis

These changes reflected the broader postwar transition from a simple dominant central city/dependent suburbia relationship to a far more complex intrametropolitan structure whose urban elements were scattered almost randomly within the regional city. In this new era of "metropolitan anarchy" (Fagin, 1958), freeways steadily eroded the regionwide centrality advantage of the CBD as suburban expressway locations became equally accessible to the whole urban area. As a result, nonresidential activities increasingly became footloose and thus able to relocate to more desirably perceived outlying sites. With a rapidly growing number of manufacturers and office employers choosing deconcentration, a widely dispersed metropolitan economic network emerged in the 1970s as many suburbs came to perform singly a myriad of functions that hitherto had operated as a bundle in the central city.

Within today's transformed metropolis, city and suburb have therefore assumed new roles. The central city is becoming more specialized as an elitist service center and the home of the metropolitan disadvantaged, while the suburbs comprise a band of diversifying urban development involving the gamut of once exclusively downtown-bound activities. As this outer city attained economic independence from the central city that spawned it, suburbanites increasingly avoided the old metropolitan hub. The concomitant breakdown in ring-core social interaction, exacerbated by diverging interests and outlook in each place, has produced considerable mutual suspicion and misunderstanding.

To no small degree, this intrametropolitan schism is an outcome of the accelerated postwar emigration of whites from big cities as an equally rapid influx of blacks replaced them. The prewar black migration to the central cities intensified in the two decades following 1945, and also widened to include the urban South and West as well as the Northeast and Midwest. By the time both flows slackened in the early 1970s, the nonwhite population of large cities had reached sizable proportions and even dominance in a growing number of cases. Although many observers suspect that this racial turnover is the result of "white flight," it should be noted that recent research demonstrates that the century-old pull of suburbia is much the stronger dispersive force (see Guterbock, 1976, esp. pp. 154–155).

The intracity expansion of the black ghetto in the Freeway Era was speeded by several social forces (Berry, 1975a, pp. 179–183). Because its postwar housing suited neither their lifestyles nor their aspirations, upwardly mobile central city whites began to suburbanize in record numbers. With an insufficiency of lower-income whites to inherit their neighborhoods, the high-density black inner-city population quickly expanded into this residential vacuum propelled by both the dislocating effects of slum clearance and the 1954 school desegregation ruling, which improved nonwhite mobility inside the city. However, many of the older white neighborhoods that filtered down to blacks were taken over by a poorer population. As rental incomes fell, landlords reduced their property expenditures, especially maintenance. The ensuing deterioration soon led to abandonment in many of the oldest inner-city housing areas, thus forcing the outward relocation of poor blacks. To maintain their social distance from the underclass as well as to partake of better housing opportunities, the growing black middle class, in turn, shifted to outermost city neighborhoods. As both push and pull processes continued through the 1970s, middle-income blacks began to spill across the city line. However, as we shall discover in Chapter 3, these inner suburban advances are modest, because white unwillingness to share social space with blacks is being expressed in the intensification of racial barriers.

The intrasuburban grouping of population by voluntary congregation has also undergone important changes in the later postwar era, which will be elaborated in Chapter 3. Class differences not only persisted but magnified with the greater scale of locally uniform residential area construction in the 1945–1965 period. Since the late 1960s, however, suburbanites have increasingly withdrawn into an even more fragmented and specialized mosaic of insulated neighborhoods (a trend also reshaping the social organization of the central city). Although this newest episode of internal suburban partitioning continues and has yet to be completely understood, Vance (1977, p. 416) attributes the trend to a search for individual and small-group identity within immense suburban realms that have now become unmanageable in social size:

> . . . people are seeking a [local] place with which to identify. . . . The long commuting journeys, the high costs of some suburban living, and the acceptance of a composite [nativist] culture are all prices people pay, not to flee the city, . . . but rather to gain a sustainable identity . . . in a vast metropolitan city.

Summary

This chapter has reviewed the evolution of America's suburbs within the framework of the four intrametropolitan transport eras, elaborating the cumulative social and economic consequences of each major urban transportation innovation. However, while these inter-linked stages are a useful way of tracing the history of suburbanization through succeeding time periods, they were used here largely for organizational convenience. As we have repeatedly seen for each era, transportation has not been the only force shaping the internal structure of suburbia, which was also very much the product of social and individual values, land and capital resource availability, private market actions, and nontransport technologies (Tobin, 1976).

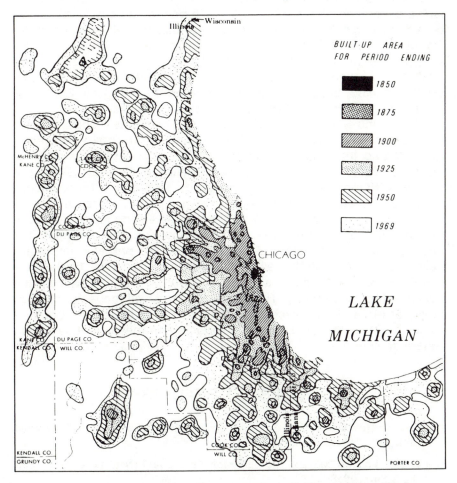

Figure 2.10 The suburban expansion of metropolitan Chicago since the mid-nineteenth century. (Source: Reproduced by permission of the Center for Urban Studies, University of Chicago.)

Our historical survey has necessarily been limited to a generalized overview of the dynamics underlying suburban development since 1850. A more detailed map analysis of Chicago's suburban growth over the same 125-year period, however, shows the broadness of this treatment (Figure 2.10). Suburbanization is revealed as something more complex than a simple continuous outward thrust, as we observe considerable developmental ebb-and-flow pulsation expressed in numerous examples of leapfrogging, backfilling, and frontier stagnation. Nonetheless, good correspondence is also seen between the four-stage growth model and the pattern of Chicagoland's expansion: the compact pre-1875 pedestrian city with its nascent horsecar suburbs is clearly discernible; the 1900 development frontier sharply defines several streetcar and rail corridors; the interstitial infilling of the Recreational Auto Era is quite evident in the 1925–1950 spreading of the built-up area; and the massive expressway-controlled urban deconcentration of the Freeway Era dominates the metropolitan form of the last two decades.

The suburban patterns of each of the four eras discussed here can be viewed as expressions of a cumulative intraurban deconcentration trend that has been marked by five characteristics since at least the 1850s. They are: higher peripheral growth rates, leveling of density differentials, absolute population loss at the core, decentralization of middle- and upper-income groups, and increasing work-trip lengths (Jackson, 1975). Yet, it would be erroneous to conclude that the contemporary urbanization of the suburbs is simply the end product of this century-long evolutionary process. Important new deconcentration forces emerging since the late 1960s have clearly accentuated and hastened suburbanization as well as the decline of the central city. The rest of the book will focus on this synthesis of old and new forces and the transformation of metropolitan social and economic life they are producing on the current suburban American scene.

SUGGESTED READINGS

CHUDACOFF, HOWARD P. *The Evolution of American Urban Society* (Englewood Cliffs, NJ: Prentice-Hall, Inc., 1975).

DOBRINER, WILLIAM M., ED. *The Suburban Community* (New York: G. P. Putnam's Sons, 1958).

DOUGLASS, HARLAN P. *The Suburban Trend* (New York: The Century Company, 1925; reprinted by Arno Press, 1970).

GANS, HERBERT J. *The Levittowners: Ways of Life and Politics in a New Suburban Community* (New York: Vintage Books, 1967).

HOLT, GLEN E. "The Changing Perception of Urban Pathology: An Essay on the Development of Mass Transit in the United States," in Kenneth T. Jackson and Stanley K. Schultz, eds., *Cities in American History* (New York: Alfred A. Knopf, Inc., 1972), pp. 324–343.

JACKSON, KENNETH T. "The Crabgrass Frontier: 150 Years of Suburban Growth in America," in Raymond A. Mohl and James F. Richardson, eds., *The Urban Experience: Themes in American History* (Belmont, CA: Wadsworth Publishing Company, Inc., 1973), pp. 196–221.

MEINIG, DONALD W. "Symbolic Landscapes: Some Idealizations of American Communities," in Donald W. Meinig, ed., *The Interpretation of Ordinary Landscapes: Geographical Essays* (New York: Oxford University Press, 1979), pp. 164–192.

SCHWARTZ, JOEL. "The Evolution of the Suburbs," in Philip C. Dolce, ed., *Suburbia: The American Dream and Dilemma* (Garden City, NY: Anchor Press/Doubleday, 1976), pp. 1–36.

TARR, JOEL A. "From City to Suburb: The 'Moral' Influence of Transportation Technology," in Alexander B. Callow, Jr., ed., *American Urban History: An Interpretive Reader with Commentaries* (New York: Oxford University Press, 2nd ed., rev., 1973), pp. 202–212.

TAYLOR, GRAHAM R. *Satellite Cities: A Study of Industrial Suburbs* (New York: D. Appleton Company, 1915; reprinted by Arno Press, 1970).

WARD, DAVID. *Cities and Immigrants: A Geography of Change in Nineteenth Century America* (New York: Oxford University Press, 1971).

WARNER, SAM BASS, JR. *Streetcar Suburbs: The Process of Growth in Boston, 1870–1900* (Cambridge, MA: Harvard University and The MIT Press, 1962; paperback edition published by Atheneum Publishers, 1974).

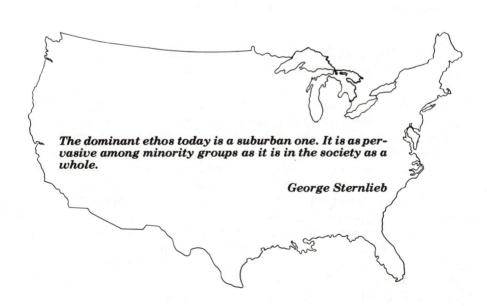

chapter 3

The Social Organization of Contemporary Suburbia and Its Human Consequences

The dominant ethos today is a suburban one. It is as per-vasive among minority groups as it is in the society as a whole.

George Sternlieb

In the evolution of the modern American metropolis, four interrelated and overlapping forces have shaped the distribution of population in general and the social structure of the suburbs in particular: (1) the steady decentralization of all but the lowest-income groups; (2) the concentration of most new housing at the urban periphery, and lately the increasing agglomeration of commerce and industry in the outer city; (3) the differentiation of population in residential space according to socioeconomic criteria, which has created considerable variation among communities of different income and social groups; and (4) the steady immigration of the rural poor to the central cities, a flow that became predominantly nonwhite during the last generation (Danielson, 1972, p. 145). This chapter focuses on contemporary patterns and problems of suburban social organization, and will review the formation of residential congregations, the racial and economic segregation of disadvantaged groups, and its human consequences.

THE RESIDENTIAL CONGREGATIONS OF MAINSTREAM SUBURBAN AMERICA

Although all but the lowest-income and certain minority groups have been able to form residential congregations in the outer city, we have seen that the American suburban experience has been a varied one, as populations from the beginning have been rigidly stratified in residential space according to their socioeconomic status. At the neighborhood scale this geographical sorting by class has produced locally homogeneous social congregations, most of which persist with remarkable stability. They continue to attract socially similar newcomers, searching for the best available housing in just such a uniform social niche or community of interest populated by people sharing the same attitudes, values, and aspirations. In the overall social mosaic seen at the metropolitan scale, however, the heterogeneity of sharply different achievement-related communities dominates the suburban residential map. Income is a primary indicator of this social diversity, and the spatial distribution of per capita income at the municipal level

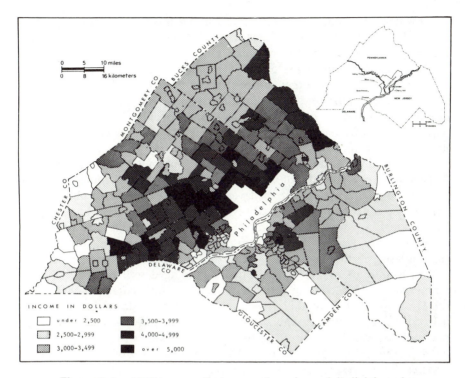

Figure 3.1 1970 per capita income by minor civil divisions in the suburban ring of the Philadelphia SMSA. (Source: Reproduced by permission of the Department of Geography, University of North Carolina at Chapel Hill, and the Association of American Geographers.)

in the Philadelphia SMSA (Figure 3.1) clearly shows the very typical socioeconomic smorgasbord encountered in the suburban ring of any large city.

Class Congregations in Suburban Social Space

Despite the superficial chaos of the geographically fragmented pattern observed in Figure 3.1, it is possible to discern a good degree of spatial order. Berry (1973a, p. 103) suggests the following allocation scheme whereby social classes generally arrange themselves in suburban space. *Upper-income* groups cluster in areas possessing both physical isolation and the choicest environmental amenities around water, trees, and higher ground; *middle-income* populations concentrate as closely as possible to the high-status residential enclaves of the most affluent; *moderate-income* families occupy

63

the less desirable housing of old industrialized towns in rail and river corridors that radiate from the central city, and the aging innermost suburbs that largely contain multiple-dwelling units; and the *low-income* and the *poor* live in isolation in the decaying centers of old towns as well as the dilapidated housing of other out-of-the-way poverty pockets. Since desirable and undesirable residential conditions are widely scattered instead of evenly distributed in geographic space, the considerable socioeconomic balkanization observed in Figure 3.1 develops as the overall population mosaic is built up.

The residential clustering of income groups of the same level in the Delaware Valley suburbs of Philadelphia (Figure 3.1) is quite consistent with this model: high-income enclaves are localized in areas well endowed with environmental amenities and historical prestige (the well-known Main Line extending west from Philadelphia; Valley Forge; Swarthmore); middle-income groups attach themselves to every upper-income cluster (particularly north and south of the prestigious Main Line); moderate-income suburbanites are concentrated in the aged mill towns of the old Pennsylvania and Reading Railroad (now ConRail) corridors which line the Delaware and Schuylkill Rivers (as well as in the farm-dominated exurbs to the far northwest and southeast); and the lowest-income suburban populations, too thinly spread to be captured at this scale, are tightly clustered in the dying cores of smaller satellite cities (Camden, New Jersey; Chester, Pennsylvania) and many scattered outlying pockets.

The suburban myth of Chapter 1 notwithstanding, social science research has established that central city/suburban differences in living patterns are almost entirely accounted for by the different socioeconomic composition of the two populations (Hawley et al., 1975, pp. 54–56). Indeed—allowing for the more dispersed settlement fabric, lower residential densities, higher average income, and greater emphasis on class distinctions in suburbia—the social heterogeneity of the suburbs, as shown in Figure 3.1, is quite reminiscent of the central city. Thus, we are not dealing with two separate urban worlds, and suburban social patterns can generally be regarded as the most recent manifestation of the overall intraurban residential sorting process that has shaped metropolitan society since the early nineteenth century. However, traditional income-based class distinctions have become less important in postwar society. Widespread economic prosperity in the 1950s and 1960s has pushed the entire socioeconomic hierarchy upward, and class strata are now increasingly cross-cut by such social criteria as ethnicity, occupation, and especially lifestyle (Berger, 1960, p. 93).

Thus, the broad partitioning of suburban residential space based exclusively on congregation-by-income is now evolving into a much more internally refined sociospatial structure dominated by stratification according to lifestyle. Since 1970, this trend is being hastened and accentuated by the emergence of a new complex of urbanization forces. These are having a considerable impact on the physical expression of residential preferences in the metropolitan social landscape, particularly in suburbia, with its more affluent population readily able to act upon the attractively perceived choices offered by contemporary social trends and lifestyles.

Changing Urbanization Influences in Late-Twentieth-Century America

Increased metropolitan scale and high population mobility, together with declining intraurban population and activity densities, are the hallmarks of ongoing change within urban America (see Berry, 1973b, pp. 38–48). Underlying these trends is the rise of a new urbanism, distinctly different from that of the recent past. Berry (1973b, pp. 48–56) attributes this metamorphosis to a combination of five mutually reinforcing contemporary urbanization forces: (1) maturation of the postindustrial economy; (2) progressive erosion of core-city centrality through intrametropolitan time-space convergence with the improvement of communications technology; (3) the growing linkage between social and spatial mobility; (4) the efficient performance of the suburban housing industry; and (5) emergence of a truly national American society. The first two dimensions relate more to the restructuring of suburban economic activity and will be treated in Chapter 4. The last three, which signify a powerful reassertion of the nativist culture complex (pages 20–25), directly involve the behavioral and institutional bases of the contemporary social organization of the suburbs.

The connection between upward social and spatial mobility noted in Chapter 2 is today a more forceful social dynamic than ever. The deeply ingrained cultural drive for achievement nurtures a vigorous pursuit of higher socioeconomic status. It is expressed geographically by spending one's earnings on the most expensive home affordable in the best possible residential area. Once one attains a higher-status mode of living, one joins in efforts to protect the neighborhood against the entry of status-challenging lower-income groups. Should these efforts to defend against the downgrading of the neighborhood fail, one may find it necessary to pull out in order to avoid the social stigma of eventually being identified with the lower-status newcomers.

Suburban developers, realtors, and lenders for the past several decades have supported, with a high degree of efficiency, these desires to maintain social congregations according to income and social status. Highly sensitive to market demand conditions, the suburban housing industry, with the approval and financial support of the federal government, has readily and profitably responded by providing a wide variety of spatially discrete, uniform residential enclaves catering to the preferences of every class group. Builders, particularly, have made every effort not to disrupt existing social patterns, as they face uncertainty and must rely on their own previous experience (see Baerwald, 1978a). They, like their customers, are constantly reaching upward and seek to construct the highest-income housing possible on their development tracts. Yet, because they specialize in giving people what they want, builders are also quick to adapt to changed social trends. Thus, today's emphasis on lifestyle and neighborhood image—as shown in the suburban real estate section of any Sunday newspaper—expresses itself in the amenities, housing styles, and layout of the *total living package* offered by major builders to increasingly specialized residential groups.

With the recent emergence of a national American society—abetted by such space-converging technological breakthroughs as nationwide television, rapid jet travel and long-distance telephone communications—suburban social congregations are increasingly being structured at the intermetropolitan scale. Sustained by high rates of urban population mobility through the recent past, "archipelagos" of similar suburban communities, with outliers in every metropolitan ring, now extend from coast to coast. Thus, families and individuals can easily move and "plug in" again within these sets of interchangeable nationally-linked residential enclaves, with minimal uprooting and disruption of their accustomed living patterns and daily social rhythms. In fact, specialized relocation consultant services have recently materialized to assist companies and individuals to transfer to compatible communities in destination metropolitan areas, as have nationwide realtor networks such as Red Carpet, Century 21, and ERA, which now make it possible to market houses throughout the United States (Figure 3.2).

The Emerging Mosaic Culture and Its Suburban Lifestyle Communities

Collectively, these three contemporary urbanization forces—sociospatial mobility, housing industry performance, and the attainment of a national society—have intensified the cultural pluralism of the American population and spawned a trend toward much more narrowly defined urban communities. In part, this is a reaction against today's vast and complex metropolitan structure whereby people feel it necessary to carve out for themselves lesser and more experientially manageable social worlds. More important, as we saw at the end of Chapter 2, this trend reflects a powerful need for small-group identity within the increasingly incomprehensible and tension-ridden society of the late twentieth century. That urge is expressed spatially by each group's identifying with a specific portion of metropolitan turf, and the resulting rise of a mosaic of such specialized social districts has all but

Figure 3.2 A truly national society: houses may now be marketed throughout the U.S. according to this advertisement that appeared in United Airlines' *Mainliner* magazine in 1977. (Source: Reproduced by permission of ERA.)

replaced land rent (overall accessibility) in shaping the morphology of urban settlement (Vance, 1972, pp. 205–210).

The perceived need of individuals to find a refuge from potentially antagonistic rival groups by withdrawing into a territorially defended enclave inhabited by like-minded persons possessing similar attitudes and goals, reinforces the formation of these detached communities of interest and identity. Thus surrounded by formidable social barriers, these self-selected communities achieve a high degree of insularity and foster the growth of equally limited social networks that greatly reduce contact among individuals of different socioeconomic background (see pages 68–69). This system tends to feed on itself as future mobility then occurs among similarly isolated residential enclaves. In fact, at the intermetropolitan level it is already possible "to be a solid citizen of metropolitan New England, San Diego, or Philadelphia and yet be utterly oblivious to the historical cultural identity of those places" (Zelinsky, 1975, p. 112).

Paralleling and complementing this trend toward the territorial detachment of dissimilar social groups absorbed in their own interests is the nationwide emergence of the *Mosaic Culture*. This new American form of macrosocial organization consists of a number of subcultures distinguished by sharply contrasting lifestyles which, although quite divisive for society as a whole, at the local level produces mutual harmony "by mutual withdrawal into homogeneous communities, exclusion and isolation from groups with different life styles and values" (Berry, 1973b, p. 66). The overall reorganization of cultural space is likened by Zelinsky (1975, p. 113) to a multilayered sandwich composed of strata of varying thicknesses stretching across the country: where a certain stratum or subculture thickens markedly, the dominant group has created a *voluntary region* of its own in that locality.

Defended Suburban Turf: Retirement Communities for the Elderly

As Figure 3.3 shows, residential congregations are increasingly expressed in the suburban landscape as unsubtly defended neighborhoods. Such territorial behavior not only asserts that local turf is claimed by a group with its own identity but also physically proscribes social barriers that make it inaccessible to all others. Barricades such as guarded gates, palisade fences, and other "keep out" symbols are typical of today's turfing messages, which signify an expanding private-place-making movement which one planner recently called "creeping expulsionism" (Clay, 1973, pp. 162–175).

Suburban retirement compounds for the affluent elderly are also classic examples of new specialized communities of interest, in this

Figure 3.3 The entrance to Leisure Towne, a community for the elderly located twenty miles east of Philadelphia. This coastal region of Southern New Jersey has become a leading retirement center for the Northeast since 1970. Its often heavily defended compounds have led one local publication to irreverently christen this type of settlement "Fort Geritol."

case the growing trend toward congregation-by-age-group, with strict enforcement of "seniors only" housing policies. Their great appeal lies in the *total-care* living package they offer, as a typical advertisement proclaims: ". . . retire to a residential home in the outer suburbs and live graciously, without loneliness, and peacefully in a secure haven." The adult-village concept was innovated in the suburbs of Los Angeles and San Francisco in the early 1960s and then swept east; judging from the number of waiting lists they command, their popularity reached a high point in the late 1970s. These communities are now proliferating in the suburban rings of most metropolises and may well account for the recent slowing of elderly migration to the so-called Sunbelt, which many retirees now perceive as "boring." Rossmoor-Maryland in Washington's northwest suburbs exemplifies the genre: 5000 senior residents living in a walled-off 900-acre, 2300-unit condominium complex of detached and semidetached housing that is readily accessible to surrounding high-quality shopping, recreational, and medical facilities. So far, developers have managed to keep dwelling prices within the $50,000 to $60,000 range, but rapidly rising costs associated with land parcel assemblage and compliance with local zoning and environmental regulations may well restrict this type of suburban settlement to the wealthy in the future.

The maturation of the fragmented Mosaic Culture is an outstanding symptom of the growing American trend toward parochialism and societal balkanization (see Phillips, 1978). This new national turning inward is most strikingly evident in the heightened sense of localism and satisfaction that prevails in the communities just described, a burgeoning neighborhood movement that, as we shall presently see, can be expected to intensify as population mobility slows in the near future. Even disadvantaged minorities are not immune, as a new black sentiment to go it alone is reshaping that ethnic group's approach to racial integration (this will be discussed later in the chapter). While dissimilar groups mutually withdraw, new dispersed social networks are being forged among those with specialized self-interests, be they occupation-, sex-, or age-related. These new communities of identity are particularly active at the national level, with their regular publications sustaining communications and their annual or more frequent gatherings, which may last only a few days, constituting ephemeral voluntary regions of considerable importance. Significantly, convention attendance has increased briskly, at a rate of more than 5 percent annually since 1970. The experience of the 6000 or so U.S. professional geographers is typical: whereas only 20 percent of the membership of the Association of American Geographers attended the 1974 annual meeting, participation rose steadily through the mid-seventies to reach 53 percent in 1978.

Before surveying the residential forms of the Mosaic Culture, let us examine more closely that social complex we call "lifestyle," which has quickly become the overriding basis of today's class stratification. Each lifestyle involves a unified group behavior pattern consistent with a central and pervasive life interest, and the lifestyles of each social class can be contrasted according to a number of variables: occupational status, stage in the life cycle, leisure time availability, importance of family versus career objectives, local versus cosmopolitan outlook, and a host of lesser environmental and ecological factors (Feldman and Thielbar, 1975; Bensman and Vidich, 1975). With rising affluence, the lifestyles of all but the underclass have evolved "in terms of a logic dictated by the values and needs of families in each class as these interact with the increasing resources and possibilities available" (Rainwater, 1975, p. 373). Not surprisingly, as we shall see, lifestyles increasingly vary within social classes as suburban living alternatives (condominium apartments, townhouses, retirement communities, etc.) proliferate. This trend is accentuated as the Mosaic Culture takes root and affiliations with its subcultures intensify. As this occurs, hastened by the persistent unwillingness of different lifestyle groups to share social space, great numbers of similar people are now congregating in potential communities of every sort. More than ever before, people know exactly what they are looking for in the residential environment, and builders, as we saw, are quite eager to respond in kind to such purposeful behavior. A high degree of satisfaction is therefore widespread as this new social matrix congeals, particularly in the suburbs, which to residents have long been the embodiment of lifestyles desired before settling there (Hall, 1968, p. 138).

Although much more detailed research into the Mosaic Culture phenomenon is needed, it is possible to delineate a broad subcultural typology and discuss each of its four constituent lifestyle community types. The following framework (Suttles, 1975, pp. 265–271; Berry, 1973b, p. 65) can be used to classify these community forms: (1) exclusive suburb/affluent apartment complex concentrations; (2) middle-class family areas; (3) lower-income working-class/ethnic-centered/ghetto communities (the last to be treated separately in the next section); and (4) cosmopolitan centers. The level of generalization intended is at the scale of what Suttles (1975, pp. 264–265) calls the *minimal named community*, a defended social area equivalent to the suburban housing development or older ethnic colony, which is enclosed by popularly recognized neighborhood boundaries. These communities are products of the established residential congregation process and their lifestyles devolve from a fairly uniform population that has faced similar preferences and socioeconomic opportunities. Most, however, contain sizable minorities of residents with varying preferences, who do not participate heavily in the locally dominant lifestyle but who tolerate it because little else is available. All four community types are much in evidence in the socially diversifying contemporary suburban scene, and each will now be reviewed.

Exclusive Upper-Income Suburbs

The high-income suburbs are distinguished by exclusive class-reinforcing social interaction in a local setting dominated by the elegant private schools, churches, and distinctive traditions that are the hallmark of the upper-class lifestyle and character structure (Baltzell, 1958, p. 174). Since houses are built on large properties and screened off by trees and shrubbery, neighboring is physically difficult and people keep in touch by participation in local social networks. The latter are tightly structured around organizations such as churches and country clubs, and newcomers to the community are carefully screened for their social credentials before being accepted. Since many are not accepted, mutually exclusive communication networks can and frequently do develop among affluent groups possessing nearly equally high status (e.g., the ethnic *nouveau riche* and the long-time wealthy Anglo-Saxon Protestant residents). This local social-space partitioning can readily be identified physically in landscape taste and artifact differences (Duncan, 1973).

As has been the trend for the last century, most of these detached prestige suburbs are found in the outer exurban fringes (although notable exceptions do exist in the cases of such elite older inner suburbs as Grosse Pointe, Michigan, and Beverly Hills, California), where the settlement pattern is characterized by even more widely spaced housing, quaint classy villages, and semirural landscapes dedicated to the "gentleman" farming of fox hunting and horse raising (Hart, 1975, pp. 184–185). Old ways of life may slowly be changing, however. Financial hard times have recently persuaded many country clubs to relax their tight admission standards. Outer suburban development in the Northeast is displacing fox hunts even farther into the country. Local community interaction may also be liberalizing: a 1977 Christmas-tree-lighting ceremony in Beverly Hills attracted nearly 10 times the turnout of past years.

A recent offspring of this elite suburban lifestyle is the growth of luxury apartment complexes that are attracting rising numbers of highly affluent singles, families, and senior citizens. Usually operated as condominiums, these swank high rises—veritable vertical country clubs—offer a complete array of first-class services and facilities. Highest-status locations are sought out, and the skylines of many a new suburban minicity (for example, International Village in Schaumburg, 25 miles northwest of downtown Chicago) and prestigious historical landmark (Valley Forge, Figure 3.1) have become dominated by these imposing residential structures.

Middle-Class Family Suburbs

The needs and preferences of the nuclear family unit shape modes of social interaction in middle-income residential areas. The management of children is a central group-level concern, and most local social contact occurs through such family-oriented formal organizations as the school PTA, Little League, and the Scouts. However, despite the closer spacing of homes and these integrating activities, middle-class suburbanites, like their turn-of-the-century streetcar suburb ancestors, are not communally cohesive to any great degree. Emphasis on family privacy and freedom to aggressively pursue its own upwardly mobile aspirations does not encourage the development of extensive local social ties. Neighboring (mostly child-related) is limited and selective, and even socializing with relatives is infrequent. Most social interaction revolves around a nonlocal network of self-selected friends widely distributed in suburban space. The insular single-family house and dependence on the automobile for all trip making accommodate these preferences and foster a strong matching or *congruence* between lifestyle and the spatial arrangement of the residential environment (Michelson, 1976, pp. 26–27, 79–87).

The long-standing casualness of local social involvement by future-oriented middle-income families assumes a central role in the emerging community forms of the Mosaic Culture. The widely dispersed life spaces of middle-class suburbanites, who increasingly participate in social networks that function with little regard for distance or territoriality, typify the unhitching of communities from geographically fixed localities (see Webber, 1968). As this kind of spatial behavior proliferates, most suburban social activity occurs beyond the local neighborhood. Thus, the territorial community has been eclipsed by the community of interest formed through voluntary association. For the suburban resident these dispersed social networks now comprise *macrocommunities* of metropolitan-wide dimensions (Figure 3.4). Yet in spite of the recent expansion of macrocommunities of interest, the overriding societal trend toward narrower defended residential enclaves and intensifying subcultural affiliation have given rise to *microcommunities* that are equally important for understanding the social organization of middle-income family suburbs.

The contemporary microcommunity may be defined as "an instrument of environmental control requiring a rather low level of contact" (Hawley et al., 1975, p. 71). Well suited to the upwardly mobile behavior of middle-class residential areas, these *communities of limited liability* require only a minimum of local group involvement (see Suttles, 1972, pp. 44–81). This largely entails episodic social mobilization for defending neighborhood turf when it appears to be externally threatened. Microcommunities, as secure residential havens worthy of individual social and property investment, expect their inhabitants to help defend local social space, provide

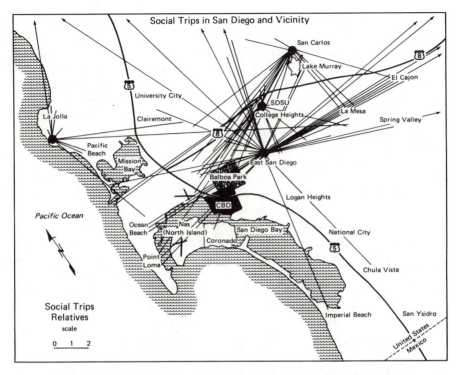

Figure 3.4 The widely dispersed social networks that comprise today's macrocommunities are shown in the map pattern of trips to visit relatives by residents of four San Diego suburbs. (Source: Stutz, 1977, p. 5. Reproduced by permission of the Association of American Geographers.)

goodwill, and, above all, evince *predictable behavior*. On the other hand, families may leave on short notice should the opportunity arise for a move to a higher-status neighborhood.

As was the case with elite upper-income suburbs, middle-income family areas are also accommodating alternative lifestyles as multiple-dwelling housing proliferates. Propelled by skyrocketing land and building costs, suburban apartment construction doubled during the 1960s to more than 6 million units nationwide; in the same period suburbia's proportion of total SMSA multiple-unit dwellings rose from 22 to 33 percent; and by 1972 as many suburban apartments as detached housing units were being started. Besides lower upkeep costs, the new multiunit lifestyle attracts middle-income suburbanites for the same reason that it attracts their wealthier counterparts: the need for less living space in an era of smaller families and working wives, extra services such as tennis courts and swiming pools, and a full array of social facilities. Although the rise of apartment living has altered the physical character of many residential areas, its social impact has been to accentuate rather than diminish class divisions within the suburban socioeconomic fabric: income and status levels of apartment buyers are overwhelmingly similar to those of surrounding neighborhoods that may, in fact, often supply many of the new multiple-unit dwellers (see Dingemans, 1975).

Apartment-based lifestyles support and are being supported by the growing movement away from nuclear-family childrearing as the special residential character of middle-income suburbs. The postwar suburban generation has produced a steadily rising number of young people and childless couples, who require smaller living quarters and who prefer to reside in the same social setting they were raised in. Apartment life is also increasingly attractive to single persons (a group that also owns more than 5 million suburban houses), who have already organized intricate social networks and voluntary regions of their own throughout the outer city. In addition, "empty-nester" households of older couples whose grown children have left home require less living space, and this group's continued strong preference for socioeconomically similar neighborhoods further diversifies the local suburban social scene.

Working-Class Suburbs and the Poor

Suburban working-class neighborhoods have steadily multiplied since the end of World War II. Before 1945 they were confined mainly to polluted narrow factory-town rail sectors (in which they still predominate), but with increased auto ownership and prosperity moderate-income blue-collar families have begun to disperse from industrial corridors and peripheral central city neighborhoods. Although by no means able to penetrate affluent residential areas, working-class families have moved into many modestly priced suburban housing tracts (often near newly dispersed manufacturing facilities) as well as to the innermost, preautomobile suburbs, whose older attached housing selectively filtered down to those spilling across the city line.

Although working-class suburbs vary according to the state of their local economies, age of housing stock, ethnic composition, and threat of racial change, their lifestyles are quite similar. Unlike the carefully structured modes of socializing in middle-class macro- and microcommunities, working-class ethnic-centered neighborhoods are characterized by a broad social interaction of informal groups congregating at such local meeting places as the church, tavern, street corner, or door stoop. Local group acceptance and integration is the dominant social value, and communal life stresses the availability of a satisfying peer-group society, similar neighbors, maintaining easy access among people well known to each other, and collective defense of neighborhood respectability (see Rainwater, 1966, pp. 24–25; Michelson, 1976, pp. 66–71). Thus, much tighter local social cohesion and control dominates suburban working-class neighborhoods. Moreover, local area attachment is reinforced by a person-oriented rather than a material- or achievement-oriented outlook: working-class suburbanites have no great hopes of getting ahead in their largely blue-collar jobs, have few aspirations vis-à-vis upward social mobility, and therefore view their present home and community as a place of permanent settlement (Berger, 1971, p. 169).

Working-class lifestyles are most congruent with high-density residential environments that facilitate the intensive use of outdoor space for local social interaction. This need for a low degree of spatial separation between people explains the continuing affinity of these groups for older factory-town rail corridors that contain most of suburbia's moderately priced attached housing.* The physical and social character of these working-class communities, which Lieberson (1962) found to be virtually identical to blue-collar central city neighborhoods, offsets them sharply from surrounding higher-income suburbs. The focus of outdoor street life is the opposite of middle-class family areas, which emphasize the privacy of the detached house. Residents of working-class neighborhoods tend to economize on housing to spend their modest incomes on other needs and interests; thus, whereas home interiors are meticulously well kept, neighborhood appearance is a low-priority concern and accounts for the frequent unattractiveness of these communities. Social network patterns are also quite different: whereas middle-class suburbs stress the nuclear family unit, socialization with friends, and a minimum of local contact, working-class neighborhoods accentuate the extended family, frequent home entertaining of relatives rather than acquaintances, and a great deal of informal local social interaction outside the home.

A more socially ambitious upper stratum of the suburban working class has been emerging outside these factory-town enclaves since the 1940s and lately shows signs of making the transition to lower-middle-class lifestyles. Understandably, the upward passage of this group is marked by the acquisition of new behavior patterns as well as the retention of some old ones. The working class has always had its more ambitious sector of strivers willing to get ahead by forsaking traditional communities and lifestyles. Through hard work and careful saving these families have managed to buy their own homes in lower-middle-income areas. Once settled, a perception of residential permanency again takes over: the family is fully satisfied that

---

*Increasingly, these towns contain little else as thriving, highway-oriented nearby shopping centers pull away retail customers and force local stores out of business. In many such near-abandoned centers, the X-rated movie theater is the only visible sign of life.

it has "finally made it" and any remaining aspirations are transferred to the children, who will continue to advance via higher education. As a result, these newer lower-middle-class suburbs have become quite stable; for example, Levittown, Pennsylvania, near U.S. Steel's Fairless Works just northeast of Philadelphia, still contains well over 25 percent of its original 1952 residents (Bittan, 1972, p. 80). Also promoting the stability of these residential areas is the in-migration of extended family members of the earlier settlers, as later upwardly mobile emigrants from traditional working-class communities first come to know through frequent visits and then prefer the immediate vicinities of their relatives' homes.

Former working-class residents of lower-middle-class family areas tend to adopt many of the customs and attitudes of their new neighborhood. They desire detached houses; prefer home owning to renting; seek to obtain appliances and creature comforts; keep up the house exterior and yard as well as the indoors; and practice selective neighboring. But at the same time, many of the old ways persist: extended family visiting dominates social interaction; they participate minimally in formal groups; and they live very much in the present and with little class consciousness (see Dobriner, 1963, pp. 57–59).

Because there has not been much research on the subject, we know relatively little about suburban ethnicity and its spatial structure. Undoubtedly, the ethnic consciousness movement of the 1970s has been widely felt in suburbia and is an additional source of its intensifying social fragmentation. Because of their long stability and similarity to blue-collar central city neighborhoods, traditional suburban working-class communities are likely to be centers of strong ethnic identification. Particularly where traditional ethnic kinship structure diverges from the American nuclear family norm—such as extended family households containing several unmarried adult male relatives—detached-dwelling family areas do not favor such old-fashioned working-class living arrangements, not only because of strong local disapproval but also because government home loan guarantee policies overwhelmingly favor single-family houses (Hahn, 1973). Ethnic concentrations are also proliferating in suburban sectors outside factory-town corridors. We have already noted the geographical tendency of nontraditional upper-level working-class groups to cluster around their relatives' homes. These kinds of migratory ties also appear to be widespread among certain middle-income ethnic groups: for example, in the Philadelphia suburbs, perhaps because of the need to minimize distance to few existing houses of worship, Jews, Ukrainians, and Greeks have often preferred to stick together with fellow ethnics in their upward social and spatial mobility. Moreover, some suburbs have even acquired national recognition as ethnic centers, including Skokie, Illinois, outside Chicago (Jewish); Union City, New Jersey, across the river from New York City ("Little Havana on the Hudson," the largest cluster of Cubans outside the Caribbean); and Hamtramck (a Polish enclave surrounded by the city of Detroit).

In addition to its moderate-income population, suburbia also contains a surprisingly large underclass. In 1970, 21 percent of the nation's poor were located there as opposed to 30 percent in the central cities. However, unlike the sizable concentrations of the central city, the suburban poor are widely dispersed among the deteriorated poverty pockets of old mill towns and the far corners of many wealthier municipalities (recall that in Figure 3.1 this scattering was so wide that the outer city's underclass could not be captured on a metropolitan-scaled income-distribution map). In many ways suburbia's all but hidden poor are worse off, because they are voiceless within a balkanized political mosaic that almost always makes them a tiny, ignored, and walled-off minority in their home municipality (in some, many affluent residents are totally unaware of their presence!). Thus, social services are minimal, and life a continuing hardship. These problems are particularly severe in the many instances when the suburban poor also happen to be black, an ethnic group whose suburbanization will be looked at closely in the following section.

Suburban Cosmopolitan Centers

Cosmopolites are talented, well-educated persons with broad national rather than narrow local horizons; they judge people and situations liberally according to objective criteria; and they participate in far-flung intra- and intermetropolitan social networks and communities of interest (see Michelson, 1976, pp. 87–91). Professionals, intellectuals, students, artists, writers, and mutually tolerated misfits who are spatially oriented to the high-culture life of the metropolis inhabit cosmopolitan neighborhoods. As theaters, music and arts facilities, fine restaurants, and other cultural activities continue to deconcentrate from the central city's downtown, cosmopolitan centers are now spreading throughout suburbia. To be sure, suburbanites have always heavily supported center city cultural events by supplying large audiences (as in the case of New York's theaters, symphony orchestras, and opera companies) and crucial financing (Main Line matrons and the Philadelphia Orchestra). The suburbs have also been havens for talented artists (New York's periodic exurbia of the central Hudson Valley, easternmost Long Island, and upper Bucks County in nearby Pennsylvania).

The new suburban cosmopolitan community, however, is a contemporary phenomenon and involves the voluntary residential congregation of people of similar interests in their own social district. University suburbs, which already contain a critical mass of cosmopolites, are particularly favored, and more often than not, towns such as Ann Arbor, Boulder, and

Princeton provide a cultural life almost as rich as that of their nearby central cities. Others achieve national leadership in certain specialized functions, such as Wheaton, Illinois, outside Chicago, whose Wheaton College has attracted the headquarters of most of America's Christian evangelical organizations. College communities are rapidly proliferating in the outer city as a number of downtown universities are successfully decentralizing some of their educational programs to suburban branch campuses. In addition to their usual college-age populations, these branches are also serving local demands for continuing education. The nation's most respected adult education facility, New York's New School for Social Research, opened its first suburban outlet in Westchester County in 1976. Besides its recent growth in college towns, the cosmopolitan lifestyle is also attracted to the vicinities of once-exurban writers' and artists' colonies that have been engulfed by advancing suburbia, and to prestigious new suburban performing arts centers (e.g., the Wolf Trap Farm Park music–dance–theater complex in Vienna, Virginia, outside Washington, D.C.) that are springing up in every region of the country (see Vasiliadis, 1976).

A Socioeconomic Comparison of the Four Lifestyle–Congregation Types

Selected socioeconomic characteristics of each type of residential congregation within the subcultural typology, as reported in the 1970 census, are displayed in Table 3.1. These municipalities were carefully chosen from the meager literature on individual suburban profiles to facilitate a direct empirical comparison of representative lifestyle communities; for example, suburban San Francisco's Milpitas was the town studied by Bennett Berger in the late fifties as the quintessential working-class suburb. Whereas it is hazardous to generalize very far from so limited a sample, observations useful to the present discussion can nonetheless be made and readers are encouraged to extend these findings to similar residential congregations in the suburbs of their home metropolis.

The social and income gradients observed in Table 3.1 are quite consistent with the Mosaic Culture community classification scheme. Two middle-income family suburbs were chosen to show the wide internal differences among communities within this most populous social rank as class distinctions are increasingly cross-cut by lifestyle variations; indeed, Darien and Levittown, even though belonging to the same suburban New York ring, are seen to be two very different places. Perhaps most surprising about both is the relatively low turnover of population between 1965 and 1970. Darien, in fact, was singled out by Packard (1972, pp. 35–45) as the classic revolving-door suburb in a supposedly hypermobile society in which everyone moved at least once each 5 years, but in the context of these data that choice has scant basis in fact! Perhaps the least surprising repre-

Table 3.1 Selected socioeconomic characteristics of representative suburban lifestyle community types, 1970

| Variable | Exclusive upper income Grosse Pointe Shores, Mich. | Middle-income family | | Working class Milpitas, Calif. | Cosmopolitan suburb Princeton, N.J. | Black suburban types | | |
		Upper Darien, Conn.	Lower Levittown, N.Y.			Spillover Glenarden, Md.	Colony Kinloch, Mo.	Satellite city Chester, Pa.
Median family income	$32,565	$22,172	$13,083	$11,543	$12,182	$12,544	$5,916	$8,511
Percent families > $25,000	60.4	41.9	5.7	1.7	18.0	2.2	1.9	1.6
Percent families < $15,000	19.1	29.6	64.0	75.8	59.8	65.8	91.4	86.4
Percent families in poverty	2.1	2.4	3.0	5.3	5.2	4.7	32.6	16.2
Percent black	0.2	0.5	0.1	5.2	10.0	87.2	99.1	45.2
Median age	41.3	32.1	24.0	20.9	28.4	20.8	21.3	28.0
Percent population < 18	30.3	35.5	41.4	46.4	16.3	45.6	44.2	34.0
Percent population > 65	12.4	7.8	3.6	2.1	10.6	2.4	10.5	10.6
Percent same address, 1965	59.5	60.3	75.1	31.5	34.2	43.0	67.1	62.0
Percent population 3–34 in school	80.3	71.0	63.0	55.3	67.4	58.9	58.3	33.8
Percent high school graduates	83.1	83.1	64.2	63.6	76.5	66.7	16.6	10.2
Percent women in labor force	20.8	34.5	41.9	45.5	49.4	66.0	46.4	43.7
Percent professional and technical workers	28.3	25.7	13.6	16.9	37.6	25.9	4.5	9.1
Percent managerial/administrative workers	31.6	25.2	9.4	5.2	7.5	41.1	0.3	3.5
Percent operatives	0.8	4.3	7.6	18.5	2.8	3.5	17.0	21.6

SOURCE: 1970 Census of Population.

sentative community is suburban Detroit's Grosse Pointe Shores, one of the nation's wealthiest residential enclaves. Its extreme affluence, high median age, and low percentage of working women are typical of elite suburbs found—for some reason almost always in the northwestern sector—in every metropolitan ring. Milpitas, everyman's working-class suburb, appears to have acquired a much more fluid and upwardly mobile population, a contradiction in a heretofore bellwether community that almost begs to be restudied a quarter-century later. Princeton, as befits this famous cosmopolite college suburb midway between New York and Philadelphia, is a true mongrel of a community, with its wealthy as well as its dominant moderate-income elements in addition to sizable local elderly and black populations (university students are not counted as Princeton residents). Childless professional couples are especially evident in the high turnover of population, very low percentage of children, and the higher proportion of working women. The three black suburbs also exhibit striking variations and will be considered in a later section. Taken together, the socioeconomic qualities of these communities probably raise more questions than they answer, and clearly offer fascinating raw material for badly needed future research into the suburban residential fabric of the 1980s.

The Intensifying Heterogeneity of Suburban Society

As the Mosaic Culture matures, those living in its new community forms appear satisfied. More than ever before, individuals and families are able to select both the lifestyle most suited to their preferences and a corresponding suburban social district that best caters to their specific needs and interests. Easy mobility within the Mosaic enhances its attractiveness, and the predilection of younger people to pick up and discard lifestyles at will augurs for continuing subcultural fragmentation in the future (see Rainwater, 1975). Yet while the Mosaic Culture promises further heterogeneity, its recently emerged communities are firmly established and will anchor the suburban societal fabric of the late twentieth century. Socioeconomic persistence has long characterized most suburban residential areas (see Farley, 1964), and it is likely that even less neighborhood turnover will occur in the future. With the exception of old industrial-rail corridors and aging inner preautomobile suburbs bordering the central city, downward filtering of housing to lower-income groups does not occur widely in the outer city. If anything, many middle- and upper-income neighborhoods built since 1945 are now appreciating in value. This housing trend is increasingly reinforced by persistent price inflation that is rapidly putting a new home beyond the financial means of all but the most affluent (see Sternlieb, 1972; Breckenfeld, 1976), a matter we shall consider later in this chapter.

Although most individuals and families enjoy the many advantages of living in the subcultural communities of the Mosaic Culture, their increasing tendency to mutually withdraw into tightly knit interest groups and insulated residential enclaves is divisive for suburban society as a whole. As we saw in the case of new specialized communities for the elderly, today's social districts are carefully delimited in a pervasive spirit of every-group-for-itself that seeks to defend local turf against all outsiders who are perceived to threaten the socioeconomic status quo of the congregation. With more and more social interest groups deliberately walling themselves off, their resulting isolation promotes tertiary interaction whereby groups behave toward one another as if oversimplified mass-media class and ethnic stereotypes were true. Thus, local separatism has become the new social reality as small loyalties and outlooks replace broader ones, a trend that Phillips (1978) views with alarming consequences for the future course of American civilization.

For suburban society as a whole, sharply defined cleavages in social interaction reflect a basic geographical incompatibility among contemporary lifestyles as well as their corresponding communities. The intensifying fragmentation of social space therefore buttresses duplication of function within an exceedingly partitioned suburban land-use pattern that caters to each income and subcultural group and encourages decreasing participation in the larger society. Schaeffer and Sclar capture the full essence of the sociospatial status quo:*

> With massive auto transportation, people have found a way to isolate themselves; a way to avoid confrontation; a way to privacy among their peer group . . . they have stratified the urban landscape like a checker board, here a piece for the young married, there one for health care, here one for shopping, there one for the swinging jet set, here one for industry, there one for the aged, here one for the rich in their fifties, there a ghetto for the *Untermensch*—be they poor or racially despised. When people move from square to square, they move purposefully, determinedly. . . . They see nothing except what they are determined to see. Everything else is shut out from their experience.

THE DISADVANTAGED AND SUBURBIA: RACIAL AND ECONOMIC SEGREGATION IN THE OUTER CITY

We have seen that mainstream suburban America is dominated by comfortable neighborhoods whose relatively affluent residents are decidedly satisfied with the forces that produce contemporary social congregations. There is, however, another side to residential suburbia, which is composed

*Schaeffer and Sclar, 1975, p. 19. Copyright © K. H. Schaeffer and Elliott Sclar, 1975. Reprinted by permission of Penguin Books Ltd.

of involuntarily segregated concentrations of disadvantaged groups that are becoming an increasingly important element in urban social geography. Whether for reasons of race, insufficient income, or both, these populations are widely refused access to the voluntary congregations of mainstream suburbia and are compelled to cluster behind powerful social barriers in the least desirable living environments of the outer city. This section will treat suburbia's unwillingly separated residents by focusing on the causes and current dimensions of racial and economic segregation in the outer city.

Black Suburbanization Trends

Among nonwhite minorities, perhaps no group has encountered more imposing suburban social barriers than blacks. Pervasive racial segregation is deeply imbedded within the fragmented society of the outer metropolitan ring to the extent that the spatial isolation of blacks is repeatedly the most pronounced pattern observed on suburbia's residential map. Whereas blacks in 1970 comprised 11 percent of the total U.S. population and more than 12 percent of its metropolitan residents, they account for only about 5 percent of the nation's suburbanites. Let us now examine the black suburban experience according to its historical trends, contemporary community forms, mechanisms that perpetuate racial cleavages, and human consequences.

Twentieth-century black suburbanization trends (Figure 3.5) reveal that such popular suburban epithets as "lily white" and "white noose" have some factual basis. It would certainly not be an overstatement to claim that blacks largely have been denied entrance to the suburbs. Prewar patterns are insignificant because comparatively few blacks lived in the North, but postwar trends clearly show a rapidly widening divergence in the presence of whites and blacks in the suburbs. Both graphs in Figure 3.5 indicate a stable black suburban population over recent decades. A goodly proportion of this population still inhabits tiny, widely dispersed, and highly segregated traditionally black areas with settlement histories of five decades or more. In other instances, large enclaves of similar age are present in satellite towns adjacent to large central cities(e.g., Evanston, Illinois; Pasadena, California; and Mount Vernon, New York). Together, these black suburbs have accounted for a stable 3 percent of the total population in the outer rings of the nonsouthern SMSAs since the 1920s (Farley, 1970, pp. 513–514), and modest postwar growth has intensified residential densities within such older pockets. Very recently, however, black population increases have also resulted from selective expansion of central city ghettos into contiguous inner suburbs—a potentially significant trend for future suburban social geography.

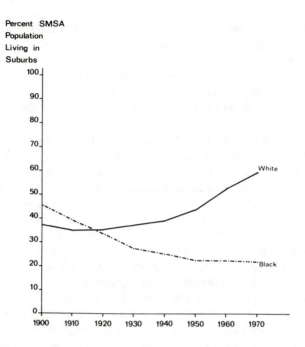

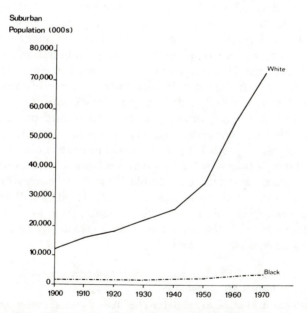

Figure 3.5 Black suburbanization trends, 1900–1970. (Source: Reproduced by permission of the Association of American Geographers.)

An overview of the latest census data indicates that America's suburbs are still all but closed to blacks. During the 1960s the percentage of blacks in the suburban population of SMSAs (as defined in 1970) increased imperceptibly from 4.78 to 4.82.* Although 800,000 blacks did enter suburbia in the sixties, their gains were all but obliterated by the more than 15.5 million whites who constituted 95 percent of the decade's new suburban migrants.

Viewed from the slightly different perspective of the total black population itself, census findings are similar. From 1960 to 1970 the percentage of this group residing in the suburbs increased only from 15.1 to 16.2 percent, compared to the 35.4 to 40.4 percent rise for whites; in terms of percentage increases whites (+14 percent) again led blacks (+7.2 percent) by a wide margin. By region, the West (25.6 to 29.5 percent), North Central (11.6 to 12.8 percent), and South (14.2 to 14.8 percent) gained in black suburban population, whereas the Northeast held a constant 18.7 percent (Pendleton, 1973, p. 173). On the other hand, black concentration in central cities during the sixties increased notably (52.8 to 58.0 percent) at a time when the corresponding white population declined (from 31.5 to 27.8 percent). By 1977, nearly three-fifths of all blacks were residents of the central city as opposed to only 24 percent of U.S. whites.

Because of the much smaller absolute number of suburban blacks in the 1960 base data—2.8 million to 56.3 million whites—suburbanization rates during the 1960s are deceptive (29 percent growth for blacks, 28 percent for whites). Nevertheless, every region recorded modest black gains except the South, where overall black suburban population declined from 12.6 to 10.3 percent. This trend must be balanced against the conclusive findings of a study undertaken by the Federal Reserve Bank of Boston (Glantz and Delaney, 1973), indicating that black suburbanization in the sixties did not result in any meaningful progress toward racial integration. Specifically, this study concluded that (1) there was very little change in the distribution of blacks both between and within central cities and suburbs during the 1960s; (2) new suburban black migrants were overwhelmingly moving into widely scattered already-black neighborhoods with almost no penetration of white residential areas; and (3) despite small absolute and proportionate nonwhite suburban SMSA increases from 1960 to 1970, intermunicipal segregation in the decade actually increased by an average of 15 percent in 14 large SMSAs surveyed.†

---

*According to census estimates, that very modest advance continued into the seventies and reached approximately 5.0 percent in 1975.

†These included all 11 of the largest SMSAs (see Table 4.1) except Washington, D.C., plus Dallas, Atlanta, Birmingham, and Greensboro–Winston Salem–High Point. Only New York City and Los Angeles recorded decreases; suburban Chicago, Detroit, Baltimore, Dallas, Atlanta, and Birmingham all recorded intermunicipal segregation index increases in excess of 20 percent.

Thus, in the 1980s suburbia remains largely off-limits to nonwhites, and Rose (1976, p. 58), in fact, underscores that the black suburbanization phenomenon is confined to fewer than a dozen SMSAs that contain central cities with large growing nonwhite populations. For those blacks who do manage to enter the few relatively undesirable suburban neighborhoods abandoned to them by whites, "it has meant little more than exchanging one hand-me-down neighborhood for another," as improvement in the quality of life over the inner-city ghetto is usually negligible (Delaney, 1974a, p. 278). Before treating this restricted suburban access of higher-income nonwhites, we will discuss the types of black suburban communities that have emerged.

Black Suburban Settlement Types

Spatial patterns of black suburban settlement are intricately tied to the urban ghettoization process that concentrates blacks in a limited number of residential areas that are avoided by whites. Often completely sealed off, these communities are typically surrounded by powerful social barriers maintained through constant external pressures. Rose (1972) has classified these outlying racial concentrations into two distinct spatial forms: (1) colonized, and (2) ghettoized black suburban enclaves (Figure 3.6).

Colonized black suburbs tend to be small stable residential pockets that have persisted for several decades, originating as outlying shacktowns on the then rural/urban fringe.* In the Northeast these communities are commonly attached to old commuter rail corridors (such as suburban Philadelphia's Main Line) and are direct descendants of local nineteenth-century servants' quarters, usually relegated to undesirable trackside locations, that housed the black domestic employees of wealthy landowners of the period. Always segregated, these mostly low-income black colonies have become completely isolated by the social barriers erected as modern suburban development engulfed them. Kinloch, Missouri (discussed in detail by Kramer, 1967; Ernst, 1976), just outside St. Louis, is the classic example:

> It is a desperately poor community surrounded by affluent white suburbs. Kinloch's single-family homes are in various stages of deterioration; its streets are largely unpaved; and at the same time it has the highest rate of school taxes in the county, the lowest tax base, and the worst schools. Kinloch survives as a community simply because no other area is willing to absorb it and its problems. Meanwhile everything is done to isolate the black suburb from its wealthier neighbors.

---

*Ward (1971, p. 142) points out that the original nucleus of black central city ghettos was often an inner suburban locality in the late-nineteenth-century metropolis. Rooming and lodging houses built by rich whites were taken over and soon became overcrowded, deteriorating residential areas. New York City's Harlem best exemplifies this type of ghetto development.

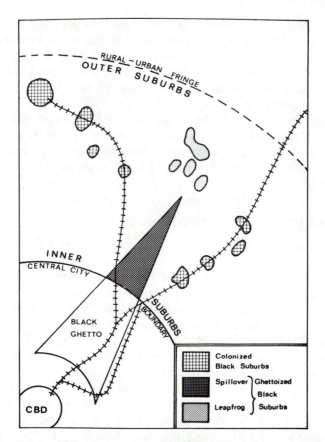

Figure 3.6 Major types and spatial forms of black suburban settlements. [Source: This figure is adapted from "The All Black Town: Suburban Prototype or Rural Slum?" by Harold M. Rose; originally published in *People and Politics in Urban Society* (Urban Affairs Annual Reviews Vol. 6), Harlan Hahn, Editor, copyright 1972, p. 408. By permission of the Publisher, Sage Publications, Inc. (Beverly Hills, CA/London)].

Roads from the next community actually stop one foot before Kinloch's borders, and while a full-scale wall like that in Berlin has not been constructed around the community, the northern community of Berkeley has built a chain-link fence all along Kinloch's border (Palen, 1975, p. 175).

Colonized suburbs can sometimes achieve considerable scale when they occur in the aging industrial satellite cities of the largest SMSAs (see Clay, 1977). The phenomenon is most widely developed in that quintessential suburban state, New Jersey, particularly in deteriorated old manufacturing centers located within rail corridors that emanate from New York and Philadelphia, such as Newark, Paterson, Elizabeth, New Brunswick, Trenton, and Camden. The colonized black suburb writ large is exemplified in the socioeconomic data for Chester, Pennsylvania (Table 3.1), a dying suburban shipbuilding and metals fabrication satellite of 56,000 located 10 miles downstream from Philadelphia (Figure 3.1). The black population is concentrated in the most blighted half of the small city, and the dismal social and income positions of Chester's residents match Kinloch's (adjacent column of Table 3.1) quite closely.

Although most colonized black suburbs are characterized by aged dilapidated housing, stagnant or declining underclass populations, and a deteriorating quality of life, there are a growing number of exceptions. Despite their unsatisfactory living environments, these communities increasingly attract middle-income blacks because they are perceived to be a geographical point of entry into suburbia with at least the potential opportunity for residential expansion into surrounding areas. These in-migrants not only build on the few remaining vacant residentially-zoned properties that were bypassed, but also upgrade existing housing. The latter may well become a critical social issue in the 1980s because such upgrading or *gentrification* of neighborhoods by more affluent newcomers—in identical fashion to the movement occurring in selected inner-central-city ethnic communities (see Cybriwsky, 1980)—usually results in displacement of the existing low-income residents. In a broader sense, this brewing social conflict is an understandable by-product of the recent emergence of the black middle class, which is now coming to include nearly half of the nation's blacks: as with most ethnic groups before them, the new achievers of higher economic status now wish to maintain social distance from their own underclass (see Masotti and Hadden, 1974, pp. 80–81, 280–281). Colonized black suburbs, however, are far too few and crowded to absorb anywhere near the steadily rising black demand for good-quality suburban housing. To accommodate these wishes, penetrations into formerly all-white residential suburbia have become increasingly necessary in the postwar era, thus giving rise to a much larger black suburban form.

That settlement type is the *ghettoized* black suburb, most commonly observed as an advancing spillover community. This is a direct result of the sectoral expansion of the central city ghetto across city lines into adjacent suburban territory (Figure 3.6). As poorest city blacks are forced to abandon unlivable dwellings at the inner edge of the ghetto, they move outward to the nearest available housing. This housing, in turn, has been abandoned by less-poor blacks seeking better housing in outer ghetto neighborhoods. The more favorable residential environment of the inner suburban margins of the advancing black community has attracted a middle-class population of better-educated, young black families. This spillover process is well advanced in many cities, such as Cleveland, St. Louis, Washington, D.C., Chicago, Atlanta, Miami, Los Angeles, and parts of the New York metropolis (the last documented in Sternlieb and Beaton,1972). Glenarden, Maryland, just beyond the northeastern city line of Washington, D.C., is typical of black communities in the inner suburban spillover zone. Here, local black political control enabled annexation of nearby unbuilt land for development in detached and garden apartment dwellings that have attracted hundreds of upwardly mobile nonwhite families.* Glenarden's socioeconomic position (Table 3.1) compares favorably with Kinloch and Chester. With respect to the other suburban lifestyle communities, Glenarden ranks approximately with lower-middle-class Levittown. Yet the economic struggle to maintain that lifestyle in Glenarden, by a minority population having access to fewer opportunities than whites of equivalent social rank, is underscored by its much higher proportion of professional, technical, and managerial workers, lower median income, and the significantly higher percentage of women who must work in order to afford suburban residence.

The other form of ghettoized suburb is the *leapfrog* type, most often an exclave located byond the spillover ghetto (Figure 3.6). This is a newly emerging phenomenon, and Rose (1972, pp. 411–414) has identifed three such clusters in central Long Island, as well as a fourth in East Palo Alto, California. These black pockets are relatively undesirable residential areas and almost always consist of deteriorating, cheaply constructed early-postwar tract housing that whites have abandoned (see Kaplan, 1976b, pp. 28–30).

Although middle-income blacks have made recent progress in gaining access to housing in the outer city, there is no guarantee that an additional supply of inner suburban housing will continue to become available to absorb this growing upwardly mobile minority group. Later in this chapter we shall see that currently changing conditions affecting overall suburban residential mobility, fueled by the astonishing and unremitting inflation in the price of new and used housing, may well work to intensify segregation and all but halt the limited racial turnover of selected suburban neighborhoods. The prospect of racial minorities being refused further entry into suburbia is not a pleasant one, particularly in light of the deepening class schism between the haves and have-nots within the metropolitan black community. Admittedly, this outlook contrasts with more optimistic assessments of the black suburban future (see as an example, Grier and Grier, 1978), but the harsh reality of the mechanisms that perpetuate racial segregation which are surveyed in the following section—*given the sociogeographical context of the maturing Mosaic Culture*—cannot lead to any-

*There is some evidence that new higher-quality middle-class black suburbs are expanding in the late 1970s, particularly around still developing Sunbelt cities [see Ford and Griffin's (1979) study of the San Diego ghetto]. Nonetheless, these improved residential environments are just as heavily segregated as older black urban communities.

thing but a pessimistic conclusion. No matter what promise some observers think it may hold, we must again stress that to date

> Black suburbanization . . . simply represents another settlement phase, and not a major reordering of the way blacks acquire residential access and subsequently access to the preferred quality of life package that is available to others possessing the same [socioeconomic] status (Rose, 1976, p. 263).

Mechanisms Perpetuating Suburban Racial Segregation

Thus, suburban blacks live in residential areas that are quite different from those occupied by whites. Even when blacks are able to find suburban housing outside their colonized and ghettoized enclaves, they tend to be tightly segregated at the block level. A tally of such microscale 1970 census data for the suburban component of the Philadelphia Urbanized Area, using all census tracts containing seemingly integrated black proportions of 17.5 to 50 percent, showed that no less than 52 percent of 1600 blocks surveyed were completely white, whereas 59 percent of the remaining black-occupied blocks possessed ghettolike concentrations of 50 percent black or higher. A comparison of housing conditions in suburban black neighborhoods reveals further disparities: blacks own fewer dwellings (50.2 to 67.8 percent), whose standards and values are significantly lower ($16,430 or 65 percent of the $25,087 white 1970 average) (Pendleton,1973, pp. 180–181). On the whole, there are far fewer blacks in the suburbs than are warranted by this group's rising income levels, and the consensus among researchers in the late seventies is that the basic cause of this residential segregation by race has been and continues to be not class differences but private and public discrimination (this argument is summarized by Taeuber, 1975, esp. pp. 90–92). The *de facto* dual housing market and *de jure* exclusionary zoning mechanisms that perpetuate suburban racial segregation merit closer examination.

The Suburban Dual Housing Market

White refusal to share residential space with blacks has nurtured a discriminatory *dualistic housing market* that systematically excludes non-whites and preserves the racial segregation of the suburbs. Berry (1975b, p. 169), in his discussion of these market mechanisms and their spatial consequences, defines a dual housing market as "one in which there is residential segregation by race, and in which a white majority preempts the outlying areas of new construction and existing zones of superior residential amenity, while the black minority is left the existing housing stock, usually within the central city, and frequently in the zones of greatest environmental risk." Numerous agencies are responsible for the maintenance of this system of housing discrimination.

1. *Subdivision developers* regularly attempt to influence the social composition of their housing tracts through various screening devices. Levitt, for instance, was well known for personally scrutinizing his buyers in order to keep out "undesirable" class and racial groups (his success is abundantly evident in the Table 3.1 confirmation of the virtual nonexistence of blacks in Levittown, N.Y.).

2. *Realtors* very carefully screen prospective home buyers and usually "steer" whites to one listing of houses for sale, and blacks to another. Furthermore, through their local realty boards, realtors control access to house listings and are often accused of denying them to minority real estate brokers. Although one might assign the primary responsibility to the real estate industry for perpetuating segregation by steering blacks away from white areas, its agents, as local business people, feel they have no choice but to cater to the social preferences of their communities.

3. *Individual sellers*, assisted by realtors, builders, and other local groups, still adhere to protective racial and ethnic "covenants." These deed restrictions, declared legally unenforceable but not outlawed by the Supreme Court in the famous *Shelley* v. *Kraemer* case of 1948, continue to be widespread and are frequently used by realtors and sellers as unofficial guides in the transfer of residential properties (Foley, 1975, pp. 172–173; Shafer, 1977, pp. 142–144). In larger southern metropolises such as Atlanta, traditional "gentlemen's agreements" may determine the overall geographical extent of black residential expansion (Hartshorn et al., 1976, p. 51); and in metropolitan Houston, where zoning is nonexistent, powerful local "civic clubs" constantly police neighborhoods to monitor conformity to deed restrictions (Palmer and Rush, 1976, pp. 117–119).

4. *Lending institutions*, through spatially discriminating methods of "redlining," financially support the stability of a chosen set of residential areas. At the same time, by denying mortgage and home improvement loans, they allow the ensuing self-destructive disinvestment process to ruin entire nonfavored neighborhoods.

5. The *federal government*, through the early 1960s, encouraged and heavily subsidized policies creating white suburbs and black central cities by explicitly forbidding home construction loans that fostered racial integration. The Federal Housing Administration prac-

ticed redlining, and the agency's handbooks prior to the Kennedy administration specifically warned against the "infiltration of inharmonious racial groups" and "the presence of incompatible racial elements." Since then the federal government has benignly tolerated segregation by often neglecting to enforce newly enacted fair housing and other equal opportunity legislation.

6. *Local government*, as we shall see in the following section, zealously uses its land control powers to enforce exclusionary zoning ordinances. Many suburban municipalities even try to destroy their black enclaves by rezoning them as commercial or industrial, or to isolate them totally by surrounding them with noxious nonresidential "no-man" zones (Kaplan, 1976b, pp. 27–28).

7. *Society*, by continuing to tolerate without widespread protest this entrenched system of unequal treatment, gives every indication of its satisfaction with the status quo.

Ironically, the failure of recent attempts to reduce racial inequality in shopping for suburban housing comes at a time of steady expansion for the black middle class and its supposed ability to buy its way into good-quality residential areas. Denied access to the mainstream suburban housing market, middle-class blacks seek to congregate in peripheral neighborhoods containing the best available housing. With the concentration of an increasing number of upwardly mobile middle-income blacks at the outer edge of the spillover ghetto (Figure 3.6), the demand for better housing exerts constant pressures to widen the inner suburban foothold. Shunning both militancy and publicity, those behind these efforts probe until the least-resistant surrounding racial barriers begin to yield. Once a breach occurs, word rapidly diffuses through the black community and the new residential pocket is quickly filled. However, this amounts only to a temporary relaxation in the high pressures of "pent-up" demand, as there is only a tightly limited supply of good suburban housing available to blacks at any one time. Moreover, this housing is overwhelmingly limited to lower-quality residential areas, as Sternlieb and Beaton (1972, p. 47) amply documented in their detailed analysis of Plainfield, an emerging spillover suburb in central New Jersey:

> Is minority-group purchasing geographically concentrated within the community? At first glance a wide distribution of minority purchasers seemed evident. Where, however, the blighted sections of the city are superimposed on areas of minority group purchase, a much more distinctive pattern emerges. The bulk of these purchases are immediately peripheral to the blighted sections of the city. The reverse is true for white purchases.

These efforts aimed at enlarging the black suburban presence notwithstanding, the results are hardly noticeable when we consider 1960–1970 census change data. Berry (1975b) underscores the ineffectiveness of suburban integration attempts in analyzing the Chicagoland dual housing market, which, it is fair to say, is quite typical of conditions prevailing in other large metropolitan areas. During the boom period of the sixties—a time when accelerated downward filtering of housing enabled nonwhites to gain access to many decent-quality outer neighborhoods in the central city—the black proportion of families migrating to the Chicago suburbs was only 4.6 percent; when dwelling-unit data are considered, the black share of newly constructed suburban houses (1.9 percent) and apartments (3.3 percent) was even lower. In the far less prosperous economy of the post-1970 period, in which housing supply has markedly tightened, prospects for immediate improvement of this situation are at best remote.

White Resistance to Suburban Integration

White resistance to racial integration is all but universal, with skin color the *master status-determining trait* as white suburbanites at every income level perceive blacks to be a direct threat to their own social position (Berry et al., 1976, esp. pp. 246–260). White animosity toward blacks is expressed no more clearly than in the testimony of a former chairman of (suburban) Baltimore County's Human Relations Commission to the federal civil rights organization that prepared the 1974 report *Equal Opportunity in Suburbia* (p. 14):

> Generally, I would say that the attitude of [white] people is negative. A great many people are without personal knowledge of black people. They respond to stereotyped ideas that we have all been brought up to inherit in a segregated society. We have a great many residents in the county who have had experiences in neighborhoods in the city where the real estate industry has abandoned areas once change has begun, and they feel that they have been hurt, and to them racial change means great difficulty, it means dissolution of neighborhoods, and they don't recognize the great harm and the great hurt that is done to black people who are caught up in this process as well.

The inevitable result of such attitudes is that whites overwhelmingly avoid sharing social space with blacks and continually work to preserve geographical separation of the races.

Low- and moderate-income suburban working-class neighborhoods are especially blunt in their hostility toward nonwhites. The lack of upward-mobility aspirations found in these communities reinforces neighborhood attachment and the desire to maintain an image of respectability, thus eliciting a passionate defense of residential turf. Vandalism and even full-scale rioting often accompany attempts by pioneering black families to penetrate these white communities, whose unity is often accentuated by tight ethnic clannishness. Upper-income residential suburbs handle similar conflicts in a more refined but just as effective manner, usually through adroit maneuvering by sellers and realtors. Consider the response of the affluent Main Line district west of Philadelphia to a recent Pennsylvania fair housing law designed to curb excesses in the state's real estate industry: in the first year following implementation of this legislation nearly two-thirds of local house turnovers were transacted privately without any official involvement of a realtor, and the social status quo of this wealthy area remained unaffected (Kron, 1973). There is also intense resistance to black entry into acutely class-conscious, upwardly mobile middle-class suburbs, particularly since social status is almost always derived from the externally perceived image of one's neighborhood. Only in a very few middle-income suburbs is there even reluctant acceptance of a limited number of black households, which results in "salt-and-pepper" integration—insignificant sprinklings of blacks here and there—frequently characterized by the "Ralph Bunche syndrome" of welcoming one respectable black family to the street but not two or more (Delaney, 1974a, pp. 279–280).*

Some proponents of suburban integration are seizing upon this entrée into certain "liberal" middle-income suburban communities by attempting to devise programs for the orderly influx of more blacks while preventing the flight of white residents common in situations of rapid neighborhood racial change. The belief underlying these schemes is that whites might well wish to remain in a community if firm assurances can be given that the entry of blacks will be controlled so as to guarantee a large local white majority. At issue is the size of the critical mass of black immigrants or the *tipping point*, purported to be in the 20 to 30 percent range, beyond which whites pull out and the entire neighborhood rapidly turns all-black. The inner middle-class Chicago suburb of Oak Park has recently been attempting to draw up this kind of "social compact" ordinance whereby a maximum of 30 pecent black population would be mandated (Farrell, 1974). Prior to 1974, only 2 percent of Oak Park's residents were nonwhite. Local fear of an imminent spillover from the adjacent Austin neighborhood—the leading edge of Chicago's expanding West Side ghetto—and the subsequent likelihood of black "flooding" followed by white abandonment, has prompted Oak Park to explore the controversial black quota solution. Although it is

---

*The racial exclusiveness of the outer city even applies posthumously, as blacks also encounter great difficulty in obtaining sufficient suburban land to bury their dead. Moreover, white cemeteries openly discriminate against racial minorities, a practice still legal in many states.

too soon to tell if such a scheme can work to integrate a large suburban community, the initial results have not been productive. So far, blacks have been segregated within Oak Park and are mainly concentrated in neighborhoods bordering the city line which directly face the Austin ghetto, and the community remains redlined (Kaplan, 1976b, pp. 32–33). Nonacceptance of the social compact idea has been widespread, especially in black quarters, where several community leaders have been particularly outspoken in their opposition to the quota concept. As a result the quota has been tabled, and a policy of selective discrimination prevails (Berry et al., 1976, p. 238). For the moment whites appear to be staying, as the black proportion of Oak Park's population had reached only an estimated 6 percent by 1978. At the same time, local government is so confident that community decline is not imminent that, beginning in late 1977, residents were actually offered the chance to buy insurance policies against deterioration of their property values!

Rising Black Frustration

The immovability of suburban racial barriers is now resulting in such rising black frustration that nonwhite pressures to enter suburbia are declining in many metropolitan areas. Endless obstacles thrown up by dual-housing-market mechanisms have greatly increased black cynicism in the 1980s. Black home-seekers are constantly reminded of racial discrimination in newspaper advertisements containing such wording as "exclusive," "secluded and private," and "country club," which are interpreted as cues that minorities are unwelcome (Outtz, 1974). Nonwhite buyers are seldom given a chance to negotiate or "sleep" on a price without having a house suddenly disappear from the market. When they are able to enter a newly opened suburban area, middle-class blacks may often still be forced to share residential space with socially dissimilar lower-income blacks, thus considerably reducing perceived levels of neighborhood quality (Caldwell, 1974; Willie, 1975). Despite ongoing attempts to modify these conditions, little change is taking place because

> ... by preventing the minority person from being able to shop for housing in the way that is normal for his white peers, a permanent barrier to residential desegregation has been created which may be beyond the power of positive law to reach (J. H. Denton as quoted by Foley, 1975, p. 174).

With heightened black suburban disillusionment in the 1970s has come an intensified aversion to "pioneering" formerly all-white areas, always a distressing practice involving exposure to white hostility and frequently physical violence. Even after penetration, however, blacks are usually never accepted by local whites and can expect more-or-less continual harassment.

In a mid-sixties study of suburbs outside Seattle, Norwood and Barth (1972, pp. 118–123) concluded too optimistically that initial opposition to blacks might subside over time. They even proposed a multistage assimilation model (preentry, entry, accommodation) leading toward residential integration. However, a newer analysis of the Philadelphia suburbs by Cottingham (1975, esp. pp. 277, 281) paints a more accurate picture of the contemporary metropolitan reality. She finds an increasing reluctance among central city blacks—regardless of income level—to move beyond their established neighborhoods. In particular, avoidance of white suburbia is reflected in consistently low black suburbanization rates: 3 percent for all blacks vs. 32 percent for nonblacks, and 6 percent for upper-income blacks vs. 57 percent for affluent whites in the 1965–1970 period. One recent demonstration of the new reality that Cottingham described is the 1977 failure of a vigorous campaign by progressive local white groups to recruit more middle-income black residents for outer Los Angeles' San Fernando Valley. In spite of aggressive advertising efforts in the black Los Angeles broadcast and print media, central-city and suburban blacks shunned the "Move On Into the Valley" appeal, with less than 100 informational inquiries, because the area was perceived as hostile residential turf (*Time*, Oct. 31, 1977, pp. 16, 21).

Exclusionary Zoning and the Persistence of Closed Suburbs

Powerfully reinforcing *de facto* racial barriers encountered by blacks seeking access to housing in the outer city are *de jure* mechanisms that foster economic segregation. Leading among these legal impediments is *exclusionary zoning*, which enables the suburban municipality, through local land control powers, to enforce various ordinances which guarantee that the sale and rental prices of properties are not affordable by low- and moderate-income individuals of any social group.

In Chapter 2 we saw that the historical roots of economic segregation extend back at least as far as the late nineteenth century. The desires of the newly emerging and suburbanizing middle class to maintain social distance from the immigrant underclass of the inner city were quickly expressed in an abiding concern with defending newly won suburban territory against all outside challengers of lower social status. In the 1920s, zoning was widely adopted to reinforce this exclusionism because property owners in the early automobile suburbs clearly recognized it as an effective tool for preserving single-family housing, suburban neighborhood character, and the existing class structure. Thus,

> Instead of becoming a useful tool for the rational ordering of land in metropolitan areas, zoning became a way for suburbs to pirate from the city only its desirable functions and residents. Suburban govern-

ments became like so many residential hotels, fighting for the upper-income trade while trying to force the deadbeats to go elsewhere (Jackson, 1973, p. 210).

Although now stripped of some of its most discriminatory excesses, this exclusionary system or *suburban filter*, institutionalized in almost every community through suburbia's fragmented local government structure, has persisted essentially unchanged since zoning was first introduced after World War I. Current exclusionary zoning practices (reviewed by Rubinowitz, 1974, pp. 27–44; and Fried, 1972, pp. 41–49) assume a variety of forms, the general thrust of which overwhelmingly favors expensive one-family homes on large lots, thus pricing out and defending against nonaffluent populations. The number and location of multiple-family units, if permitted at all, are tightly controlled by piecemeal zoning. This practice limits land parcel size in order to prevent construction of large apartment complexes by assigning sites next to obnoxious land uses, which usually deters builders, and by restricting apartment size, which holds the school-age population down ("hysterectomy" zoning). Other less costly housing, especially mobile homes, is almost universally banned in middle- and upper-income suburbs.* Municipalities justify large-lot zoning of ½ acre or more as a way to control local growth, preserve low population densities and good environmental quality, and avoid urban problems that emanate from over-crowded conditions. Should development conditions change, many local zoning boards will also not hesitate to *upzone* minimum residential lot sizes into even larger land parcels. Moreover, most municipalities also enforce housing codes whose standards are so high (and so costly to meet for building permit approval) that critics refer to them as "Cadillac" requirements. Among these are extravagant structural and material stipulations, lavish minimum-floor-space requirements, and sidewalk and sewer tie-in regulations. Although many communities recognize that their zoning and building ordinances result in an exclusively middle- and upper-income local population, they argue that preservation of the municipal tax structure would be impossible if lower-income housing were suddenly permitted, because of the huge burden that such an influx of people would place upon social and other public services.

The results of half a century of suburban economic segregation are increasingly evident. 1970 census data on metropolitan housing available to low- and moderate-income groups reveal a striking disparity between central city and suburbia: for owner-occupied homes valued at less than $12,500 the city proportion (31.2 percent) was almost double that of the

---

*Despite exclusion from higher-status residential areas, mobile home parks have grown steadily around lower-income suburbs. These types of suburban dwellings doubled in number during the 1960s and continue to proliferate as attractive housing alternatives for moderate-income groups.

suburbs (17.6 percent), and for rentals of less than $80 per month the differential (23.8 versus 13.7 percent) was almost identical (Downs, 1973, pp. 191–192). The outlook for narrowing this divergence is not promising when one considers zoning data on undeveloped suburban land. The metropolitan New York case is typical. In 1971, Davidoff et al. (1974, p. 136) observed that 90 percent of the remaining open residential land within the New York state suburbs was zoned for single-family homes; in northern New Jersey 82 percent of such land was zoned for ½-acre or larger lots; and in southwestern Connecticut at least 75 percent of the available land was zoned for lots of an acre or more. Suburban Philadelphia is similar: 64 percent of developable residential land is zoned for 1 acre or larger lots, with one-third exceeding 2 acres; 38 percent of suburban municipalities prohibit multiple-family housing; and 42 percent of those that permit such housing restrict the number of bedrooms per apartment unit (Anastasia, 1975).

Perhaps the most telling impact of the suburban filter in recent years is the inevitable overall housing shortage in the outer city caused by artificial limitations on dwelling-unit supply. Zoning thus greatly reinforces the upward spiral of both land and home construction costs, so much so that middle-income groups are increasingly unable to compete in certain segments of the suburban housing market at the present time. In the early seventies, only 20 percent of all the families residing in the New York metropolis could afford a new house (versus 70 percent in 1950); significantly, this proportion would rise to 47.5 percent if suburban zoning were to change and 57.5 percent if mobile homes were more widely permitted (Caldwell, 1973, p. 19). Recession and the climbing of already high mortgage interest rates through the mid-1970s have combined to erode further the financial position of middle-income households. Even such mass builders as Levitt and Sons claimed in 1975 that they could not sell a new house to families earning under $17,000 annually. In some suburban communities this new reality is finally raising doubts as to the long-run effects of the exclusionary system. This concern, however, is not for disadvantaged outsiders but is rather one of self-interest: residents are becoming aware that the expense of local housing is forcing out their own elderly and young married populations. Thus, limited, moderate income, multiple-unit housing plans are tolerated in a growing number of suburban municipalities, but almost always on the condition that eligibility be restricted to senior citizens and others already living in the community.

The Continuing Legal Struggle to Open the Suburbs

To the American public at large, exclusionary zoning is most widely known as a term referring to the ongoing legal battle to break the economic segregation system of the nation's suburbs (for a general review of this movement, its attendant issues, and important legal decisions through the middle seventies, see *Newsweek*, 1971; Babcock, 1973; Masotti and Hadden, 1974, pp. 112-175; Platt, 1976, pp. 20-23; R. Williams, 1978).

Through the mid-sixties legal decisions on local zoning strongly supported suburban exclusionism. Since zoning originated from enabling acts passed by state legislatures, cases were usually confined to the state courts. Federal courts rarely heard such cases; the U.S. Supreme Court has not ruled on municipal zoning since it approved this method of local land-use control in 1926, and still refuses to hear such cases a half-century later. In recent years, however, the growing financial commitment of the federal government to local planning and community development, an outcome of wide-ranging social legislation passed by Congress since 1963, has increased the involvement of the federal judiciary in exclusion cases. At the same time, the legal record has become less one-sided as certain decisions have been rendered in favor of opening the suburbs to lower-income populations. As yet, many legal contradictions remain to be resolved. Opponents of exclusionary zoning have gained mostly moral victories to date, and the closed suburban system persists. Rather than review the full record of exclusionary zoning adjudication since 1960, let us briefly examine four cases of the mid-seventies which are pertinent to the future of present forms of suburban exclusionism: (1) Mount Laurel Township, New Jersey; (2) Petaluma, California; (3) metropolitan Hartford, Connecticut; and (4) metropolitan Chicago (see pages 98–102).

Mount Laurel, New Jersey

The Mount Laurel, New Jersey, case (Anastasia, 1975; Trillin, 1976; Rose and Rothman, 1977) involves the most important state-level decision yet rendered, and deals not only with the narrow question of restrictive municipal zoning but also the wider issue of how local government may use its powers to shape the socioeconomic composition of its community. Ruling in 1975 on Mount Laurel's township ordinances that banned apartments and single-family homes on lots smaller than ¼-acre, the New Jersey Supreme Court struck down exclusionary zoning statewide. The Court felt that restrictive zoning went beyond the powers that the state legislature had intended to give local governments, and directed that every such municipality must change its land-use regulations to "make available an appropriate variety of choice in housing." More important, the Court also found that any developing community shares with its neighbors a legal and social obligation to provide a fair share of housing for low- and moderate-income families. Thus, a New Jersey municipality now had a regional responsibility for people living outside its boundaries, and may no longer enforce local housing plans that operate exclusively for the financial advantage of its taxpaying residents.

The Mount Laurel decision was upheld later in 1975 by the U.S. Supreme Court, which refused to hear this appealed case based exclusively on state law. Courts in other states are bound to be influenced and may well be persuaded to take a more active role and render similar verdicts. Yet, in realistic terms Mount Laurel is a hollow victory and will hardly result in meaningful immediate change. Whereas New Jersey law now states that lower-income housing is required, public funds are not available to subsidize its building, an absolute necessity because this type of suburban construction is a money-losing proposition for private builders. Moreover, the Mount Laurel decision has been diluted by later court rulings in New Jersey that limit its impact to those municipalities not already built up as single-family residential areas.

Petaluma, California

The recently resolved legal conflict over zoning in the outer San Francisco suburb of Petaluma (Fosburgh, 1975) centered around a municipality's right to determine the need to slow its own growth, and act accordingly by sharply limiting the supply of new housing for nonresidents. A local zoning ordinance restricted new housing to only 500 units annually for 5 years in order to "shape orderly growth" and safeguard the "small-town character" of the community. A coalition of builder organizations initiated the Petaluma case in 1972 after the ordinance was approved in a local referendum; since the lawsuit was brought on constitutional grounds it was pursued in the federal courts. In 1974 the U.S. District Court of San Francisco ruled in favor of the plaintiffs and declared the ordinance unconstitutional because it abridged the Fourteenth Amendment equal-protection-under-the-law provision by denying citizens the right "to travel and to settle wherever they wished." On the first appeal, however, the U.S. Appellate Court in 1975 overturned the lower-court ruling and let the original ordinance stand on the ground that Petaluma's "public welfare" as a community overrode the more general societal right to travel. By deciding on final appeal to refuse to intervene in the case in 1976, the U.S. Supreme Court upheld the appellate court decision and legitimized this use of zoning to limit new housing.

Although the Petaluma case was essentially an environmental clash between builder and conservationist interests, the final court decision was significant because it appears to remove a community's obligation to provide for regional housing needs in planning its future development. By further restricting supply, the cost of housing in Petaluma will become that much higher and effectively exclude all but the affluent. Moreover, scores of other suburban communities watched the case with interest, and many in California are following suit by implementing their own "grow slow" zoning ordinances (Jensen, 1976). This slow-growth technique is also gaining popularity in other states, most prominently in Boulder, Colorado, near Denver, which in 1977 instituted a highly publicized yearly quota of only 450 new dwelling units in order to restrict local growth to 2 percent annually.

Hartford and Its Suburbs

The growing federal involvement in the legal struggle to open the suburbs is underlined in the case of Hartford, Connecticut, and its suburbs (Fellows, 1975; 1976). In 1975, the central city successfully obtained a federal district court injunction to prevent payment of more than $4 million in community development funds which had been awarded to seven suburban towns by the U.S. Department of Housing and Urban Development (HUD). Hartford's lawsuit claimed that 90 percent of the metropolitan poor were concentrated within its boundaries and that these federal funds should therefore be used to relieve some of that city's heavy regional burden of public housing and to provide social services for low-income families (the suburbs intended to use this federal aid for building new sewers, roads, and parks). The local U.S. District Court sided with Hartford in 1976 by making the original temporary injunction permanent, but on the narrow ground that HUD had violated the federal Community Development Act of 1974 by waiving application requirements on projections of low-income population growth in the suburban communities. The waiver was permitted by HUD because appropriate data were difficult to obtain, a liberty the court refused to sanction since the 1974 law "clearly states, as one of its objectives, the spatial deconcentration of lower income groups, particularly from the central cities" (Fellows, 1976, p. 58).

Since HUD was processing at least 3000 applications for community development assistance from all parts of the United States in 1975, many of them involving similar city/suburb competition, the Connecticut decision could have had wide impact. However, as one judge in the Hartford case conceded, the communities involved were eligible to reapply for the same funding provided that they attached the necessary low-income projections, and some of these suburban municipalities have indeed done so after making the required revisions in their applications. Although the city of Hartford again challenged these reapplications by suing the suburban towns to provide fully detailed information on their declared intentions to provide low-income housing, the U.S. Supreme Court in 1978 terminated the matter by declining to review a 1977 appellate court decision which ruled that Hartford had insufficient legal interest concerning internal planning in municipalities lying outside the central city.

Metropolitan Chicago

The increasing federal presence and the widening of the legal movement to open the suburbs through nonzoning cases is further demonstrated by the U.S. Supreme Court's 1976 decision in *Hills* v. *Gautreaux* (Farrell, 1976). The black plaintiffs had brought suit against HUD and the Chicago Housing Authority in 1966 on the grounds that the agencies, by restricting construction of low-cost housing almost exclusively to black inner-city neighborhoods, had perpetuated racial segregation in that city. The unanimous Supreme Court ruling in the Gautreaux case agreed that this government confinement policy violated the constitutional rights of blacks, and affirmed that federal courts can order HUD to locate subsidized low-income housing in white suburbs to relieve urban racial segregation. HUD had argued that it had no authority to interfere in local government affairs by locating public housing in suburban communities, especially when the latter had not been found guilty of practicing racial or economic discrimination. The high court, rejecting the notion that the central city/suburb border is a barrier to remedies for segregation, maintained that HUD could intervene because suburban municipalities were still free to exercise fully their local land control powers through zoning.

The last qualification, of course, allows each suburb to block low-income housing and therefore renders the Gautreaux case but another hollow victory that is unlikely to open the suburbs in the near future. HUD cannot require suburbs to accept low-cost housing, and the burden of proof still rests with the litigant to show that the federal government has practiced discriminatory use of housing subsidy monies (Oser, 1976). A more recent Supreme Court action involving the Chicago suburb of Arlington Heights reinforces the Gautreaux ruling. In question was a zoning ordinance that prohibited construction of multiple-family housing. When a local religious order brought in a builder to construct a low- and moderate-income apartment complex on its own land, the village refused to permit rezoning. The builder and two local black residents eligible to move into the planned complex then filed suit charging unconstitutional race discrimination (Arlington Heights in 1970 contained just under 65,000 whites and 27 blacks). Nevertheless, the Court in 1977 ruled against them on the grounds that local government actions were not unconstitutional solely because they resulted in a racially disproportionate impact. Thus, once again, proof of discriminatory intent, notoriously difficult to obtain in such cases, was required to reverse the zoning status quo. The Supreme Court, however, did not totally reject the arguments of the open housing advocates: the case was, in part, returned to the lower courts for reconsideration as a possible violation of the 1968 federal Fair Housing Act. But a major legal breakthrough is not expected because Arlington Heights is a narrowly drawn case affecting only federally subsidized public housing, for which little funding is likely to be available in the foreseeable future.

Thus, the question of suburbia's regional role in sharing in the solution of central city problems is still unresolved. Emotions run high because suburbs wish to preserve the present character of their neighborhoods. As a result, a growing number of suburban municipalities are forgoing application for large sums of federal community development aid which is contingent upon planning for local low-cost housing (a few of Hartford's suburban communities chose not to reapply for federal funds rather than prepare low-income population projections). One danger inherent in the widening suburban nonparticipation in federal housing programs is that large cities may be the ultimate losers, because if the suburbs no longer apply, their congressional representatives (who constitute a sizable voting bloc in the House) will increasingly vote not to appropriate community development funds.

The Future Legal Outlook

Although the Mount Laurel, Petaluma, Hartford, and Chicago cases represent the latest confrontations in the continuing legal struggle against suburban exclusionism, no clear pattern has emerged from these decisions. The refusal of the U.S. Supreme Court to consider Mount Laurel's final appeal confines exclusionary zoning matters to the state courts for the foreseeable future. Perhaps state-level efforts can eventually result in more open housing if new legal mechanisms are vigorously enforced. Besides fair housing laws, a number of such innovative tools have emerged in the 1970s. One increasingly common technique in Pennsylvania and a few other states is the use of *curative amendments* to remedy local zoning ordinances: if a litigant can demonstrate that an ordinance is exclusionary (more liberal standards than the strict-constructionist Supreme Court interpretation have so far applied), the courts will alleviate grievances by granting the property owner a "cure" to nullify that land-use restriction.

As the recent legal record has shown, the involvement of the federal government as the leading funder of low-income housing is growing steadily. Even though large additional commitments toward constructing public housing are politically unlikely, Washington can and does exert considerable local influence in the disbursement of community development monies. At this writing, the Carter Administration's Department of Housing and Urban Development is pursuing this leverage more aggressively than its predecessors in order to encourage wider zoning of suburban land for lower-income housing. However, even if successful, this effort alone will probably not result in any dramatic change in the status quo (Figure 3.7). Thus, the major legal conflict over low-income housing is certain to continue in the absence of a landmark court ruling, and the issue of open versus closed suburbs is likely to remain one of the nation's major metropolitan crises for some time to come.

'Patience, it'll melt. It's only been 200 years.'

Figure 3.7 One view of HUD's legal effort to open the suburbs to lower-income groups in the 1970s. (Source: © Tony Auth, *The Philadelphia Inquirer*, April 22, 1976.)

The Failure of Voluntary Housing Programs to Open the Suburbs

As the legal struggle over exclusionism has intensified since the late 1960s, a simultaneous movement involving local housing programs to open the suburbs voluntarily has been under way in certain urban areas. At the state level, Massachusetts and New York have been prominent. The former has endorsed mixed-income publicly subsidized housing projects as well as a 1969 "antisnob" zoning law which aims at a one-tenth low-income dwelling proportion in new developments, and the latter developed an ambitious plan for massive aid to open wealthy Westchester County through the state's Urban Development Corporation. Metropolitan-level programs have also been announced, with some modest initial successes reported for Minneapolis–St. Paul, Indianapolis, and Washington, D.C.'s Maryland suburbs. Although planning strategies abound (see as an example, Downs, 1973), these and other less publicized efforts for reducing suburban economic segregation have been isolated and in the aggregate have accomplished very little. After 5 years under the new zoning law, almost no progress had been made in Massachusetts' suburbs toward meeting lower-income housing goals. In New York the much heralded Westchester campaign was abruptly canceled in 1973 in face of that county's overwhelming opposition. Indeed, resistance to lower-income housing has become so pronounced that by the late seventies not only were suburban municipalities around the nation giving up federal community development funding, but many local officials working to open their jurisdictions were being recalled and even harassed by vandalism and threats of physical violence.

The most advanced open housing plan of the 1970s has been implemented in metropolitan Dayton (Gruen and Gruen, 1972). This "fair share" plan was adopted in 1970 when, under the aegis of the Miami Valley Regional Planning Commission, the area's suburban municipalities reluctantly agreed to accept a limited amount of low- and moderate-income housing. By the end of 1974 more than half of the planned 14,000 residential units were open and occupied by lower-income families who had relocated from Dayton. These housing developments, widely scattered across many outlying communities, were given such typically suburban names as "Chevy Chase Village" and "Northlake Hills," and consist of a number of garden apartment complexes. As might be expected, there was considerable local resistance to the newcomers (Delaney, 1974b), and although many of them were enthusiastic about the extra living space, good schools, and recreational facilities, they were also bewildered by their new surroundings and the challenge of adjusting to them. Of particular concern were fear of going out at night, the absence of city-style social services, and mobility problems (public transportation was found to be useless and total reliance on the automobile was an experience new to most). Although long-time suburban residents have expressed surprise that their new neighbors appear to be taking good care of their properties and that only a small minority are black, there is much resentment and total avoidance of social contact with the lower-status newcomers.

A similar but far less ambitious experiment of this kind was being undertaken in suburban Chicago in the late 1970s (Reinhold, 1978). As a result of the Gautreaux decision, HUD, assisted by a private open housing organization, is placing a very limited number of low-income black Chicago families (21 per month) in apartments throughout suburbia with federal financial aid used to make up the higher rent differential. With only 376 families relocated through May 1978, the initial results were inconclusive and HUD was optimistic about expanding the program to New York and other metropolises. Nevertheless, negative feedback was reported from the first wave of new suburbanites. As with suburban Dayton's lower-income newcomers, coping with the hostile social environment, lack of sensitivity toward those on public welfare, and the automobile-based existence were proving difficult. Heightening these burdens in the outer-Chicago-ring experiment, of course, was the added element of racial bias. Besides harassment encountered by the newcomers themselves, their unwelcome institutional benefactors also faced difficulties in finding sufficient dwelling units in the context of the dualistic housing market and a total lack of cooperation from local suburban governments.

By the mid-seventies it had become evident that voluntary housing programs were not succeeding in opening the nation's suburbs to lower-income groups, a conclusion endorsed by a 1975 conference of leading urbanologists at California's Center for the Study of Democratic Institutions (Lindsey, 1975). Failure to increase the access of low- and moderate-income families to suburbia was attributed to the unremitting resistance of middle- and upper-income communities whose residents feared property value losses, erosion of suburban lifestyles, and the proliferation of violent crime and other serious urban problems; recent government actions and court decisions that allow exclusionism to persist; the policies of federal administrations and actions of Congress that have practically eliminated lower-income housing subsidies; and the recent spread of the nationwide grass-roots "slow-growth" movement. Looking ahead, the conferees were pessimistic that meaningful progress toward open housing would be achieved in the foreseeable future, and based what little optimism they had upon vague hopes of massive new federal aid combined with the development of more effective instruments of metropolitan government.

In the late seventies, harder-nosed assessments have produced an even gloomier outlook concerning these efforts to alleviate suburban economic segregation. The consensus today (see Chow, 1980) is that housing programs which break ground for lower-income people regardless of their social and employment needs are unlikely to produce stable communities, certainly one lesson learned from the suburban Dayton and Chicago experiences. If the concept of equal opportunity in housing is to have a fair chance of succeeding, it must include realistic measures that will reduce the income, training, and employment disparities to be discussed later in this chapter.

Housing Price Inflation and the Reinforcement of Closed Suburbia

Sharply accentuating the already formidable racial and economic barriers encountered by disadvantaged metropolitan groups seeking to enter residential suburbia is the unremitting price inflation that has dominated the suburban housing market since the early 1970s. We are about to see that this additional obstacle makes even more remote the already dim prospects for lessening suburban segregation in the social milieu of the Mosaic Culture's new localism. This growing problem has been fleetingly considered at several places earlier in this chapter: let us now take a closer look at the dimensions of the current housing crisis and its already decisive impact on overall residential mobility.

We have seen that exclusionary zoning has always artificially depressed the supply of most good-quality suburban housing that was warranted by market demand, but the present shortage of such residential accommodations is intensified by mutually reinforcing economic trends which have emerged since the late 1960s. Rapidly escalating costs of labor, materials, financing, and particularly land have together produced a doubling in the price of a new house from 1969 to 1977 (Figure 3.8). Nonetheless, housing demand continues to grow, with the building industry hard-pressed in many areas to keep new house starts at the desired level. The most extreme acceleration of the inflationary spiral can be observed in suburban California: many housing developers are faced with overnight campouts by hordes of prospective buyers, bribery, and even the need to run lotteries in the selling of their woefully undernumbered new single-family homes, and as competition drives up prices and appreciates real estate values in lightning-like fashion, more and more homeowners are turning into speculators ready to speedily resell for an immediate profit. Throughout the nation an overriding psychological force threatens to further exacerbate the problem today and in the future:

> Americans have come to look on a home of their own—and a pretty big, detached, single-family house at that—as not just a desire but a

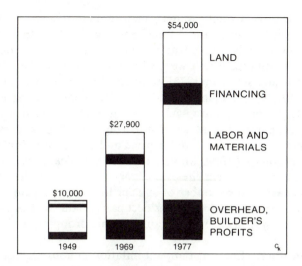

Figure 3.8 The skyrocketing costs of the single-family house since the end of the 1960s. (Data source: National Association of Home Builders.)

need and almost a right. They are being unrealistic. To shelter the entire nation in spaced-out, single-family houses near metropolitan centers would be a physical impossibility; to house even a substantial portion that way is turning out to be enormously expensive (*Time*, Sept. 12, 1977, p. 53)

In the late seventies, the housing price situation was so fluid that any attempt to gauge its ultimate directions would soon become outdated. Instead, we present a brief statistical portrait as of early 1978 (based largely on the 1977 survey undertaken by the Harvard–MIT Joint Center for Urban Studies [see Frieden et al., 1977] and summarized as the feature article in the September 12, 1977, issue of *Time*), which should be compared to existing trends at the time this is being read. From 1970 to 1976, in spite of the Great Recession of 1973–1975, new house prices rose by 90 percent and should come close to tripling for the decade as a whole, while used house prices increased 65 percent and will probably reach 100 percent by 1980; for the same 1970–1976 period, personal incomes could not keep pace and increased by just under 50 percent. By 1978, the national average price for a new house exceeded $56,000 (versus $24,000 in 1970, $36,000 in 1974, and $45,000 in 1976), while the mean for a used home was $39,000 (about double its 1970 level). Regional price variations reveal the selectivity of inflation in the costs of housing: the most expensive areas were southern California (average new house price $83,200, with an astonishing median of over

$110,000 in Orange County alone), metropolitan Washington, Houston, Chicago, Seattle, Denver, and Minneapolis, while Atlanta and the urban Northeast and Florida ranked at the lower end. As for housing styles, multiple-unit dwellings, which were so popular early in the 1970s (50 percent of all housing starts in 1973), were steadily giving way to a major resurgence of single-family homes and by 1977 accounted for only slightly more than 30 percent of nationwide housing starts. Nevertheless, suburban apartment occupancy was at an all-time high in 1978, and multiple-unit dwellings were experiencing similar price and rental inflation in the most popular metropolises (*Time*, May 1, 1978, p. 43). The latter may well be a result of some of the recent lifestyle changes we noted earlier, particularly the great increase in the number of smaller households occupied by never-married and divorced singles; recent occupancy data for Los Angeles confirm that trend, with dwellers per housing unit dropping from 2.2 in 1970 to 1.9 by 1975.

The immediate effects of rampant inflation in housing costs during the seventies may well become permanent. At this writing, no end of the upward spiral was in sight, and by the early 1980s the national average price for all detached houses was expected to climb beyond $80,000, with only 40 percent of the population able to afford one. With the peak of the postwar "baby boom" population cohort (people born between 1946 and 1968) about to enter the housing market, the dwelling-price problem is certain to continue intensifying. Moreover, even if a prosperous economy prevails, a monumental housing shortage is anticipated, because it is unlikely that the 10 million new dwelling units required nationally by 1985 can be built in time. Indeed, some signs of the growing dilemma are already visible: 50 percent of 1973 home-buying activity involved purchases by first-time owners, a ratio that declined more than one-third by 1978. The future outlook, then, is hardly encouraging, as it will soon be almost mandatory that one have equity in a dwelling place in order to survive in the fiercely competitive suburban housing market. In fact, people are already making adaptations to the changed housing situation: spending too large a proportion of their income on housing and forgoing other expensive purchases, such as furniture and recreational vehicles; assuming second jobs; putting off having children; and even "doubling up" with other families. Builders are also trying to offer cheaper accommodations where they can. In Orange County's Irvine, recently opened large houses actually contain nearly invisible partitions that separate the building into three attached townhouse units. Popular, too, is the single-story "no-frills" two- or three-bedroom house, but its prices vary considerably depending on local land values and omnipresent zoning restrictions (such a house in 1975 cost less than $20,000 in Florida but $25,000 and $40,000, respectively, in the suburbs of Pittsburgh and Washington).

The likeliest longer-term impact of the suburban housing cost crisis is the slowing of spatial and upward social mobility as individuals and families will be forced to delay or even set aside aspirations to move into increasingly unattainable, more expensive neighborhoods. Unable to afford such moves for several years, people will have little choice but to remain where they are. On the beneficial side, recommitment of financial and other resources to improve their present homes and residential enclaves will undoubtedly help to renew and even upgrade the existing suburban housing stock; another positive effect will surely be the strengthening of attachment to the microcommunity and perhaps the locality beyond, as already seen in the recent proliferation of such new well-attended social events as town picnics and holiday celebrations. However, as social congregations develop stronger internal ties, they can also be expected to intensify their defense of local residential turf against the entrance of undesirably perceived minority and lower-income groups. Within the congregation, too, people may become more cautious and family-centered as a "home-as-fortress" mentality hardens, making neighborhoods more conservative and even more hostile to socially unalike outsiders of all kinds (see *Time*, Nov. 4, 1974, p. 102).

Thus, reduced sociospatial mobility is the bottom line of the housing crisis, with the probable freezing in place of the outer city's current residential congregations only serving to enhance the balkanized suburbia-wide social structure of the Mosaic Culture. Census reports already indicate a significant slowing in the hypermobility of the 1950s and 1960s, which saw people move an average of once every 5 years. From 1970 to 1977 the annual percentage of movers in the U.S. population slipped from 19.1 to 17.7 percent, an especially meaningful drop since it heavily involved the most mobile, higher-educated professionals at a time when supposedly hypermobile post-college-age adults belonging to the postwar demographic-bulge cohort were constantly increasing their proportion of the nation's labor force (*Time*, Nov. 28, 1977, pp. 107–108). There is also evidence that besides the new economic constraints introduced by housing-price inflation, other forces are serving to heighten the shift in national values that is fueling the new trend toward immobility in the American population (*Time*, June 12, 1978, pp. 73–74). Among these are a renewed desire to sink local community roots, perhaps a natural by-product of the social maturation of the large portion of residential suburbia built in the early postwar period; younger family heads refusing corporate transfers, with the growing acquiescence of the companies themselves; more spouses than ever holding jobs, which means two careers affected by a possible move; older empty-nester households hanging onto their homes long after their living space needs decline; and once again, regional house price differentials (a recent transferee refused his new assignment when he discovered that the $80,000 he could sell his New Jersey house for would be only half the price of equivalent accommodations in southern California).

THE HUMAN CONSEQUENCES
OF SUBURBAN EXCLUSIONISM

The persistence and likely intensification of forces that maintain suburban racial and economic segregation is requiring disadvantaged metropolitan nonwhite and lower-income groups to concentrate even more heavily in the central cities. This is reflected in the continually widening income disparity between the residential populations of the central and outer city: in 1969 the central cities' percentage of suburban-ring median family income was 83.2—$9,157 to $11,343, but slipped to 81.0 percent in 1974—$11,003 to $14,007 (U.S. Bureau of the Census, 1975). Berry and Dahmann (1977, pp. 32–33) further reported that the 1970 differential between average family income in central city and outer ring, 17.8 percent, had enlarged by 1975, with the suburban mean advancing 4.6 percent while the average for central cities dropped 0.3 percent. They also observed an increasing localization of poverty in the central cities, whose proportion of national poverty rose by 3.2 percent from 1970 to 1975, with 10 percent of their families now receiving some form of public assistance payments as opposed to less than 4 percent in suburbia. Since suburban exclusionism is becoming even more deeply entrenched, the socioeconomic gap between the inner and outer segments of the metropolis is liable to widen further. The present and future human consequences of that trend now need to be weighed.

The Growing Geographical Mismatch between Metropolitan Housing and Employment Opportunities

For the underprivileged, the growing geographical disparity between housing and employment* within the contemporary metropolis has now reached crisis proportions (for a discussion of the issue, see Gold, 1972; Cox, 1973, pp. 62–66; Masotti and Hadden, 1974, pp. 311–318; Christian, 1975). The blue-collar and nonspecialized service jobs most compatible with the limited education and skills of low- and moderate-income central city residents, are precisely those which are suburbanizing the fastest without commensurate growth of replacement jobs in the city. Thus, with a shrinking employment base for workers with modest skills in the central city's economy, those jobs which have traditionally served as points of entry into the metropolitan labor force for the unskilled are simply disappearing.

Residential adjustment by this central city population to the dispersing job market is largely prevented by suburban housing barriers. A double standard often prevails in the outer city, where municipalities want high-

*The suburbanization of jobs is discussed in Chapter 4.

tax-ratable industries but not their lower-income work force. The Princeton, New Jersey, vicinity is typical: *The Wall Street Journal* reported that the surrounding 400-square-mile area contains land zoned for an additional 1.2 million manufacturing and research jobs, but only enough residentially zoned land to house 144,000 more workers (Harvey, 1972, p. 22). As a result, blue-collar city laborers must commute longer distances to keep up with the widening separation between residence and workplace. This is mirrored in the steady rise of reverse commuting, which nearly doubled in the largest SMSAs during the 1960s, and the trend has surely continued unabated since. Nonwhites seem to be especially affected: one study (McKay, 1973) based on data from six large SMSAs showed that the black inner-city rate of suburban commuting was fully 40 percent higher than that for whites.

Reverse commuting inconveniences abound (see Collura and Schuster, 1971; Miller and Garfinkle, 1973). As trip lengths increase, so do the money and time costs of the daily work journey. In many urban areas these costs have become so restrictive that they foster absenteeism. High job turnover rates also result, and in many metropolises the job retention rate following city-to-suburb relocation is as low as 10 percent. Moreover, there is usually little incentive to engage in reverse commuting because no opportunity to improve one's job status is involved; in other words, the same old job offers the same meager financial reward but now requires a more burdensome work trip. Community cohesion is threatened as well because out-commuting has a destructive impact on inner-city working-class neighborhoods, whose social unity relies on local friends and acquaintances being employed together at nearby factories (Westcott, 1977). Mobility problems also aggravate metropolitan spatial injustices for low- and moderate-income city residents, particularly blacks (see Rabin, 1973). These groups own far fewer automobiles, a critical factor since more than 90 percent of all suburban travel is by car. Because universally inadequate public transportation in the suburbs is accessible to only a tiny fraction of dispersed expressway-oriented employers, non-car-owning transit riders find job opportunities drastically limited in the outer city.

Despite these serious movement constraints, better transportation access to the suburban labor market is not the answer to improving the underemployment situation of inner-city workers. Recent studies (e.g., Bederman and Adams, 1974) have demonstrated that the journey to work is hardly the most important problem faced by lower-income central city residents. Rather, other obstacles to employment must be overcome, such as generally low and weakly marketable skill levels, a deficiency most correctable by intensive and widespread job-training programs, and racial and other biases in hiring practices (see Masters, 1975). Although specific research on *dualistic job markets* has yet to be undertaken, several studies show that as job opportunities suburbanize, residential and employment discrimination become mutually reinforcing. DeVisé (1976), in his survey of 19 Chicago suburbs employing blue-collar blacks, found that in a color-blind suburban housing market 25,000 more nonwhites would be employed beyond the 82,000 already at work. That finding extends the earlier work of Christian (1975), which demonstrated the tendency of manufacturers relocating from Chicago's ghetto between 1965 and 1971 to choose distant suburban sites (nearly two-thirds moved at least 10 miles away) in communities that contained negligible black populations (93 percent of the relocated jobs went to municipalities that were less than 1 percent black). Both studies support Harrison's (1974) arguments that even if blacks were freely able to residentially suburbanize, they still would not have access to the same employment opportunities as whites, because blacks would only be offered the same lower-quality jobs in suburbia that they are now offered in the central city. And even when blacks do possess white-collar job skills, discrimination is still apparent: Rose's (1976, p. 218) map of commuting destinations for Glenarden's workers (see occupational structure in Table 3.1), quite unlike neighboring white communities, shows a decided bias in favor of the city of Washington rather than workplaces in the better-paying Maryland and Virginia suburbs.

Also more important than transportation constraints are communication barriers that impede central city residents seeking work in the suburban ring: information flows on job openings are almost always restricted to suburban newspapers and employment agencies, and job searches in suburbia are virtually impossible without an automobile. Overall, the multiplicity of these hindrances amounts to considerable inequality in access to suburban job opportunities. Without programs to train the disadvantaged in the job skills required in today's changing metropolitan economy, their future outlook in the labor force is bleak because, as we shall see in Chapter 4, less-skilled manufacturing employment is becoming increasingly scarce in the dawning postindustrial era. One immediate result is that a growing number of potentially employable city residents simply give up, and if present trends persist, inner-city blue-collar neighborhoods are certain to become expanding areas of chronic unemployment.

Other Consequences

A whole array of secondary impacts flows from the tightening residential concentration of lower-income groups in general, and blacks in particular, in the nation's central cities (see Cox, 1973, pp. 59–62; Rubinowitz, 1974, pp. 18–25). There are strong indications today that the trends identified in the late-1960s report of the President's Commission on Crimes of Violence have not been redirected and are indeed now producing the anticipated further metropolitan social fragmentation, heightened segregation by class and race, and polarization of attitudes on an increasing variety of urban issues. Moreover, the persistent lack of freedom of residential choice by minorities and the central city underclass who cannot meet the standards of the suburban filter means, in effect, that the outer ring of the metropolis is dictating living conditions to the inner.

Thus, what is beginning to emerge is the form of metropolitan social organization which the National Advisory (Kerner) Commission on Civil Disorders foresaw in 1968:

> [an overall] trend toward predominantly black cities surrounded by almost entirely white suburbs—the geographic manifestation of "two nations, one black and one white, separate and unequal" . . . Within two decades [of the mid-1960s] this division could be so deep that it would be almost impossible to unite . . . [and would entail] a conclusive repudiation of the traditional American ideals of individual dignity, freedom, and equality of opportunity.

In fact, to a growing number of observers we have already become two societies, separate and unequal. *New York Times* columnist Tom Wicker (1977) saw the New York City blackout riot of July 13, 1977, as the fulfillment of the Kerner Commission's prophecy, the result of promises made to the black community in the late sixties that went unkept in the economically unstable seventies as whites came to realize the complexity of the problem and the degree of commitment, sacrifice, and discomfort required to solve it. It is still too soon to gauge the overall impact on black America of the arrival of a fully dualistic society. One immediate response, according to former N.A.A.C.P. executive director Roy Wilkins (U.S.N.W.R., 1976), is that we are now headed for a (largely nonviolent) racial showdown because change for the better in housing, jobs, income, and education is coming too slowly for the upwardly mobile segment of the younger black generation.

Increasing black loss of faith in the system is occurring despite the spillover suburbanization of middle-class blacks in certain metropolitan areas. As we have seen, racial change here is not accompanied by the lowering of housing barriers between whites and blacks. George Sternlieb (U.S.N.W.R., 1971, p. 45), a leading student of the inner suburban zone of emergence, puts it this way:

> The prime question which is not being approached in our day is this: Will this old suburb serve as a satisfactory safety valve for the [black] guy or will it over a period of time convince him that all this business of trying to make it in America really doesn't work? I am afraid that the odds right now are on the later.

A corollary of this trend is the crucial implication it has for the fate of the central city, an issue to be treated at the end of Chapter 4. With increasing white middle-class abandonment, the problem of retaining the middle-income *black* in the city may eventually loom large, because the only thing keeping that group there now is that there is no better outer residential area currently available.

Summary

This chapter has surveyed the changing structural organization of contemporary suburban society and its negative human consequences. The dynamics that shape residential congregations are now becoming more complex as new urbanization influences emerge in the final quarter of the twentieth century. These forces are no longer restricted to the relatively simple formation of broad social groupings by economic class alone, but now operate to produce a highly refined spectrum of much more specialized communities of interest. This fragmentation into new, staunchly defended social districts is most clearly seen in the lifestyle communities of the Mosaic Culture, whose major congregation types were contrasted and compared. Residential suburbia also contains concentrations of the racially and economically disadvantaged, who are involuntarily segregated from their surrounding congregations by powerful social barriers. Their presence is hardly surprising because

> The fundamental process at work in American [metropolises] are those of congregation and segregation. . . . In times of striking change, both are jointly at work so that a new congregation (an active process) leads automatically to a new segregation (a passive process). It is in this distinction that the basic injustice of segregation is to be found (Vance, 1976, p. 44).

Black suburban trends and settlement types are dominated by the persistence of dual housing markets that residentially separate the races. White refusal to share social space with blacks is universal, and rising nonwhite frustration is nurturing a new inwardness that also augurs against rapid future territorial expansion of the metropolitan black community. Exclusionary zoning fosters the much wider economic segregation of all low- and moderate-income groups, a social status quo unlikely to be modified by legal actions in the foreseeable future. And precisely because this system has been so successful for the sizable majority of metropolitan households able to benefit from it, we can hardly expect suburbanites to voluntarily initiate change. Finally, disastrous inflation in the price of housing in the outer city is certain to reinforce the suburban filter as an already strong movement toward reduced mobility is accentuated and suburbia becomes less susceptible than ever to social change of any kind. The immediate human consequences of the new metropolitan reality are a growing spatial mismatch between housing and employment opportunities and the realization of a nearly complete racially dualistic society. Without major public and private intervention, the longer-term urban future may hold in store even more serious problems and social impacts.

Most of suburbia's intensifying social problems stem from the growing inequities catalogued throughout this chapter. Within the ever more heterogeneous and balkanized residential fabric of the outer city, less-advantaged groups encounter mounting difficulties in their effort to obtain the amenities that contemporary suburban life has to offer. Besides blacks and those with incomes insufficient to pass through the suburban filter, other racial minorities and under-privileged groups are increasing their presence in the outer metropolitan ring. Chow (1980) has studied the access of suburban San Francisco's Chinese, Filipino, and Japanese residents to housing and employment opportunities in the Bay Area and found barriers almost identical to those encountered by blacks. Across the continent, New York City's Puerto Rican community is experiencing both spillover suburbanization of the middle class from the North Bronx into southernmost Westchester County and the refusal of whites in those aging inner suburbs to stay and share local social space with the newcomers (Severo, 1977). Thus, pending confirmation through badly needed additional research, it may well be that the black suburban experience is typical of conditions faced there by all ethnics of color (see also Siembieda, 1975). In addition to minority groups, suburbia contains a growing proportion of the nation's elderly—21.5 percent in 1970—many of whom are nonaffluent (see Taylor, 1976). And, although often discussed in local and regional transportation, housing, and community plans, suburbia's youth, women, and handicapped are among additional groups experiencing various social problems.*

Viewed in juxtaposition to the central city, other potential social problems come into focus. While lower-income groups are increasingly concentrated in the old metropolitan core, the costs of the growing city/suburban income disparity are not borne equally. The central city is hit harder because it must increase social services as

---

*The transportation problems resulting from limited automobile access for each of the group categories identified in this paragraph, with some emphasis on the suburbs, are reviewed in Muller (1975).

its local tax base shrinks. However, fragmentation of suburbia's political map also causes cost inequities within the outer ring because municipal tax-service ratios can and do vary enormously from one jurisdiction to another. Quality of local services usually ranks higher in the outer city, but steadily rising property and other taxes are necessary to keep abreast of inflating costs in their provision. Demographic change foretells further dissatisfaction: falling enrollments necessitate education program cutbacks and even closing schools, often beginning in the more affluent municipalities into which today's younger families cannot afford to buy. Many observers are also predicting that as the urbanization of the suburbs proceeds apace, central-city-type urban problems such as violent crime will intensify, although the on-going renewal and upgrading of older suburbs may well help ameliorate that threat.* A greater acceptance of planning in suburbia would undoubtedly help solve problems caused by disorderly development, but the widespread rejection of such current planning concepts as new towns and cluster housing is resulting in a growing vacuum as the planners retreat in many parts of the nation.

Suburban society and its social problems are also increasingly influenced by the massive and unremitting intrametropolitan deconcentration of urban activities that has been under way since the 1960s. The final chapter will survey the dimensions and implications of that transformation, and the emerging economic structure of the late-twentieth-century American metropolis.

SUGGESTED READINGS

BERGER, BENNETT M. *Working-Class Suburb: A Study of Auto Workers in Suburbia* (Berkeley: University of California Press, 1960).

BERRY, BRIAN J. L. *The Human Consequences of Urbanisation* (New York: St. Martin's Press, 1973), Chap. 2.

BERRY, BRIAN J. L., CAROLE A. GOODWIN, ROBERT W. LAKE, AND KATHERINE B. SMITH. "Attitudes toward Integration: The Role of Status in Community Response to Racial Change," in Barry Schwartz, ed., *The Changing Face of the Suburbs* (Chicago: University of Chicago Press, 1976), pp. 221–264.

DOWNS, ANTHONY. *Opening Up the Suburbs: An Urban Strategy for America* (New Haven: Yale University Press, 1973).

---

*The latest crime data still show a persistently significant difference between central city and suburban criminal activity, with less violent crimes against property predominant in the metropolitan ring.

FARLEY, REYNOLDS, HOWARD SCHUMAN, SUZANNE BIANCHI, DIANE COLASANTO, AND SHIRLEY HATCHETT. "Chocolate City, Vanilla Suburbs: Will the Trend toward Racially Separate Communities Continue?" *Social Science Research,* 7 (1978), 319–344.

FISCHER, CLAUDE S. *The Urban Experience* (New York: Harcourt Brace Jovanovich, Inc., 1976).

KAPLAN, SAMUEL. *The Dream Deferred: People, Politics, and Planning in Suburbia* (New York: The Seabury Press, 1976; paperback edition published by Vintage Books, 1977).

MICHELSON, WILLIAM H. *Man and His Urban Environment: A Sociological Approach* (Reading, MA: Addison-Wesley Publishing Company, Inc., 2nd rev. ed., 1976).

OWENS, BILL. *Suburbia* (San Francisco: Straight Arrow Books, 1973).

ROSE, HAROLD M. *Black Suburbanization: Access to Improved Quality of Life or Maintenance of the Status Quo?* (Cambridge, MA: Ballinger Publishing Company, 1976).

SUTTLES, GERALD D. "Community Design: The Search for Participation in a Metropolitan Society," in Amos H. Hawley amd Vincent P. Rock, eds., *Metropolitan America in Contemporary Perspective* (New York: Halsted Press for Sage Publications, 1975), pp. 235–297.

VANCE, JAMES E., JR. "The American City: Workshop for a National Culture," in John S. Adams, ed., *Contemporary Metropolitan America,* Vol. 1: *Cities of the Nation's Historic Metropolitan Core* (Cambridge, MA: Ballinger Publishing Company, 1976), pp. 1–49.

chapter **4**

The Suburbanization
of Economic Activity
and the Rise of the
Multicentered Metropolis

*Regional [shopping] centers have turned into minicities.
. . . The result has been a little-remarked but momentous
change in urban geography. The economic magnetism of
[these] great centers has split asunder the functions of
most large cities. . . . Instead of a single nucleus there
are several: the old downtown and a band of satellite
centers on the periphery.*

Gurney Breckenfeld

While suburban social congregations are evolving into important new community forms, it is the more dynamic forces shaping the location of nonresidential activity that are mainly responsible for the growing intra-metropolitan dominance of the outer city. The suburbanization of commerce and industry, under way for the first two-thirds of this century (Figure 2.6), has accelerated strikingly since the early sixties, and its intensification in the 1970s has resulted in a complete restructuring of the metropolitan economy. Retailing and the rapid rise of the catalytic regional shopping center led this latest and most vigorous episode of intraurban activity deconcentration. Following close behind was the dramatic upsurge in the suburbanization of employment, not only in manufacturing but increasingly in the metropolitan office industry, which constitutes the heart of today's postindustrial economy. Once content to locate at any interchange or other site convenient to the freeway network, suburban activities now gravitate toward each other. Accordingly, multifunctional urban cores or *minicities* have emerged swiftly in the outer city, and these major nodes now confer a greater degree of spatial order on the heretofore centerless distribution of production in the suburbs. This chapter will trace the individual paths whereby retailing and employment have dispersed through the outer city since 1960, the recent formation of minicities and their impact on the geographical organization of suburbia, and the rise of the multicentered metropolis in an age of tightening energy supplies.

THE SUBURBANIZATION OF RETAILING

Although rooted in the twenties and thirties, as we saw in Chapter 2, the suburbanization of retailing is essentially a postwar phenomenon. Growing slowly at first, intraurban decentralization of shopping activity advanced steadily through the 1950s. By the early sixties the takeoff point was reached, and there followed more than a decade of massive suburbanization that wholly transformed the retail trade function of the central city vis-à-vis its no

Table 4.1 Selected data on the suburbanization of economic activity in the 15 largest SMSAs

SMSA	Percent suburban share total jobs		Percent suburban share total SMSA retail sales		Percent suburban share total SMSA manufacturing employment	
	1960	1970	1963	1972	1963	1972
New York	28.8	35.9	32.9	55.2	19.1	53.4
Los Angeles*	47.8	54.3	58.7	60.0	63.9	64.0
Chicago	32.2	47.5	43.1	56.8	41.0	57.4
Philadelphia	37.0	51.8	56.6	66.7	50.5	59.3
Detroit	43.3	61.4	57.3	74.1	59.3	67.6
San Francisco	44.9	50.0	52.0	63.3	53.3	62.3
Washington, D.C.	36.2	54.9	57.9	76.3	55.8	64.7
Boston	55.5	62.2	68.8	76.3	71.8	78.2
Pittsburgh	64.0	63.7	65.9	77.0	70.0	76.1
St. Louis	39.3	58.0	62.5	77.2	50.3	62.0
Baltimore	34.1	49.9	41.9	61.5	45.4	68.3
Cleveland	28.3	46.0	45.2	69.0	39.7	51.3
Houston*	15.7	24.4	17.6	29.0	28.8	34.3
Minneapolis–St. Paul	23.6	41.1	38.5	62.9	32.7	45.3
Dallas*	24.4	29.0	28.8	58.6	21.2	53.6
Average	37.0	47.6	48.5	64.2	46.8	59.9

*Annexation of suburban territory since 1960.

SOURCES: Rosenthal (1974); 1963 Census of Business; 1972 Censuses of Retail Trade and Manufacturing; 1972 County Business Patterns.

longer subordinate outer metropolitan ring (see columns 3 and 4 in Table 4.1 and retail employment data in Table 4.2). We now review these stages in the recent evolution of suburban retailing dominance.

Postwar Shopping Center Development, 1945–1970

The expansion of postwar suburban retailing is really the story of the arrival and diffusion of the large shopping center. In the late forties and early fifties outlying retail centers spread slowly, particularly in the older metropolitan areas of the North and East, as consumer and retailer ties to the central city CBD were relinquished reluctantly. During those years only modest-sized neighborhood and community shopping centers appeared. However, once the final break with downtown was made by 1960, the much larger scale

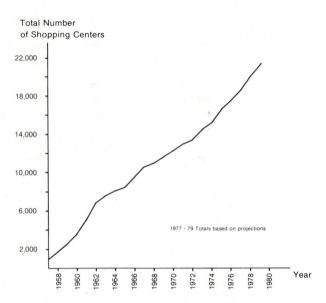

Total Number
of Shopping Centers

1977 - 79 Totals based on projections

Year

Figure 4.1 The growth of shopping centers in the United States, 1957–1979. (Data source: International Council of Shopping Centers.)

regional center quickly came to dominate suburban retailing. The spread of shopping centers during the last quarter-century is shown in Figure 4.1, with large regional centers (exceeding 250,000 square feet of selling space) accounting for a consistent 5 to 7 percent of each yearly total. The rapid takeoff at the end of the 1950s coincides with the shift from the *consequent* to the *catalytic* stage of postwar shopping center evolution, or the transition from stores passively following a decentralizing urban population to the dynamic leadership of center developers actively shaping the growth of the outer suburban ring by attracting people and other activities to locate around their new malls (Epstein, 1967).

The consequent stage of retail deconcentration (1945–1960) entailed the leisurely outward drift of stores in the wake of new suburban residential development. A pronounced reluctance of retailers to move large stores into the suburbs characterized this period. The continuing success of downtown stores did not immediately require testing the unknown waters beyond the city line. Mass-merchandising concepts themselves were relatively new in early postwar America, and the large chains wanted more experience in refining these selling approaches at established city locations before undertaking major commitments in the untried suburban market. As a result, through the late fifties most outlying retail centers were small isolated clusters of moderate-order convenience goods establishments interspersed with a few widely scattered concentrations of high-order shoppers goods stores.* The typical commercial development of this period was a highway-oriented grouping of retail facilities usually strung out haphazardly along a major artery leading out of the city. In the absence of serious competition from the major chains, local retailers thrived on these highway strips, where the formula for success involved little more than a main-road location, a salable product, and free parking at the front door.

Although small shopping centers and commercial strips dominated, innovative consequent-era developers began to achieve success with their relatively few regional centers built in the inner suburbs before 1955 (prototypes such as Boston's Shoppers World, Seattle's Northgate, and Los Angeles's Lakewood). This message, however, spread very slowly in the 1950s, as "safe" market development strategies prevailed and big suburban stores were opened only after an outlying area was settled and threshold demands were comfortably surpassed.† As department stores began to enter suburbia in the late fifties, they cautiously avoided each other. However, when they saw that their competitors chose nearby locations which quickly divided business in the local market, they soon concluded that it made better sense to congregate in bigger single centers and meet the competition head-on as they had always done downtown. This learning process completed, the consequent era came to a sudden end in the early 1960s as the regional shopping center transformed suburbia's retailing.

The shift to the catalytic stage of retail decentralization (1960–1970) was accomplished swiftly with the recognition of the full economic potential of the expanding suburban marketplace, increasingly settled by the more affluent segments of the metropolitan population. Steadily rising real incomes, fueled by the booming aerospace-led economy of the middle and late sixties, created a virtually insatiable suburban demand for durable consumer goods. With almost no preexisting retail facilities in the burgeoning outer suburbs, huge capital investments were easily attracted from life insurance companies and other major financial institutions. Not surprisingly, regional shopping centers quickly sprang up at the most accessible highway junction locations as their builders strived to make them the focus of all local development.

The catalytic strategy was highly successful, and most new malls indeed became magnetic attractions in their suburban sectors. Typical of this new

---

*The order of a good is its geographical range or the distance that consumers are willing to travel to purchase it; a hierarchy of such ranges exists, so that higher-order goods draw customers from wider surrounding areas than do lower-order goods. Low-order *convenience* goods are everyday items such as food, newspapers, and gasoline, which are in frequent demand; high-order *shoppers* goods are expensive items such as furniture, major appliances, and automobiles, which are demanded less often and involve comparison shopping.

†The *threshold* demand is the minimum number of potential customers residing within the geographical range of a retail good to enable the sale of that good at a profit.

growth pole function was the Rouse Corporation's large suburban Philadelphia shopping facility at what is now Cherry Hill, New Jersey (Figure 4.12),
which opened in 1961 and immediately drew big shopping crowds as well as
the attention of sightseers and developers throughout the Northeast. Locally,
Cherry Hill Mall sparked the rapid urban growth of South Jersey and provided a much-needed focus for this otherwise sprawling residential area; in
fact, the surrounding community was so impressed that its citizens voted to
rename their municipality in honor of the new shopping center. Through
widely repeated expressions of this sort, suburban residents were signaling
their growing perception of new shopping malls as pacesetting, prestige-laden
places. These sentiments were not lost upon commercial developers, who by
the end of the 1960s were openly capitalizing on the now glamorous images
projected by suburban retail centers.

These developers preferred larger sites in the more distant suburbs, not
only to take advantage of lower land costs but also to resist encroachment by
parasitic discount houses and other highway strip facilities, which had by
now gravitated to roadsides leading to regional centers in the older inner
suburbs. Huge parking lots as well as a number of architectural and atmo-
spheric innovations (more important location factors than shopping trip
length in the all-but-frictionless freeway metropolis) were introduced in the
fierce competition to lure shoppers from ever-widening catchment areas.
Inevitably, mall size itself became a primary attractive force. No longer
content to merely repeat the familiar dual anchor department store/temper-
ature-controlled, enclosed two-level mall—innovated at Victor Gruen's
Southdale center outside Minneapolis in 1956—shopping center builders by
1970 had significantly broadened both the scale and range of functions of
their facilities and in the process helped revolutionize the geography of the
outer city.

The Superregional Shopping Mall
of the 1970s and 1980s

With increased mall size the leading criterion, most of the regional centers
built after 1970 are more aptly labeled *superregional* shopping facilities. At
the end of the decade, Woodfield Mall (Figure 4.3) in suburban Schaumburg,
Illinois, just northwest of Chicago's O'Hare International Airport was the
nation's—and the world's—largest. Its vital statistics underscore the
grandiose scale of these contemporary retail centers: four enormous anchor
department stores and 230 smaller shops occupying more than 2.2 million
square feet on three levels; 10,800 parking spaces serving over 100,000 visitors
daily; and an annual sales volume approaching $200 million.

Apart from its enlarged scale, the superregional shopping mall of the
eighties can also be distinguished from its forerunners by a subtle but critical
shift in primary emphasis from mass selling to serving a much wider spectrum

of the needs of suburbanites. Today's bigger retail centers have become convenient all-purpose places to go, and suburban lives are increasingly organized around them. After home and work, malls are now the third most popular place for spending one's time in the outer city:

> These meticulously planned and brightly enclosed structures . . . have taken the concept of one-stop shopping, as old as the ancient public market, and turned it into a virtual one-stop culture, providing a cornucopia of products nestled in an ecology of community, entertainment and societal identity (Kowinski, 1978, p. 33).

These new cultural, social, and communal functions of shopping centers merit closer attention.

As was noted above, the growing importance of the retailing environment itself in attracting shoppers became apparent to mall builders late in the catalytic era. By 1970 they had fully recognized that in addition to bigness customers most desired an enclosed, protected, predictable, and socially comfortable shopping space, and this quickly became the standard for their new superregional centers (see Harris, 1975). The most successful of these malls—such as Houston's Galleria (Figure 4.2) and Woodfield (Figure 4.3)—

Figure 4.2 Houston's Galleria, the last word in sumptuous mall architecture and environmental comfort. Built around an olympic-sized skating rink, this huge retail complex encompasses three anchor department stores, 200 high-quality shops, four office towers, two hotels, 18 restaurants, three nightclubs, four cinemas, a private athletic club, and a seven-level garage for over 10,000 cars. (Courtesy of the Galleria Center Association, Inc.)

Figure 4.3 The suburban shopping center as cultural focus: the Chicago Symphony Orchestra in concert at Woodfield Mall, Schaumburg, Illinois, 1974. The size of the audience attending this event was more than fifteen times the capacity of Orchestra Hall, the Symphony's downtown Chicago home base. (Source: © Robert M. Lightfoot III; courtesy the Chicago Symphony Orchestra.)

carefully blended this formula with striking architectural designs, so as to give renewed and strengthened meaning to Victor Gruen's (1973) earlier maxim that centers must be busy, colorful, stimulating, and full of variety and excitement. Some recent observers have even elevated the suburban mall to the status of major cultural event, an hypothesis elaborated by Kowinski (1978). In this view, shopping centers may appear as a pile of blocks from the parking lot, but once inside one enters a world of magic and entertainment. The mall is likened to a movie sound stage or Disney theme park (many new malls literally incorporate amusement park rides), a manufactured and manipulated environment in which only the best features of metropolitan life are retained while everything negative is filtered out. Management control is the key: not only is the right mix of stores crucial for shopping ambience, but constant vigilance over tenants maintains their immaculate appearance as well as a collective image of mall glamour. Whether or not the perception of "mall as culture" is of lasting significance remains to be seen, but there is no denying that it powerfully integrates the three ideal American community forms of village green, Main Street, and suburbia (see Meinig, 1979). Having demonstrated that superregional malls are the suburban counterparts of Main Street, we now further consider their equally important role as the outer city's village greens.

As malls have evolved into entertainment-filled shopping parks, their patrons are drawn as much by leisure-time activities as they are by retail goods for sale. Center managers, once reluctant to promote nonbuying behavior, now enthusiastically endorse recreational functions as being good for business. According to a Woodfield Mall spokesman

> We encourage housewives to come out and shop, have lunch, have their hair done, see a movie, shop some more, then meet their husbands after work for dinner—to spend their entire day here, in other words (U.S. N.W.R., 1973, p. 46).

To be sure, organized entertainment has always been a part of the suburban shopping center scene, as parades, exhibits, petting zoos, fireworks displays, and celebrities—many of whom travel the now nationwide mall circuit full-time—were used as "traffic builders" to increase sales. However, the diversity and richness of leisure-time experiences at malls today far transcends this trivia, as the superregional center has truly become the suburban equivalent of the central city downtown (Breckenfeld, 1972). This new cultural "hub" function is best typified in Figure 4.3, which shows the Chicago Symphony Orchestra and part of the crowd of 40,000 onlookers during a concert at Woodfield Mall. At other suburban malls around the nation one finds live theater, first-class restaurants, college courses, luxury high-rise apartment buildings, and tourists from around the world (the Galleria is Houston's leading attraction). Among the myriad of other nonretailing activities that are now commonly found at suburban shopping centers are religious services, psychological counseling, dentists, ice skating, tennis courts, voter registration, political campaigning, dieting and smoking-withdrawal seminars, health salons, library branches, public buildings of every sort, and just plain people-watching. The universal lifting or ignoring of local blue laws in the late 1970s has resulted in malls opening Sundays across the country—the last major chain holdout, Sears, yielded in 1978. This is but the latest testimony that these facilities have fully emerged as the social focal points of the suburban ring.

Long favored as informal gathering places, large malls are now becoming true community centers for their surrounding residential areas. At the same time, because of their outstanding accessibility, the superregionals are performing a similar role for the much wider outer urban realms they both serve and anchor. These communal functions are undoubtedly enhanced by the fact that malls are the only common turf in suburbia, one of the very few places anywhere in the outer city that encourage the coming together of large numbers of dissimilar people. Historian Neil Harris (1975, p. 24), in fact, attributes mall popularity to a direct reaction to the compartmentalization of residential suburbia, and psychologist Robert Coles observes that frequent visits to them is a necessary community ritual in which usually isolated individuals share common experiences, if only to see people and be seen by them (Warner, 1977, p. 16). For local municipalities malls now actively seek to enhance community spirit through such gestures as the offering of rent-free halls for lectures or social events, and free space for such activities as charitable fund drives, arts and crafts displays, and scouting events (including the use of mall corridors for overnight campouts). Shopping centers also cater to specific age groups. Although the conventional wisdom has it that teenagers cause widespread trouble, Millison (1976) exploded that myth in a comprehensive survey in which he found that fewer than 5 percent of the nation's mall owners reported problems with adolescents, and those who did conceded that they were minor. Far from discouraging that affluent suburban cohort, most owners seek to encourage teens to develop adult buying habits. Many centers sponsor special events for young people, such as the use of public rooms for dances. In fact, malls are now believed to be the most common place for meeting members of the opposite sex; the Galleria, for example, has a *national* reputation for this second to none! The elderly are another population courted by malls, even though less affluent seniors are far more likely to "hang out" rather than shop. Nonetheless, several centers arrange shopping trips for retired groups, offer them special sales hours, and provide equipment such as coin-operated machines for measuring blood pressure.

Undeniably, the trend toward larger regional malls has been one of the most spectacular successes in American suburban history: mall sales have nearly tripled since 1965, and the nation's 20,000-plus shopping centers now account for well over 50 percent of total U.S. annual retail trade. Moreover, superregional malls are so strong economically that they easily weathered the Great Recession of the mid-seventies without a single failure. The emergence of the outer city as America's retail pacesetter is also seen in the increasing attempts of central cities to emulate the suburban superregional (Warner, 1977). Large mall-type facilities have recently opened in a number of CBDs, most notably Boston (Faneuil Hall Market), Chicago (Water Tower Place), New Orleans (Canal Place One), and Los Angeles (Broadway Plaza). However, despite the badly needed infusion of new shopping activity downtown, these malls do little to improve the central business district's overall economic position: most are walled enclaves that do not fit well into the CBD environment, and they siphon off shoppers from other center-city retail-clusters while being unable to draw in suburban customers from beyond the central city's inner metropolitan realm. There is even evidence that these malls can have a negative social impact, as in the case of Chicago, where racial bifurcation of the CBD has occurred, with whites gravitating to the new shopping node around Water Tower Place while the old Loop south of the Chicago River is increasingly abandoned to the city's blacks.

Suburban Retailing in the Eighties: Saturation, Recycling, and Smaller Shopping Malls

Although the superregional mall was still diffusing across the country and many older centers were still adding big stores at the end of the 1970s, doubts have arisen as to how much longer the supersize suburban retailing phenomenon can continue. For one thing, three-level facilities such as Woodfield and outer San Jose's Eastridge reach the upper size limit that commercial developers acknowledge as the equivalent of a three-city-block walk from one's automobile. Moreover, huge suburban sites of 100 acres or more are no longer cheaply or easily assembled, and construction costs for giant malls now exceed $100 million. The uncertain energy situation also makes building in the far metropolitan fringes a much riskier proposition than it was a few years ago, as more than one exurban center owner has discovered. Closer-in suburban trade areas, of course, are by now saturated with large regional malls, and the few bypassed markets were rapidly being filled in during the late 1970s. Finally, the federal Environmental Protection Agency and local governments are increasingly taking developers to task for the pollution they claim is caused by major new centers and the spontaneous adjoining growth they trigger (U.S.N.W.R., 1974).

In response to these new constraints as well as to the downward filtering of innovative supermall architecture and milieus, an emerging trend toward smaller shopping centers is certain to intensify in the 1980s. Much building activity is now focused at the level in the suburban retail hierarchy below that of regional center, as middle-sized malls of 50,000 to 250,000 square feet are squeezed into the less extensive lower-order market areas lying between the biggest shopping centers. Some contain only a single anchor department store, and a growing number contain no big shops at all. Moreover, a new emphasis on greater specialization often accompanies this latest retailing trend: with diminished trade areas these smaller suburban malls and their stores appeal and cater not to the masses but to the specific socioeconomic and interest groups residing in surrounding areas. Thus, the immediate and widespread success of such facilities linked to the local Mosaic Culture may well indicate a growing societal detachment in retailing, too, as more and more suburbanites now prefer to shop mainly in the company of socially similar people. The specialization trend is further reflected in the increasing tendency of smaller malls to offer individualistic themes, such as exotic, rustic, or colonial motifs. Glamorous environments and prestigious images are essential for shopping center success today, and those which do not keep pace are likely to be winnowed out by the aggressive competition.

This lesson has not been lost on older suburban retail centers, as many have recently waged successful comebacks. This is especially true of inner suburbia, where upgrading and slower neighborhood turnovers present new economic opportunities that make center recycling highly worthwhile. Developers now acknowledge that while rapid suburban growth and turnover covered mistakes in the past, success today depends on tailoring their centers to the present population. Modernization efforts usually involve physical improvements, such as new enclosures, a complete refurbishing and more parking, and better services, which include longer hours, wider acceptance of credit cards, and a more appropriate mix of stores. Older suburban towns with still viable retail areas are undergoing renewal as well. By sprucing up, carefully adding the right kind of new shops and sufficient free parking space, many have begun to recapture a local clientele lost to big malls years ago through appeals to the nostalgia of shopping in a more simplified and intimate setting. Interestingly, the recycling movement has also filtered up to all but the newest supermalls: image strengthening has become a constant force there, too, in order to maintain positions of leadership in the fiercely competitive world of suburban retailing. In the late 1970s both Cherry Hill and the Galleria underwent major expansions, and the Tyson's Corner Center in Washington's Virginia suburbs began a massive enlargement that will make it the country's largest shopping complex by 1982.

In the last 15 years suburbia has become the nation's retail trendsetter. As early as 1969, New York's fashionable Lord and Taylor's opened its own high-prestige center of 25 stores in suburban Paramus, New Jersey, and claimed: "we certainly don't consider ourselves the Main Street of suburbia—we're its Fifth Avenue" (Morris, 1969, p. 9). By 1978, it was clear that even that Manhattan street had been eclipsed by the suburbs when *The New York Times* (Hollie, 1978) conceded that Beverly Hills' Rodeo Drive—pronounced "roe-DAY-oh"—had become the wealthiest and most sophisticated shopping place in America. And why not, for where else in the world could one find a local population whose average annual spending income exceeded $35,000, enough to support, in the space of three blocks, Tiffany's, Van Cleef and Arpels, Gucci, St. Laurent, Giorgio's, the Beverly-Wilshire Hotel shops, 50 other high-fashion stores, art galleries, the Brown Derby, and an outdoor cafe—complete with $8 hamburgers—where tables for people-watching may be rented at $300 per month?

THE INTRAMETROPOLITAN DECONCENTRATION OF EMPLOYMENT

The suburbanization of employment, a trend originating in the interwar era (Figure 2.6), has greatly accelerated since 1960. The dimensions of recent shifts in the suburban ring/central city share of total metropolitan jobs are recorded in the decennial census data displayed in Table 4.1 (columns 1 and 2). Detailed investigations reveal that central city job loses in the 1960s alone surpassed those of the preceding six decades (Hughes, 1974, p. 8). Moreover, the tilt toward the outer city affected all job categories: in 101 SMSAs studied by Berry and Kasarda (1977, p. 236) the 1960–1970 gain in blue-collar employment for the suburbs was 29 percent versus a nearly 13 percent loss for the central cities, while suburbia also outdistanced the central city in white-collar job gains, 67 to 7 percent. Although comparable 1980 data will not be available until late 1982, there is every indication that the suburban employment trend not only persisted but significantly intensified during the 1970s, with the nation's suburbs pulling ahead of the central cities in total number of jobs as long ago as 1973.

Comprehensive intercensal statistics on employment suburbanization are impossible to obtain because the U.S. Department of Labor in its monthly data series unwisely classifies metropolitan jobholders by place of residence rather than work. Nonetheless, the dimensions of intraurban employment dispersal in the 1970s are strongly suggested in other federal data compilations. The most useful is the *County Business Patterns* series published by the Census Bureau,* which permits the assembling of detailed private-sector job estimates for the eight metropolises—fortunately spanning the nation's major regions—whose central cities also happen to be counties or their equivalents. These data, grouped here into the major urban job sectors, are arrayed for 1970, 1973, and 1977 in Table 4.2; Table 4.3 records percentage changes within each central city and suburban economy. Both tables indeed confirm heightened and unremitting suburbanization *in every employment category*, not only in the older metropolitan areas of the North and East but also the rapidly maturing ones in the South and West (see Muller, 1980). Moreover, this conclusion is reaffirmed in numerous other studies based on reliable post-1970 data sets; for example, Hartshorn (1978, p. 44) reports that Atlanta's suburbs overtook the central city between 1970 and 1975 by advancing from 46 to 54 percent of the metropolitan employment total.

With a critical mass—greater than 50 percent of the SMSA total—of urban jobs deconcentrating in sector after sector, it is clear that the outer city has achieved dominance in metropolitan employment activity. Journey-to-work patterns especially reflect this passing of "bedroom suburbia": today's dominant commuting flows are suburb-to-suburb instead of suburb-to-central city trips, with reverse city-to-suburb daily movements becoming ever more important. The internal distribution of jobs within the suburbs is also changing as the outer city attracts the major share of urban employment. Rather than dispersing widely, the post-1970 trend is for jobs to increasingly cluster into new suburban centers and subcenters (Greene, 1977; Gruenstein,

---

County Business Patterns data are not strictly comparable to those reported in the much more accurate decennial population census because they are based on a less comprehensive definition of employment and a broader sampling scheme.

Table 4.2 Suburban percentage of SMSA employment, 1970–1977: private-sector changes in eight large metropolises

	1970	1973	1977		1970	1973	1977
Baltimore				*Philadelphia*			
Total employment	39.3	41.6	*53.2*[a]	Total employment	48.8	*51.6*	*59.5*
Manufacturing	47.4	48.8	*55.4*	Manufacturing	*54.5*	*56.4*	*65.5*
Wholesale trade	24.6	36.7	48.9	Wholesale trade	39.7	43.4	*59.6*
Retail trade	46.9	*50.9*	*65.0*	Retail trade	*55.9*	*59.4*	*66.7*
F.I.R.E.[b]	21.3	24.2	39.5	F.I.R.E.	31.0	35.2	45.5
Services	29.2	32.2	46.2	Services	42.7	46.3	*52.4*
Business services	20.2	23.4	*54.5*	Business services	38.2	41.6	*51.6*
Health services	21.3	24.7	39.3	Health services	46.1	*51.1*	*51.6*
Denver				*St. Louis*			
Total employment	33.3	37.4	47.1	Total employment	*51.6*	*54.4*	*65.2*
Manufacturing	45.8	47.6	*54.5*	Manufacturing	*53.9*	*54.9*	*61.3*
Wholesale trade	13.1	13.6	31.2	Wholesale trade	34.7	40.1	*58.7*
Retail trade	42.6	47.2	*58.5*	Retail trade	*63.4*	*66.3*	*77.8*
F.I.R.E.	17.0	31.2	32.9	F.I.R.E.	42.7	43.8	*54.1*
Services	30.3	33.7	41.1	Services	45.4	49.9	*64.8*
Business services	24.7	28.3	38.7	Business services	29.5	34.5	*62.0*
Health services	35.3	38.1	42.6	Health services	*52.0*	*55.9*	*66.3*
New Orleans				*San Francisco*			
Total employment	27.0	28.6	41.8	Total employment	*58.9*	*60.2*	*61.1*
Manufacturing	40.9	42.1	*51.6*	Manufacturing	*71.9*	*71.8*	*76.5*
Wholesale trade	20.7	24.0	45.8	Wholesale trade	*51.5*	*53.3*	*68.3*
Retail trade	34.1	36.4	*50.4*	Retail trade	*68.3*	*70.9*	*74.0*
F.I.R.E.	10.5	14.0	28.7	F.I.R.E.	33.7	38.6	37.6
Services	17.8	19.7	32.1	Services	*54.0*	*54.3*	*57.8*
Business services	19.6	20.2	30.6	Business services	46.8	49.0	*54.1*
Health services	22.1	22.6	36.3	Health services	*66.3*	*67.7*	*66.1*
New York[c]				*Washington, D.C.*			
Total employment	45.1	47.7	*52.3*	Total employment	*54.1*	*60.0*	*65.6*
Manufacturing	*55.5*	*56.8*	*62.1*	Manufacturing	*57.6*	*65.5*	*68.0*
Wholesale trade	40.5	44.0	*53.7*	Wholesale trade	*53.6*	*60.4*	*74.3*
Retail trade	*53.4*	*56.4*	*61.4*	Retail trade	*65.7*	*72.3*	*77.4*
F.I.R.E.	25.2	28.5	31.3	F.I.R.E.	47.7	*53.5*	*57.7*
Services	38.0	41.4	45.3	Services	43.4	47.4	*54.7*
Business services	32.0	36.7	41.8	Business services	*51.9*	*57.6*	*67.9*
Health services	47.0	49.2	*52.3*	Health services	*54.6*	*59.3*	*60.5*

[a] Italic entries indicate >50% suburban share.

[b] Finance, insurance, and real estate activity.

[c] Standard consolidated area.

SOURCE: *County Business Patterns.*

Table 4.3 Central city/suburban ring percentage changes in private-sector employment, eight large SMSAs, 1970–1977

	Baltimore		Denver		New Orleans		New York[b]		Philadelphia		St. Louis		San Francisco		Washington	
	C.C.	Ring	C.C.	Ring	C.C.	Ring	C.C.	Ring	C.C.	Ring	C.C.	Ring	C.C.	Ring	C.C.	Ring
Total																
employment	-20	+41	+12	+99	-6	+82	-21	+6	-21	+22	-25	+31	+10	+20	-9	+48
Manufacturing	-29	-2	+6	+50	-26	+13	-31	-10	-39	-4	-27	-1	-22	-1	-23	+21
Wholesale																
trade	-27	+115	+6	+220	-27	+138	-27	+24	-32	+51	-36	+71	-38	+27	-44	+38
Retail trade	-26	+57	+5	+100	+1	+99	-21	+9	-17	+31	-32	+38	-2	+30	-19	+44
F.I.R.E.[a]	-5	+128	+16	+178	-7	+217	-6	+28	-10	+68	-18	+31	+26	+49	-4	+44
Services	+1	+109	+29	+106	+13	+146	-3	+31	+9	+62	-18	+82	-19	+39	+11	+75
Business																
services	-17	+295	+58	+197	+43	+155	-9	+39	+8	+140	-18	+218	+23	+64	+1	+98
Health services	+19	+181	+25	+70	+25	+150	+19	+46	+29	+60	-1	+81	+42	+41	+42	+80

[a]Finance, insurance, and real estate activity.
[b]Standard consolidated area.
SOURCE: *County Business Patterns.*

1979). The emerging geographical pattern for metropolitan Washington in 1972 is mapped in Figure 4.4, and the clustering tendency may certainly be assumed to have intensified further since that time. It is this multicentered spatial structuring of employment activity that the reader should bear in mind as we seek to explain why recent job suburbanization has assumed this particular form.

Whereas evidence signaling the arrival of the outer city as the leading zone of intraurban employment is overwhelming, there is less agreement about the forces underlying this latest episode of job deconcentration. On the one hand, many observers (especially in the popular press) claim that simultaneous city losses and suburban gains are the result of a simple decentralization process in which central city jobs merely relocate to the outer city. On the other hand, more cautious students of the urban scene insist that what appears in the raw data to be a simple outward drift of employment is actually a response to a more complex amalgam of noncomplementary push and pull forces whereby rapid absolute central city job losses happen to coincide with the vigorous expansion of new jobs in the suburbs. There can be no argument about suburban dominance of *new* employment activity— 75 to 90 percent of the metropolitan jobs created since 1960 have been concentrated in the outer SMSA ring—but more research is required to understand precisely how the overall dispersal mechanism operates.

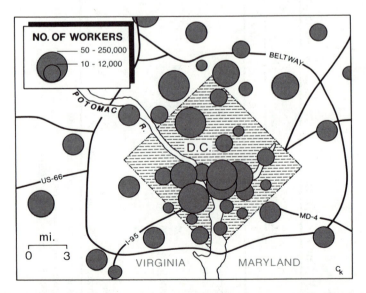

Figure 4.4 Major centers of employment in metropolitan Washington, 1972. (Source: Adaptation prepared by permission of the Metropolitan Washington Council of Governments.)

A key to the controversy is that, given the ongoing urbanization of the suburbs, there has been a pronounced erosion in metropolitan centrality as a locational attribute of the central city. This has affected different types of employment activity in different ways: whereas manufacturing has been quickest to respond to the new suburbanization forces, there are growing indications that office-based high-order service activities respond similarly. These trends are consistent with the two remaining dimensions in Berry's interpretation (1973b, pp. 48–56; see page 65) of contemporary urbanization: *progressive intrametropolitan time–space convergence* and the *maturation of the postindustrial economy*. We next treat these dimensions by considering, in turn, the locational dynamics of current manufacturing and office employment growth in the outer city.

The Suburbanization of Manufacturing since 1960

As we saw in Chapter 2, the deconcentration of manufacturing originated before the turn of the century. Centrifugal forces in and around downtown (congestion, lack of space, spiraling land values) had combined with peripheral centripetal impulses (cheap and abundant land, low taxes, good railroad access) to induce many manufacturers—particularly those engaged in the large-scale and mass production of standardized industrial goods—to suburbanize their facilities along axial intercity rail corridors. However, the great majority of lesser manufacturing operations, requiring steady contact with local buyers and other firms, as well as smaller plants whose marketing and industrial functions were geographically inseparable, remained in or near the CBD until well into the 1960s. Even the growing presence of the motor truck did not break this agglomeration pattern until certain technological advances were achieved. These breakthroughs involved factory production technology, completion of the urban freeway network, and the long-delayed attainment of cost economies in short-distance trucking operations, and their coalescence after 1965 has revolutionized the intrametropolitan manufacturing location process (Berry and Kasarda, 1977, pp. 233–234).

Industrial Location Forces in the Contemporary Metropolis

Postwar technological change in factory production heavily favored outlying areas over the inner city. Increasing automation and assembly-line fabrication in most heavy industries transformed manufacturing from a vertical to a more space-consuming horizontal operation. Sufficient land for constructing spacious one-story plants was both readily available and much cheaper in suburbia. A sizable physical plant existed outside the central city as well, in the form of almost new but now empty suburban wartime factories that the federal government was only too glad to lease or sell cheaply to decentralizing manufacturers. Moreover, improved supporting services constantly increased the attraction of the outer city: better communications, more fire and police protection, the growing concentration of machinery repairmen and subcontractors, new high-capacity utility networks, and especially the proliferation of superhighways.

Metropolitan expressway construction was largely triggered by the federal interstate highway-building effort. In 1956, the program's initial year, only 2600 miles of divided high-speed urban freeways were in operation and constituted about 7 percent of all metropolitan highways; by 1969, more than 13,000 miles were open and comprised almost one-fourth of all urban highway mileage (Stanback and Knight, 1976, p. 25). The greater ease of movement that resulted quickly wrought enormous changes for the location of industry in cities and suburbs, because goods could now be assembled just about anywhere on the expressway system, yet be equally accessible to the rest of the metropolis; one former New York City firm even discovered that the truck trip to a Brooklyn customer was faster from its new North Jersey suburban site than it had been from its old Manhattan location a short distance across the East River (Stanback and Knight, 1976, p. 25). With factories no longer required to locate in the central city, freeways simultaneously improved the access of outer-ring sites to the entire metropolitan pool of diversified blue-collar specialists, a highly mobile and increasingly suburban labor force almost exclusively tied to automobile commuting (Struyk and James, 1975, p. 13). Moreover, many other industry-related activities soon realized greater advantages in suburbia. Wholesalers, for instance, immediately recognized that improved overall accessibility meant that several smaller warehouses scattered throughout the metropolitan area could be combined into a single large freeway-oriented facility, thus transforming product distribution from a center-outward to an edge-inward operation (Vance, 1977, p. 385).

The third breakthrough—achieving cost economies in intraurban trucking—is also a direct outcome of freeway expansion as local truck flows increasingly shift away from the congested inner city to the much higher mobility of outlying superhighway corridors. Besides higher road speeds, additional time and cost savings are realized in loading operations at suburban plants, where ample off-street parking and docking facilities drastically cut turnaround times. A further stimulus to increased competition and lower truck shipment rates in suburbia was the ICC order of 1977 that extended the unregulated commercial trucking zone to 20 miles beyond the central city boundary: for the first time, small urban truckers were permitted to serve a lucrative territory which had previously required a $25,000 operating license. This modification of intrametropolitan economic geography has neutralized the former location cost differential between the central city and suburban ring, and made intraurban goods movement via truck as efficient as interregional freight transport. Suburbia has also attracted the lion's share of the latter, as its huge long-distance truck terminal complexes (and their related facilities, such as regional food distribution centers) fast replace aging downtown rail and water terminals as the dominant metropolitan freight "port," yet another signal of rapid erosion in the locational pull of the central city within its urban sphere.

The coalescence of horizontal fabrication technology, freeway orientation, and economical trucking in the 1970s has turned the urban manufacturing complex inside out. With accessibility now an all but ubiquitous good, the deteriorating inner-city industrial district no longer commands its former metropolitan centrality advantage. Entrepreneurs have responded to their new locational footlooseness by sharply increasing their activity in the suburbs since the mid-sixties (see columns 5 and 6 in Table 4.1 and manufacturing employment data in Table 4.2). Concomitantly, central city investments have been greatly reduced, especially in the old industrial cores of the northeastern Manufacturing Belt, where aging and frequently obsolescent factories predominate. The central city annual blue-collar job loss rate in the mid-1970s was nearly 4 percent nationwide, compared to 0.8 percent in the preceding decade; New York City alone lost over 300,000 or almost 40 percent of its manufacturing jobs between 1969 and 1976, and the story has been much the same in such other overindustrialized cities as St. Louis, Detroit, Philadelphia, and Cleveland. This economic unraveling can only signify that the geographical conditions that created the compact central city have now disappeared. Thus, put into proper historical perspective, these recent events represent nothing less than the final unfolding of an evolutionary process of agglomeration that began with the industrial revolution a century ago:

> The concentrated industrial [city] *only* developed because proximity meant lower transportation and communication costs for those interdependent specialists who had to interact with each other frequently or intensively and could only do so on a face-to-face basis. But shortened distances also meant higher densities and costs of congestion, high rent, loss of privacy, and the like. As soon as technological change permitted, the metropolis was transformed to minimize these negative externalities (Berry and Cohen, 1973, p. 454).

With the transformed metropolis a near frictionless area vis-à-vis internal goods movement, economic forces are becoming less important in shaping the geography of urban manufacturing as industrialists become freer to locate at the "best" metropolitan sites they can find. Noneconomic factors increasingly come to the fore in such locational decision-making, and the perceived advantages of suburbia are accentuated for just about every kind of industrial operation. Leading among these non-cost-related forces is the *prestige* factor in suburban industrial location, which may soon become central to an understanding of the contemporary spatial organization of urban manufacturing.

The importance of prestige and corporate image in the functioning of today's industrial firms cannot be understated, since manufacturers, like the general public, are highly susceptible to the latest social trends. In recent years it has become extremely fashionable to locate in booming new suburban areas, which are promoted enthusiastically by industrial realtors as high-status, style-setting centers containing the most exciting new metropolitan opportunities. Companies now spend lavishly to be in fashion, and the overwhelming concentration of these current investments outside the central city confirms that entrepreneurs widely share this glamorous perception of the outer city. As but one example of this kind of behavior, Sternlieb (U.S.N.W.R., 1971, p. 42) cites the case of a Boston firm which forsook downtown site costs of $1.25 per square foot in order to relocate to a higher-status suburban location where equivalent space sold for $4.75. Thus, industry increasingly avoids low-status areas, such as the blighted inner city, much of the urban waterfront, and even old suburban rail corridors, in favor of prestigious outlying expressway locations. The gravitation of suburban manufacturing to freeway corridors is particularly noticeable not only for their superior accessibility but also for their priceless visibility, advertising, and image-enhancement opportunities (Figure 4.5). Practically every suburban expressway in the nation is now lined with prominently displayed modern plants where site amenities (at least on the side facing the freeway) are given as much weight as production-related needs. Lately, industrial plants indicate an even stronger preference for expressway nodes, especially those possessing the most glamorous suburban addresses in the proximity of superregional shopping malls.

Industrial Parks in the Outer City

Most accommodating for all but the largest manufacturing facilities around these suburban centers are *industrial parks* (Mayer, 1964; Hartshorn, 1973), which in many ways are microcosms of the full range of locational advantages now available in the outer city. These organized industrial districts were first established in suburban Chicago in 1908 and gradually spread to other metropolitan areas through the efforts of railroads, which stood to profit doubly as both landlord and exclusive transport supplier at outlying trackside locations. It was the postwar shift to freeways, however, which led to the rapid proliferation of the industrial park, and of the nearly 3000 such facilities now operating more than half have been developed since 1965.

Figure 4.5 Volkswagen's Rabbit assembly plant at New Stanton, Pennsylvania in Pittsburgh's outer suburbs. This site is a short distance from the intersection of the Pennsylvania Turnpike (left rear) and I-70, one of the Northeast's most important expressway junctions. The factory was opened in 1978, and besides visibility also emphasizes lavish use of on-site space and harmonic integration into the high-amenity Allegheny hill environment. (Courtesy Volkswagen of America, Inc.)

Besides traditional space and cost benefits of suburban location, contemporary industrial parks offer their tenants a number of special advantages. Foremost among them are their self-contained agglomeration advantages arising from the clustering of ultramodern and automated plants that permit ready material and information linkages among firms. Sharing a large common site minimizes the costs of utilities, waste removal, and other public services, and makes possible more favorable leasing, financing, insurance, and local tax arrangements. The usually excellent accessibility of industrial parks, combined with the heightened drawing power of their multiple employment opportunities, makes them especially attractive to the increasingly diversified and skilled resident suburban work force. Moreover, the highly satisfactory working conditions in these modern surroundings reduces labor turnover, and in many suburbs the mere announcement of plans to construct a new park unleashes a deluge of job applications to the developer and prospective tenants.

Above all, the industrial park powerfully reinforces the prestige factor for its tenants by emphasizing a positive collective public image. Stylish park names as well as highly visible and glamorous main-road addresses are deliberately sought. Attractive, imaginative architecture and landscaping enhance the site, and space is used lavishly in buildings, parking lots, and loading areas. Industrial parks also provide a complete array of supporting services for tenants, among them private security and fire protection, building maintenance, executive clubs, employee cafeterias, and even recreational facilities (Tam O'Shanter Industrial Fairways Park north of Chicago is actually built around nine holes of a former championship golf course). Comprehensive site and access planning stresses maximum unity with the surrounding environment as well as harmonious integration within the local community. Nuisance activities and obnoxious land uses are excluded, and schemes to smooth traffic flows are worked out. The typical mix of companies consists of small- and moderate-sized light manufacturing, material fabrication, wholesale and warehousing firms; however, the scale of operations is increasing, with some of the newest parks employing as many as 30,000 workers.

The universal acceptance and widely admired efficiency of industrial parks in the outer city has launched an intensifying trend toward more specialized facilities. "Fly-in" parks are increasingly common around major airports, especially such regional dominants as Atlanta, Los Angeles, and Chicago's O'Hare. Suburban research and development complexes often spring up near major universities. North Carolina's Research Triangle Park (front cover) typifies the genre: a recent survy (*Fortune*, June 1977) counted 28 major private and public scientific organizations engaged in advanced research amid 5500 beautifully wooded acres that also contained a hotel and fine restaurants. Science–industry complexes particularly favor such settings (see pages 140–142). Even major government facilities now form such clusters, as we shall see later when we discuss the huge federal complexes that have concentrated in the Maryland and Virginia suburbs of Washington, D.C. Still another specialized facility type to be covered later is the now ubiquitous suburban office park.

The Suburban Science Park Complex: California's Silicon Valley

Epitomizing the linkage between suburban amenities and today's high-technology research-and-development industry is Silicon Valley, a 30-mile strip of industrial parks along the southwestern shore of San Francisco Bay that is home to much of the microelectronics industry (Figure 4.6). The heart of this complex is the 15-mile axis of

Figure 4.6 A view across Silicon Valley near Palo Alto, with San Francisco Bay in the background. (Courtesy Patricia Ulmer.)

the Bayshore Highway, which stretches northwest across Santa Clara County from the edge of San Jose to Stanford University in Palo Alto, a corridor that has been called the densest concentration of innovative industry in the world (*Time*, Feb. 20, 1978, p. 51). Here, more than 800 small plants develop and manufacture the tiny silicon chips and semiconductors that make possible the miniaturized electronics industry, which produces ever-higher-speed computers as well as such everyday marvels as microwave ovens, pocket calculators, and digital wristwatches. The growth catalyst for all of Silicon Valley is Stanford, the leader in microelectronics research and applications as well as the foremost producer of electrical engineering Ph.D.s. Although the complex first developed in the late 1950s after the transistor was innovated at Stanford, Silicon Valley did not eclipse the MIT-dominated electronics complex of suburban Boston until the chip technology era began in the early 1970s. The tie to Stanford was absolutely crucial, because constant research breakthroughs there produced such rapid progress in microelectronics production that other R&D centers were unable to keep pace. Only Stanford's graduates were familiar with the latest advanced technologies, and nearly all went to work for local companies. Fierce competition prevails in Silicon Valley: young technicians soon spawned rival companies by going into business for themselves, and employee raiding among firms is a thriving pursuit. By 1980, however, the Silicon Valley dominance was being threatened as other universities closed the research gap and the big companies of the electronics industry increasingly acquired the latest knowledge and expertise through their own developmental efforts. Competition from such giants as Texas Instruments is soon expected to have a serious impact, forcing small companies to either sell out or form their own larger corporations through mergers with local competitors. At the same time, Silicon Valley's geographical dominance is being challenged by southern California's San Diego, which has already attracted several microelectronics manufacturers as well as such Japanese majors as SONY and Sanyo (*New York Times*, March 28, 1979, p. D-13). As San Diego's skilled labor force grows steadily, it well may achieve parity with Silicon Valley, especially since it advertises cheaper housing, less traffic, more space for industry, and a less polluted environment than the lower San Francisco peninsula.

Suburban Industrial Growth Trends

The growing locational affinity of suburban manufacturers for each other as well as for certain activity nodes is a significant trend in the emerging industrial geography of the outer city. To some extent this process of concentration is a longer-standing postwar suburban phenomenon, as seen in such older outlying clusters as the electronics industry west of Boston, steel fabrication around the Fairless U.S. Steel complex northeast of Philadelphia, and aircraft manufacturing in outer Los Angeles and on New York's Long Island. However, by the early 1970s, the critical mass of intrametropolitan manufacturing activity had become so firmly entrenched in the suburbs that many industries were establishing themselves in the outer city simply because so many others had found it profitable to do so. Moreover, industries now tend to locate as closely as possible to established suburban facilities and business concentrations. Increasingly, a move by one firm will trigger similar location decisions by others: like people, industry will not locate just anywhere in the metropolis but will select sites accessible to the same services and labor force demanded by competitors (Schaeffer and Sclar, 1975, p. 59).

The emergence of suburbia as the leading zone of manufacturing necessitates a reinterpretation of classical industrial decentralization models, which view the outer urban ring merely as a reception area for companies emigrating from the central city. Wood (1974) has effectively attacked this obsolete core-dominated interpretation; by focusing instead on the metropolitan fringe, suburbia is quickly identified as a major zone of industrial expansion in its own right, in which *self-generated* growth has been primarily responsible for its current preeminence. Given the recent suburbanization of entire industrial complexes and their supporting business facilities, the outer ring now functions as the dominant "incubator" location for new manufacturing firms. Moreover, as existing companies expand they usually seek to minimize the distance of new investment, and the resulting local dispersion of branch plants provides the other major internal source of industrial growth in the suburbs. External contributions also swell the suburban total, both from in-migrating central city firms (although to a much lesser extent than heretofore attributed) as well as from the branch facilities of extraregional national corporations whose locational strategies no longer require orientation to the old metropolitan core.

Further tests of this alternative explanation of metropolitan manufacturing development are needed. Although data on industrial firm relocations are difficult to obtain, the limited information currently available indicates only modest numbers of direct city-to-suburb shifts. Indeed, James and Hughes (1973) found that in heavily suburbanized New Jersey local outlying establishment growth—complemented by plant demise in adjacent central cities—dominated the process of manufacturing employment change. At any rate, it is clear that a new reality now exists. Suburbia is home to a leading proportion of the nation's urban industrial base, and can be expected to make sizable further gains as noneconomic locational decision-making forces intensify in the future. This is true not only for the burgeoning Sunbelt suburbs, but also for such Manufacturing Belt suburban areas as Long Island, where advanced-technology aerospace, communications, electronics, and other growth industries are in the vanguard of a booming local economy (McQuiston, 1979).

The Suburbanization of the Metropolitan Office Industry and Its Consequences

Many of the same forces that shape the prestige-related deconcentration of manufacturing are also working to disperse the urban office industry. After modest early postwar beginnings, the suburbanization of office-based activities has accelerated strikingly since the mid-1960s. Pioneering sales offices of manufacturers were followed by large routine-operation insurance and other companies; they in turn were pursued by a myriad of smaller computer, research, and other service firms. In the next stage, regional offices of big national companies tested the suburban waters and found them to be so favorable that a major wave of corporate headquarters relocations soon followed. Most recently, as the nation completes its passage to a postindustrial economy dominated by information and communication-intensive activities,* the outer city has acquired a steadily rising number of once exclusively downtown-bound elitist functions (Manners, 1974, pp. 100–101).

Although the intensifying suburban office trend is well known, its precise dimensions are impossible to gauge because there is no systematic collection of office-space data in the United States. Census data are limited to selective (but incomplete) employment sectors, and perusal of *F.I.R.E.*, *services*, and *business services* proportions in Table 4.2 indeed confirms an unrelenting tilt toward the outer city. Occasionally, more specific data of unknown reliability are gathered by local agencies. Two careful recent studies—focused on Dallas and Atlanta—are briefly reported here; however, since both are "youthful" Sunbelt metropolises, it is reasonable to assume that the suburban orientation of office activities is even greater in the older urban areas of the North and West. For metropolitan Dallas, Rees (1978, p. 346) found that floor space in organized suburban office districts grew from 26 percent of the SMSA total in 1970 to 46 percent in 1976 (achieving equivalency with the central city's share), as the outer ring accounted for four-fifths of the space added and 82 of the 86 office buildings constructed during the 6-year period. The Greater Atlanta changes (Wright, 1978; Hamer, 1978) were just as noteworthy, with the booming suburbs advancing from 36 to 56 percent of total metropolitan office space between 1970 and 1977; a parallel 1970–1975 tally of sectoral changes showed consistently sizable suburban gains for banking (26 to 39 percent), insurance (40 to 57 percent), business services (47 to 70 percent), and miscellaneous services (49 to 70 percent).

Elimination of the Central City– Suburban Differential in Office Location Advantages

The information-transactional office industry has traditionally been located in the central city CBD, which possessed geographical advantages of metropolitan centrality as well as the benefits of face-to-face contact with other business people and immediate access to the ancillary services of outside specialists. As we have observed, however, this superior accessibility of downtown no longer pertains. More important, the once exclusive economic advantages of the CBD are being undercut by the changing needs of the industry, which can be better satisfied at newer, outlying business cen-

---

*Abler (1974, p. 8) has reckoned that by the mid-1970s white-collar services, information-processing, and private and public managerial workers accounted for fully 75 percent of the American labor force, a proportion that can only have grown larger in succeeding years.

ters. The result has been a rise in locational footlooseness with urban offices, like manufacturing plants, increasingly free to concentrate at amenity- and prestige-rich sites in the outer city.

Economic factors governing office location—available space, labor, and ease of communication—certainly do not inhibit the burgeoning suburban trend. Land cost and space availability in the suburbs are frequently more favorable than in the CBD because a campus-style office complex may cost as little as half its equivalent square footage in a downtown skyscraper. However, this is a relatively unimportant cost differential because rent and local taxes amount to less than 10 percent of total office expenditures (Manners, 1974, p. 98): the dominant cost component (80 to 90 percent) in running an office involves labor. Given the continuing dispersal of the metropolitan population and its overwhelming preference for commuting by automobile, the outer city now holds a commanding advantage in labor access. By locating at convenient highway sites with ample free parking space, suburban offices easily attract workers and executives whose rates of turnover and absenteeism tend to be much lower than those for counterpart CBD firms.

Despite warnings that offices would not be able to function properly at a distance from the downtown business community, firms now operating in suburbia report no problem in maintaining interoffice communication. Although it is true that chance suburban meetings are fewer and that nearly every face-to-face transaction must be planned, it often requires no more time to drive to a conference in the outer city than it does to walk or take a cab to one in the CBD. New suburban business networks themselves have adapted with surprising speed, often by successfully combining professional dealings with luncheon meetings, golf dates, or with more informal contacts at cocktail parties and barbecues (Sommer, 1975, p. 141). The radial expressway system, which, ironically, was designed to preserve the dominance of the postwar central city, has actually helped accomplish the opposite, with its peak-hour traffic jams that now make midday travel to the city infinitely more convenient (Schaeffer and Sclar, 1975, p. 54). For those suburban office firms that must maintain continuous contact with downtown, telephones have proven quite satisfactory. Moreover, the success and proliferation of such new telecommunications devices as picture phones, two-way cable TV, rapid document facsimile, and computerized information transmission networks can only allow the further substitution of intraurban communication for individual travel and loosen ties to the CBD for a greater number of office activities (Harkness, 1973). By 1982, high-speed satellite communications systems are expected to be in place, offering all these business services plus long-distance conference hookups, which will enable suburban locations to be linked directly to the entire nation and much of the world beyond (Schuyten, 1978). Finally, suburban office location also means much easier highway access to other metropolitan centers, particularly airports, an advantage universally cited by executives of companies whose activities require frequent out-of-town trips.

With the rapid emergence of the office industry in the suburbs, CBD-bound ancillary activities are now also deconcentrating. Whereas a few years ago suburbanizing firms often had to perform functions usually contracted to outside specialists, major suburban office concentrations today routinely contain a full range of legal, tax, accountants, direct mail, public relations, advertising, management consultant, and countless other supporting business services. In a survey of these operations in the New York suburbs, Darnton (1974) found that they usually consisted of small-scale firms and were run by single independent business people who sought locations in small commercial buildings close to the office complexes of larger companies. Most specialized in rapid high-quality service abetted by the availability of a large and skilled local labor pool, and one highly pleased southwestern Connecticut businessman even reported that he had just received his first order from Manhattan!

Thus, dispersion has superseded concentration as the dominant force governing the intrametropolitan distribution of office activities. With communication increasingly substituted for transportation, business transactions themselves assume new modes as indirect interactions—involving only roles—steadily replace the face-to-face contact that was so important through the immediate past. Access to ultramodern telecommunications technology is fast becoming essential as business operations expand in geographical scale, a development that further favors suburbia because of the costlier aging and often-overloaded phone and electrical networks found in large central cities. And at the national level it is already clear that there is no longer need for a single corporate and financial center to serve the postindustrial economy, a point emphasized throughout this section as we observe the persistent and widening decline of New York City's economic leadership.

The Changing Metropolitan Office Location Decision

With intraurban space, labor, and communication advantages no longer heavily favoring the CBD, the metropolitan office industry, like manufacturing before it, increasingly responds to noneconomic locational forces. Once again geographical *prestige* is the pervasive decision-making factor, accentuated all the more because business cachet has always played a dominant role in shaping the spatial evolution of urban office activity (Vance, 1977, p. 372). Thus, office companies are even more sensitive to the glamour and status-enhancing opportunities offered by fashionable new suburban commercial centers in highly visible freeway corridors, especially around superregional malls. And, as we shall presently see in a closer look at the huge office complexes of Fairfield and Westchester Counties north of New York City, many of the biggest corporations are in the vanguard of this office suburbanization movement, and their very presence has elevated this business center into the highest national ranks.

Because the decision-making structure of even the biggest office firms is usually centralized in the hands of a few individuals, management perception is a key variable in the location of white-collar companies. With executives increasingly choosing prestigious suburban sites in very much the same manner as individuals select residences, their motivations are sometimes misunderstood by those who view their actions as negative responses to conditions in central cities. Critics of recent suburban office moves often charge that personal convenience is the strongest motive: by moving the company close to home, the chief executive can minimize commuting time. Yet, such selfish behavior has rarely been documented other than to show a much more general preference for a certain suburban sector. What is overlooked, of course, is that a majority of employees are already suburbanites and that relocating their workplace to suburbia actually means greater total commuting convenience, even for those living in opposite metropolitan sectors who can use circumferential freeways to bypass central city traffic congestion. Far more serious is the charge that management's racial prejudice has governed the relocation decision process. New York City's former economic development administrator, D. Kenneth Patton, has bluntly asserted that the changing ethnic composition of Manhattan's labor force has prompted corporate moves in order to preserve what he called "social distance":

> The executive decision-maker lives in a homogenized community. Increasingly his employees in the city are from communities very different in class and ethnicity. . . . The decision-maker can't relate to the city kid; that kid doesn't look the same to him. It's an older generation in charge trying to reestablish a setting that seems to be more comfortable, more the old way (Masotti and Hadden, 1974, p. 84).

This irresponsible line of reasoning, unsupported by any available evidence (suburban companies have, in fact, been known to go out of their way to hire local minorities), is typical of the more extreme defenders of the central city, who deliberately ignore the prevailing suburban trend affecting all forms of economic activity. Patton is also wrong in depicting older executives as giving up on downtown, and this bears closer examination.

Although positive perceptions of suburbia far outweigh dissatisfaction with the CBD, the central city's image and economic position is not helped by the steady deterioration of what office managers call its *quality of life*. By that is meant a relaxed and comfortable business environment free of outside stresses which distract workers and reduce their productivity. Whatever the objective merits of this argument, a growing number of business people say they no longer need the cultural amenities of downtown, the rising frustration of commuting there, and immersion in its increasingly tension-ridden commercial life. However, older executives, who have long been part of the CBD business scene, are *least* prone to breaking their firm's commitment to the central city. Rather, it is the emerging generation of younger executives that is far more likely to prefer the calmer suburban business milieu, often because they chose to have junior executive experience with office firms in the outer city. Since a steady incoming supply of new managerial talent is seen to be essential for the successful operation of major office companies, many corporations have recently learned that it is easier to recruit and keep promising young executives at newer suburban facilities. These and the other noneconomic forces just discussed have combined, since the late 1960s, to produce a still continuing wave of corporate headquarters suburbanization. We focus next on this cornerstone of the office industry and what its deconcentration portends for the metropolitan economy.

The Suburbanization of Corporate Headquarters

International corporate headquarters are the most prestigious and highest-order office functions, and their growing predilection for suburban locations represents the fullest flowering of the intrametropolitan deconcentration of major economic activities. Whereas comprehensive geographical data on head offices are not regularly compiled, *Fortune's* fairly accurate annual listing of the nation's 1000 largest corporations reasonably suggests the kinds of locational choices that are now being made by this leading segment of the office industry. Among these companies the suburban trend is burgeoning: in 1978, 170 "Fortune 500" corporations were headquartered in the outer city as opposed to 47 in 1965, 56 in 1969, and 128 in 1974; an additional 182 of the "Second 500" firms (ranked 501 to 1000) had suburban locations in 1978, up from 161 in 1974.

Historically, American corporations have been mobile, but headquarters moves since 1970 have occurred at an accelerated pace (Meyer, 1976). Before the 1960s, agglomeration was the prevalent migration trend, with most moves involving shifts toward the largest cities, particularly New York. Deconcentration has dominated since, with about 75 percent of such relocations directed to the suburbs of these cities. Most of the remaining corporate moves have been from the North to the Sunbelt, a national-scale migration occurring for the same reasons that office suburbanization occurs at the metropolitan level. In fact, Sunbelt headquarters are most frequently situated in prestigious new suburban or recently annexed outer central city locations; they also tend to announce their arrival in bold and imaginative architectural statements (see the front cover), a practice that is increasingly noticeable in Northern suburbs, too, as we shall see when we focus on the corporate landscape of Fairfield and Westchester Counties outside New York City. But first let us take a closer look at that city, whose position as the nation's leading corporate center was continuing to erode at the end of the 1970s.

The Exodus of Corporations from New York City. The recent decline of New York City's corporate headquarters complex is shown in Figure 4.7, and reveals that by 1979 the suburbs—Westchester County and Long Island in New York State, Fairfield County in Connecticut, and most of northern New Jersey—had surpassed the city in total number of major head offices. This slippage is strongly reflected in the city's shrinking share of Fortune 500 companies: of the 138 such corporations located there in 1968, only 73 remained at the beginning of 1980. Understandably, this exodus has been a severe blow to New York's prestige, already suffering heavily since grievous fiscal problems surfaced in the mid-seventies. The city's frustration finally turned to outrage in 1976, when Union Carbide, at the height of the municipal financial crisis, announced with much fanfare that it was abandoning its famous Park Avenue skyscraper for suburban Danbury, Connecticut. A barrage of criticism from elected officials, the press, and public was swiftly unleashed, and even the Episcopal Bishop in his Easter sermon castigated Carbide and other departing companies for "betraying" the city.

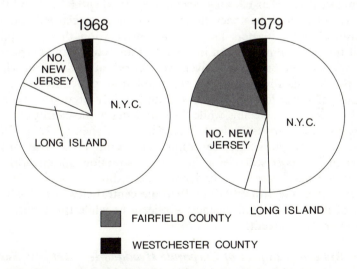

Figure 4.7 The changing distribution of large corporate headquarters in the greater New York area, 1968–1979. (Source: Adapted from Sterne, 1977; based on data compiled in Barratt, 1977. © 1977 by The New York Times Company. Reprinted by permission.)

Once the furor died down, the city launched a public relations campaign to keep corporate headquarters in town. That simply forced companies planning to leave to maintain secrecy until their moves were *faits accompli;* others tried the more diplomatic approach of suburbanizing most operations but maintaining a residual Manhattan office suite as the "official" headquarters address. New York City's media campaign in the end produced more embarrassments than successes. One of its more pathetic efforts was the 1978 breakfast at the Waldorf-Astoria, where a host of high public officials welcomed the *seventy-seven* workers of the Helena Rubinstein Company back to New York 2 years after moving to a poorly chosen suburban site. But the height of unreality was achieved by Mayor Koch that morning, who really appeared to believe the remarks attributed to him by *The New York Times:* ". . . the suburbs are a nice place for people who need sleep, but the action is here and always will be here" (L. Williams, 1978). A few months later, however, all the mayor could muster in response to the sudden departure of American Airlines for suburban Dallas was a general grumble that firms move "to put four or five top people closer to their homes and golf courses." American's relocation, a not illogical step given the airline's Sunbelt-centered route system, was also an especially bitter pill for the city to swallow because the company's president served on two blue-ribbon economic panels striving to keep business in Manhattan.

Although New York has lost nearly half of its major headquarters offices in the last dozen years, the city is still a leading center for such supporting corporate services as banking, accounting, legal specialties, and the like. However, not enough has been done to link these specialized activities to new suburban headquarters facilities, a reorientation that is required to forestall the development of an independent and competing corporate service complex in the outer city. Given New York's attitude of superiority, it will be psychologically devastating for Manhattan to acknowledge its passage from corporate leader to follower, but the only alternative seems to be unremitting economic decline while the remainder of the metropolitan headquarters complex thrives. Indeed, Drennan and Cohen (1977, p. 76) warn that the city's corporate-service community could unravel at any time. Whereas their report still views the current situation optimistically, such disintegration may already be under way according to the data series presented in Table 4.2: from 1970 to 1976 the central city lost 43,000 or 6.5 percent of its F.I.R.E. and business service jobs while the suburbs gained by 62,000 or 24.5 percent.

***The Suburban Impact of Corporate Headquarters Activity: Fairfield/
Westchester's Business Complex.*** The Fairfield County, Connecticut/ Westchester County, New York, area north and northeast of New York is the quintessential suburban corporate complex (Figure 4.8). Thirty-three of the Fortune 500 companies were headquartered here in 1978—plus an addi-

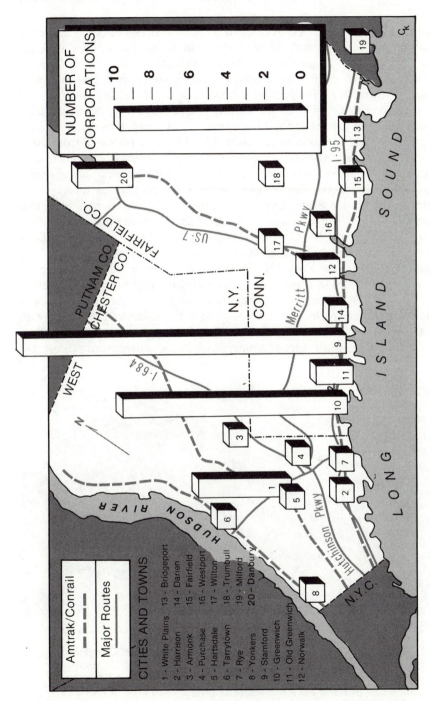

Figure 4.8 The suburban corporate complex of Fairfield and Westchester Counties, showing Fortune-1000 headquarters at the end of 1978.

tional 23 of the Second 500—sufficient to make Fairfield County alone the second largest concentration of head offices in the nation (surpassing third-place Chicago 27 to 24 for the top 500, and 44 to 43 for the top 1000). Fairfield's major corporations have been arriving steadily since the late 1960s (Figure 4.9) and the in-migration shows no signs of abating, with several dozen companies believed to be secretly assembling office land packages. Almost all have moved from Manhattan (Singer and Kennecott Copper being the two latest to announce), although a few have relocated from other cities. The natural amenities of wooded hills and seacoast combined with proximity to New York were the initial lures, and the influx of big corporations rapidly made the county one of the most prestigious business addresses in the United States (see *Time*, August 1978; *Newsweek*, 1976; and *Business Week*, 1977b). About two-thirds of the headquarters facilities, among them Xerox, Olin, Continental Oil, and General Telephone and Electronics, are clustered in the high-status Greenwich–Stamford corner of the county closest to New York City (Figure 4.8). Despite the extraordinarily high property values in these towns, there were enough new office development applications before zoning boards in 1977 to double the existing 8 million square feet of local office space; as we shall shortly see, nearly all will be rejected. Neighboring Westchester County across the state line, long one of the most glamorous suburban counties in the country (Shouma-

Figure 4.9 The corporate headquarters of CONOCO in High Ridge Park at the edge of Stamford. Continental Oil Company, the nation's 18th largest industrial corporation in 1978, relocated to this site from Manhattan in the early 1970s. (Courtesy of CONOCO.)

toff, 1979), is nurturing its own growing corporate community. That county's excellent access to Manhattan began to attract headquarters offices early in the postwar period, most notably IBM and Reader's Digest. Lately, however, Westchester has stressed its economic independence from "The Big Apple" by promoting itself as "The Golden Apple," whose core is the Platinum Mile stretch of the Cross–Westchester Expressway corridor near White Plains, which contains the home offices of Texaco, General Foods, Nestlé, and PepsiCo (Figures 4.8 and 4.10).

Despite the competition between the two that is heightened by state government rivalry, Fairfield–Westchester is becoming a well-integrated single business complex that is increasingly able to assert its commercial independence from the rest of the New York metropolis. Recently arrived corporations express a high degree of satisfaction with the area, not only for the usual reasons but also for such extra benefits as a consolidated headquarters operation (versus frequently scattered overflow offices in the CBD) and higher executive productivity (a return to a 40-hour suburban workweek versus 35 to 37 hours downtown to allow for extra commuting time). Longer-term corporate tenants are beginning to expand their suburban operations, and demand for office space by smaller companies is so brisk that several high-rise buildings are sprouting in White Plains and Stamford (Figure 4.11). Concomitantly, a large labor pool of skilled white-collar workers is accumulating and several companies have made special efforts to recruit from the local black and hispanic populations; in fact, labor supply can barely keep up with demand and the bistate suburban area enjoys one of the lowest unemployment rates in the Northeast. An even more im-

Figure 4.10 A view of Westchester's Platinum Mile. (Courtesy Schulman Investment Company.)

Figure 4.11 Landmark Tower in central Stamford is an outstanding example of high-rise suburban office development, and is the focal point of Landmark Square adjacent to the new Town Center multi-purpose activity complex. The tiered structure in the distance just to the left of the Tower is the corporate headquarters of General Telephone and Electronics Corporation. (Courtesy F. D. Rich Company.)

portant measure of the arrival of Fairfield–Westchester as a national business center is the myriad of ancillary corporate service companies that began to flock into the area in the late 1970s. At last report, this secondary ripple effect of headquarters complex development was attracting dozens of advertising agencies, law and accounting firms, and even New York City bank companies, most of whom came from Manhattan to establish permanent suburban offices from which to serve their corporate clients (Madden, 1978). As the new office complex expands to become the suburban area's dominant specialization, longer-standing economic activities began to be squeezed out. This is particularly the case for Fairfield County's older manufacturing plants, which are being displaced by office facilities in most of the industrial satellite towns that line the New York–New Haven rail corridor (Tomasson, 1978). There are other problems as well.

Since most of southwestern Fairfield County and adjoining central Westchester were already developed as wealthy residential areas, the influx of corporate offices after 1965 has had the effect of "citifying" these communities. Local traffic congestion and overloading of public service facilities have been the most serious problems, and it is not surprising that a grass-roots "slow-growth" movement has mushroomed in response. The outcry against overcrowding has been loudest in Greenwich and Stamford, where citizens fear that even a single additional large office development will totally destroy the high-quality residential character of these towns. As a result, corporate applicants are being turned down by local zoning boards and must search for alternative locations deeper inside Connecticut. There, too, local resistance is intensifying, and corporate headquarters are being admitted only if they agree to pay for near-site highway improvements and surround themselves with wide buffer zones so as not to disturb adjacent neighborhoods. Headquarter moves into exclusive residential suburbs also create problems for workers who do not earn high incomes and thus cannot afford entry into the local housing market (the 1980 *average* price for a house in Greenwich was just under $200,000). Although sufficient housing for them is available within reasonable commuting distance of lower Fairfield County, open housing groups have charged that corporations are lax in using their local leverage to ameliorate the exclusionary effects of large-lot zoning and other devices that maintain the social status quo.

Despite these difficulties, most Fairfield–Westchester communities would undoubtedly agree that the recent growth of the suburban corporate complex has had an overall beneficial impact. Ripple effects have emanated throughout the suburban economy, creating expanded employment opportunities as well as dotting the local landscape with sleek new shopping centers, recreational, and entertainment facilities. One of the more spectacular spinoffs has been the growth of higher-education facilities, and Westchester already claims to have more college classrooms and professors per capita than any other U.S. suburban county. To be sure, the suburban college boom of the late seventies is a nationwide phenomenon that is attuned to an affluent market of business people, continuing-education returnees (many of them women), and those who might never have gone beyond high school. Westchester's leadership was enhanced by its existing campus network— Manhattanville, SUNY–Purchase, Marymount, Briarcliff (now Pace), Iona, and Mercy—plus the willingness of such New York City institutions as N.Y.U., Fordham, Pace, and the New School for Social Research to compete in the suburban marketplace. Business support for higher education, in the form of tuition subsidies and on-the-job rewards for workers taking extra coursework, has been particularly strong in Fairfield County, where the Universities of Connecticut, Bridgeport, and New Haven plus Fairfield University have recently opened degree programs (Tomasson, 1977). Moreover, classes are offered right in Greenwich and Stamford at schools, community centers, and YMCAs, and schedules are designed to dovetail with the business day. Westchester's higher-education programs are more diversified, and N.Y.U. has even begun to advertise a broad-ranging graduate studies curriculum leading to Master's degrees in six arts and sciences, business, and public administration.

Spillover effects are by no means confined to the new suburban landscape; they have directly stimulated revitalization of nearby older towns as well. One spectacular example is the center of Stamford, which is rapidly completing its transition from railroad mill town to corporate showcase. Its centerpiece is the Landmark Square complex, which includes a 21-story office tower in which the cost of floor-space rentals exceeds even Manhattan levels (Figure 4.11). Adjoining developments include new corporate headquarters buildings, hotels, and Stamford Town Center, which will not only be Fairfield's largest regional shopping mall when completed in 1981 but also the site of the nation's biggest urban parking garage, with room for 4000 cars. In Westchester, a similar renewal project is under way in White Plains near the Platinum Mile, where a superregional four-level mall (containing the New York area's first Neiman-Marcus department store) is also due to open in 1981. The fact that White Plains is also the county seat has not hurt, because politicians will often try to steer growth opportunities toward suburban government centers (metropolitan Baltimore's Towson, St. Louis' Clayton, and San Francisco's San Rafael are outstanding examples). Even such aging inner suburbs as Yonkers and New Rochelle are beginning to cash in on Westchester's new commercial aura, and may well come to enjoy Stamford-like revitalization later in the 1980s as commercially zoned land becomes increasingly scarce elsewhere in the corporate headquarters complex to the north.

Suburban Office Location Types

As the suburban office industry has matured in recent years its internal distribution pattern has changed. Early-postwar suburban offices, like manufacturing plants, were usually isolated and scattered widely among outlying sites offering good highway access. Although the high-amenity business campus concept was developed by Reader's Digest in Westchester before 1950, the innovation was slow to catch on before the corporate headquarter suburbanization wave began in the late sixties. A parallel trend, also pioneered shortly after the war but not widespread until two decades later, involved the growth of specialized centers containing concentrations of smaller offices; one of the best known examples is Clayton, Missouri, in the western suburbs of St. Louis, whose central regional location stimulated its early development as a leading metropolitan office center (Kersten and Ross, 1968). By the beginning of the 1970s, however, both locational types came to dominate the suburban office scene. The business campus has now been developed to an advanced level and is increasingly characterized by high-rise structures (Figure 4.12). Smaller centers have also proliferated rapidly since 1970, particularly in the form of *office parks*, the hottest new locational concept in the industry.

Suburban office parks (Hartshorn, 1973, pp. 42–43; Daniels, 1974, pp. 184–186) include many of the same attractions as industrial parks, especially prestigious addresses, self-contained concentrative economies, and easy access to other business centers. These kinds of facilities first developed as clusters of regional offices of national corporations (which explains the particular affinity of early office parks for sites near airports), but now appeal to the entire range of small- to medium-size suburban firms. Office park development in recent years has therefore been considerable and is typified by suburban Atlanta, which grew from one facility in 1964 to 40 office parks employing nearly 25,000 workers in 1974; by the early 1980s, more than half of the total office space in the metropolis will be located in suburban parks versus less than a third in Atlanta's CBD. The internal structure and range of supporting services in newer office parks emphasizes the ultimate in prestige and luxury: imaginative combinations of buildings designed by famous archi-

Figure 4.12 The Executive Campus office facility (center foreground) in Cherry Hill, New Jersey, 4 miles east of downtown Philadelphia, counts among its tenants the regional offices of H. J. Heinz, McDonald's, and Aetna Insurance. The superregional Cherry Hill Mall is less than a mile away (center rear), with a large office park visible just to the right of the shopping center. (Courtesy of Public Service Electric and Gas Company.)

tects; elegant restaurants and visitor reception areas; and such frills as swimming pools, tennis courts, saunas, and jogging and bicycle trails. The latest office parks are also growing larger in size, with some now exeeding 4 million square feet, and are able to compete successfully for the most prized outer city locations. For example, the Oak Brook, Illinois, Park, which contains the headquarters of McDonald's, is located less than 5 miles from O'Hare Airport and two huge shopping malls, and adjoins a golf course as well as the Chicago area's largest motor hotel complex.

As office parks multiply and grow ever more sophisticated, they reinforce the position of suburbia as home for complete white-collar business concentrations. They also share with industrial parks a trend toward greater specialization. An outstanding example is the Forrestal Center just outside Princeton, New Jersey, which will open in late 1980. This 1600-acre educational–scientific research–residential complex, three times the size of North Carolina's Research Triangle Park, will contain numerous high-technology companies whose activities will be integrated with the University's neighboring James Forrestal Campus. Development of the office park, which also includes the new headquarters of Educational Testing Service, is being carefully guided by Princeton University, which will allow tenants access to its computer and library facilities. The centerpiece of the project is a luxurious international business and educational conference center called Scanticon Princeton. When the Danish developers brought in by the university were asked why so prestigious a meeting facility was situated in suburban New Jersey rather than Washington or New York City, they responded, "Princeton offers the most ideal combination of a strong reputation and a good location. . . . This is the right location with the right people and environment" (Berens, 1978).

The suburban office industry seems certain to continue its growth in the foreseeable future. As was the case with intraurban manufacturing, suburban moves by major office firms are now beginning to affect the location decisions of others. More than one corporation has recently shifted to the suburbs because its competitors have found it advantageous to do so. Although hard data are lacking, it is also likely that the sources of new suburban office activity are changing. Besides companies still leaving the CBD, it is highly probable that ongoing and near-future office growth in the suburbs will more heavily involve in-migrating firms from outside the metropolis, self-generated expansion of existing outer city white-collar firms, and the indigenous birth of entirely new suburban office establishments.

The Changing Role of the CBD Office Complex

In spite of the prevailing suburban trend, any current interpretation of the metropolitan office industry must consider the still important role of the CBD. After all, during the 1960s the centers of several large cities enjoyed an office job expansion and building boom of unprecedented proportions. The continuing dominance of the downtown business community seemed all but assured, and plans for further growth were eagerly drawn up. However, by the early 1970s much of this optimism subsided as it became clear that CBD revival had swiftly given way to a weakening trend in many metropolises. Thus, by 1975 Sunday newspapers were no longer filled with glowing economic reports on downtown; one was far more likely to read about the glut of central office space as hard-pressed commercial developers lowered rents and raised fringe benefits in the fierce competition to attain tenancy thresholds in their new skyscrapers. Increasingly, older CBD office buildings became the casualties as their former tenants took advantage of these bargains and flocked to newer quarters, and vacancy rates rose at a time when energy and other operating costs were escalating sharply. In retrospect, it is obvious that builders overreacted to the heightened demand for downtown office space, a trend that peaked at the end of the sixties and then fell steadily before it leveled off and began a modest comeback in the late 1970s. Since more than 5 years of lead time is usually necessary for skyscraper construction, developers were unable to respond quickly to the changed market situation. The glut of unoccupied space in new CBD office towers that resulted was enormous, with New York City alone recording more than 1 square mile of such vacancies in 1975. Moreover, CBD employment gains of the late 1960s turned out to be unexpectedly sensitive to economic downturns and were largely wiped out by the Great Recession of the early seventies (Kihss, 1975).

The CBD did rebound somewhat at the end of the 1970s, but its office market remains relatively weak. Whereas most new office space has been filled, this should not be taken to mean that downtown has retained its economic importance, because the shift to recently constructed buildings almost always enlarges the central zone of discarded older structures (Vance, 1977, p. 372). Detroit is a classic example: its new Renaissance Center complex, which is actually walled-off physically from the rest of CBD, has largely been filled at the expense of such older downtown office buildings. In other words, today's CBD office industry is usually in a steady state, with nearly all growth derived from the internal expansion of existing companies rather than the arrival of new ones.

The limited future growth of the downtown office complex may well follow the example of midtown Manhattan, whose excess new office space has finally been absorbed, thanks to an influx of foreign corporations and banks since 1975. Current construction trends there show that the CBD is no longer expanding 1960s-style but *imploding* toward a few high-status areas, such as Park and Fifth Avenues between East 42nd and 57th Streets. This contraction is not only occurring in response to the noneconomic force of locational prestige, but also for the decidedly economic reason that office building financing is increasingly available only at a few remaining prime-address sites (Goldberger, 1978). Since these areas are already fully developed, two novel construction concepts have been devised to accommodate the new reality. One is "shoehorning" or squeezing new skyscrapers amidst a dense cluster of existing office towers, such as Fifth Avenue's new AT&T Building. The other is "piggybacking" new high-rise structures atop smaller older buildings whose owners are eager to profit from the sale of air rights; such prestigious landmark buildings as the Museum of Modern Art and Radio City Music Hall are especially coveted, although a successful 1978 court challenge by preservationist groups has prohibited construction of a 50-story tower directly over Grand Central Station. New York's planners have been less than thrilled by the extra congestion resulting from the shoehorned overconcentration of offices as well as the architectural ugliness of piggybacking, but have so far been loath to intervene for fear of the city's losing this new business activity. This phenomenon is now widespread in other cities, too, as people and activities draw ever more tightly into downtown's shrinking "winner's circle" (Sternlieb and Hughes, 1979).

Post-1960 CBD office growth was based on supposedly unassailable centralized metropolitan business community advantages. Yet there is now much evidence that traditionally downtown-bound office functions can operate successfully at many suburban locations. One of the most geographically conservative CBD office activities—banking—is a further case in point, and a recent study (Bies, 1974) sheds light on why so many banks have remained downtown and why they, too, may now be about to suburbanize. As the intraurban population disperses, so do its banking habits, as people tend to use bank branches closest to home. Thus, the pattern for metropolitan Washington, D.C., is typical, where the central city share of regional bank deposits dropped from 73 to 50 percent in the 1960s and has probably declined at least another 10 percent since 1970 (Grier, 1971, p. 45). However, the seemingly reluctant dispersion of branch offices in a majority of metropolitan areas is not at all a locational strategy aimed at preserving CBD banking dominance: in no less than 31 states in 1974, government regulatory agencies tightly restricted the number and distribution of branches, a policy dating back to the Depression belief that overbanking contributed to the number of bank failures. These regulations obviously favor the CBD, whose recent growth of bank activity may be more the result of suburban expansion constraints and central city consolidation through closings of high-risk inner-city branches than a resurgence of downtown economic dominance. Although little noticed, a reform movement is gathering momentum in the banking industry as government rules begin to be relaxed. Several states now permit affiliation arrangements between central city and suburban bank companies, and a few (most notably New York State) have recently permitted city banks to expand more widely into the suburbs and beyond. As these reforms continue to spread, they will almost certainly weaken the CBD's role in the metropolitan banking establishment (many Los Angeles area banks are already headquartered in the suburbs). With the steady deconcentration of business, the comparative advantage of downtown as a commercial banking center will continue to erode. And the increasingly widespread use of automation, such as new methods of telephone and electronic fund transferring, will hasten that reduced dependency on the CBD.

Nowhere are these gathering deconcentrative forces more dramatically apparent than in the largest city of all: New York's sharp decline as the national corporate headquarters center in the 1970s will very likely be matched in the 1980s by a similar erosion of its Wall Street financial community. By the mid-seventies, stock brokerage houses began to signal that they were no longer bound to the lower Manhattan financial district (Phalon, 1975; Narvaez, 1976). In response to the city's steadily rising securities transfer taxes, more than a dozen major firms relocated staffs to Jersey City and Hoboken, a 10-minute subway ride just across the Hudson River in tax-free New Jersey. This new locational footlooseness was fully confirmed in 1978 when the American Stock Exchange (Amex), after a year-long search for a new headquarters site, decided to shift to another building in lower Manhattan rather than move to the suburbs. The main point is not that the Amex finally decided to stay in New York—that came about only at the eleventh hour, when the city came through with a favorable financing and tax-relief package—but that it was absolutely serious about almost accepting an even more lucrative deal to relocate to Jersey City (Sterba, 1978). Most devastating to Wall Street's dominant position, however, is the implementation of the Securities Act Amendments passed by Congress in 1975, which mandate development of a nationwide marketing system for securities transactions. By 1978, appropriate electronic technologies were perfected to initiate a pilot program called the Intermarket Trading System, which linked together the computers of six stock exchanges in New York, Boston, Philadelphia, Chicago, San Francisco, and Los Angeles. This allowed traders at all six facilities to engage in buy–sell transactions involving hundreds of different stocks, and it is only a matter of time before the complete securities listings of these exchanges will be added (Sloane, 1978a, 1978b). Moreover, the Securities and Exchange Commission in 1979 was about to approve off-board trading, which will permit member brokers to trade stocks wherever they like instead of exclusively on the exchange floor. These decentralizing mechanisms assure that New York, which has steadily lost securities business to other markets since 1970, will yield its financial dominance to a nationwide central-trading facility in the 1980s; Wall Street's expertise will guarantee it a continuing role in the industry, but it will be reduced to that of a clearing and depository service whereby at least 45,000 of its 75,000 securities-related jobs will be lost (Salpukas, 1977).

Given the changing mix of push and pull forces now reshaping metropolitan office geography, what is the future outlook for the CBD vis-à-vis the suburbs? A careful analysis by Manners (1974, esp. pp. 103–105) concludes that the central city in the future will attract only a steadily diminishing share of office activity, whereas suburban office employment will increasingly become the norm. From the more recent and wider-ranging evidence considered above, the validity of that interpretation is fully supported here. Manners builds his conclusion upon three interrelated and self-reinforcing factors. The first is that the major impact of private CBD reinvestment has already been felt. The building boom of the 1960s resulted from the desires of the private sector to preserve existing center city investments, and may well have amounted to the last defense of downtown against the persistent challenge of the economically burgeoning suburbs (which in many SMSAs added more new office space in the sixties than did the corresponding CBD). With established interests and remaining companies increasingly housed in new structures, the future of this kind of downtown growth is expected to be limited. Second, suburban offices are proving to be efficient for almost every type of urban-based office activity in the multinodal freeway metropolis, within which the CBD no longer commands a region-wide centrality advantage. And third, as we noted earlier, changing origins of the outer city's office industry heavily favors suburbia. Self-generated development by enlarging office firms already located there, the strong suburban preferences of national corporations entering from outside the metropolis, and the increasing importance of the outer city as a seedbed for newly formed white-collar companies will almost certainly combine to trigger future rounds of outlying office growth.

SUBURBAN ACTIVITY LOCATION TRENDS AND THE RISE OF THE MULTICENTERED METROPOLIS

Integration of the similar location trends shaping the suburbanization of retailing, manufacturing, and the office industry shows an increasing propensity for economic activities to gravitate toward each other. Pacesetting superregional shopping centers with their myriad social functions, complete attunement to the automobile, and metropolis-wide drawing power via freeway have become such focal points in the outer city. Their immediate vicinities assume an equally glamorous aura, and attract manufacturers and office employers whose current locational desires are fully satisfied at these prestigious sites highly accessible to skilled labor and established suburban business facilities. The result has been the post-1970 emergence of major multifunctional urban cores that are rapidly coming to dominate the geographical structure of heretofore centerless suburbia. Breckenfeld (1972, p. 80), among others, defines these suburban downtowns or *minicities* as intricate and compact orchestrations of mixed land uses, including shopping, employment, offices, wholesaling, entertainment, hotels, restaurants, and personal services such as medical facilities. Let us examine the minicity by first focusing on its internal organization and then upon its increasingly powerful impact on the overall form of the metropolis in an age of scarcer energy supplies.

The Internal Organization of the Suburban Minicity

The internal structure of the minicity is typified by King of Prussia, Pennsylvania (Figure 4.13), a major suburban core adjacent to Valley Forge 20 miles northwest of central Philadelphia at the intersection of the Pennsylvania Turnpike, Schuylkill Expressway, and three other main suburban highways. Situated at the nucleus of the complex is King of Prussia Plaza, the metropolitan area's second largest superregional shopping mall, which contains 1.8 million square feet of selling space, six major department stores (with three more scheduled to open in 1981), and 200 smaller shops. Distributed about the vicinity within a 5-minute drive of the mall are dozens of highway-oriented retail facilities, including two community shopping centers; one of the region's largest industrial park complexes (over 750 acres), containing the plants and warehouses of Western Electric, GM–Chevrolet, Sears, Borg-Warner, Philco-Ford, three major pharmaceutical manufacturers, and 30 smaller companies; one of General Electric's leading research and manufacturing facilities; a variety of office parks and buildings, among them the headquarters of Gino's (a leading Northeast fast-food chain) and the American Baptist Convention; the Valley Forge Music Fair, a year-round theater offering top-name entertainers weekly; five first-run cinemas; at least a dozen fine restaurants; one of the area's best-known cabarets; numerous superior quality high- and low-rise apartment complexes; and six large motor hotels, with a total of more than 1500 rooms, which annually host more than 300 conventions.

Although the exact formula varies, the admixture of high-order urban functions observed in the King of Prussia core is quite representative of minicities that are materializing throughout the nation's suburbs. For reasons identical to those underlying the suburbanization of economic activity, cultural, entertainment, leisure, and hotel facilities are now also gravitating toward these new metropolitan nodes. We noted in Chapter 3 that cosmopolite communities are burgeoning in the suburbs as cultural activities deconcentrate. Performing arts centers are the most visible facilities and increasingly bring to the outer city world-class evenings of opera, ballet, symphonic, and semiclassical concerts; in addition to Wolf Trap Farm Park near the Tyson's Corner minicity in Vienna, Virginia, outside Washington, similar centers have recently opened in the suburbs and New York, Chicago,

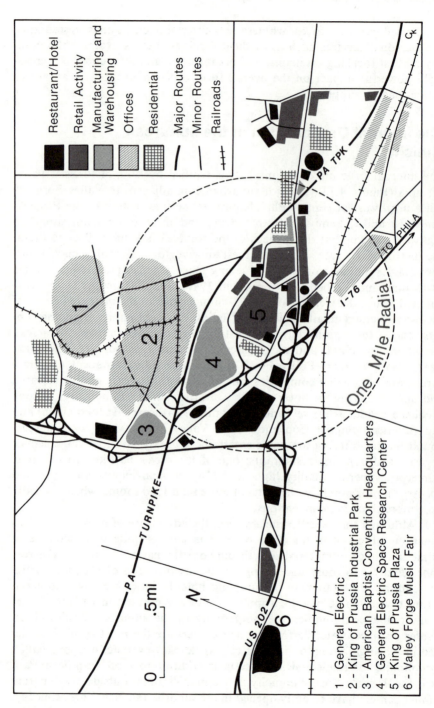

Figure 4.13 The internal activity structure of the typical suburban minicity: King of Prussia, Pennsylvania. (Source: Reproduced by permission of the Association of American Geographers.)

1 - General Electric
2 - King of Prussia Industrial Park
3 - American Baptist Convention Headquarters
4 - General Electric Space Research Center
5 - King of Prussia Plaza
6 - Valley Forge Music Fair

San Francisco, Detroit, Philadelphia, Cleveland, and Buffalo (Vasiliadis, 1976). Besides ubiquitous modern cinemas—which have all but taken over the first-run-film-showing function of the CBD—the suburban entertainment scene is dominated by a variety of live theatrical events. A nationwide circuit of ultramodern theaters, such as the Valley Forge Music Fair (Figure 4.13), sprang up in the 1970s and regularly draws huge audiences to see such performers as Frank Sinatra, Tom Jones, Liza Minnelli, and Johnny Carson; locally, dozens of first-rate theatrical companies are emerging in suburbia and are even known collectively as "the highway stage" in southern California's vast outer city; and the dinner theater, that quintessentially suburban entertainment medium, is flourishing and even making major inroads into the central city. Sometimes entire new entertainment districts emerge in suburbia, an outstanding example being Fat City just outside New Orleans, which boasts not only a jazz–dining–shopping complex to rival the French Quarter, but actually hosted the 1979 Mardi Gras celebration while the Crescent City's police were on strike! Moreover, recreational activities of every sort are attracted to suburban nodes: professional sports is the most spectacular example, and in the seventies the Dallas Cowboys, Detroit Lions, New York Giants, Capital Bullets, and Anaheim's California Angels and (formerly L.A.) Rams have been in the vanguard of a growing number of major league teams shifting from the central city to luxurious new stadium–arena complexes in the suburbs. The glamour of minicities also draws new hotels and high-quality residential development. For instance, the prestigious French Sofitel hotel chain chose suburban Minneapolis for its first American venture, and the Hyatt House chain Cherry Hill, New Jersey, for its first hotel in the Northeast (right foreground of Figure 4.12); such facilities, of course, greatly enhance suburbia as a leading site for both business conferences and larger conventions. Increasingly, the most elegant new condominium and apartment complexes are also lured near prestige-rich suburban activity centers, which now command some of the highest prices and rentals in the metropolis. High-rise structures are particularly favored by their affluent residents, whose small non-nuclear-family households are much more attuned to the centralized work, shopping, and recreational opportunities offered by minicities (Hirsch, 1977, p. 278).

Although the minicity has introduced significant economic and geographical efficiencies to the overall suburban scene, a number of corollary local problems have materialized in all but a small handful of carefully planned cores. The King of Prussia map (Figure 4.13) clearly illustrates the main problem—a lack of cohesion among component activities. This intraminicity hodgepodge pattern results from the independent actions of developers and builders, whose uncoordinated, differently-timed location decisions guarantee a piecemeal and haphazard accretion of uses as the land surrounding the nuclear shopping mall is filled in. Thus, what emerges is not a true multifunctional core but rather a loose cluster of isolated and specialized unifunctional subcenters, a development process documented by Gruen (1973, pp. 90–91) for a number of suburban minicities. Internal mobility, then, is often a major deficiency, as short-distance auto travel, usually among parking lots separated by less than a mile, is required in order to move from the site of one function to that of another. The internal minicity dispersion of activities and parking facilities also forces the dangerous mixing of slow-moving short-distance and higher-speed through traffic on interconnecting main roads as well as adding greatly to local highway congestion, the latter exacerbated by the growing size of individual enterprises that continue to cluster in and attract even more traffic to the expanding core. Occasional attempts are made to alleviate these problems through better planning, and improved traffic-flow schemes have even been mandated to get zoning board approval for enlarging such malls as King of Prussia and Tyson's Corner. Most successful are comprehensively planned unit developments (PUDs), such as Echelon near Cherry Hill, New Jersey (which won an important court test in the late 1970s), and southern California's Newport Center (Figure 1.4), where the developer owns and controls a wide zone of surrounding land in order to resist the disorderly encroachment of other activities near the central retail–employment core. However, the almost universal lack of stringent nonresidential land controls assures that most suburban minicities will remain inefficient locally structured agglomerations.

The Emergence of New Minicity Forms

As the multipurpose suburban center proliferates and matures, numerous variations of this novel urban form are emerging in the early 1980s. Several cores are becoming more specialized while others pause in their development to function as incomplete minicities; some grow superimposed on old suburban towns rather than being oriented to new highways, and many are now even abandoning compact sites to spread linearly along expressway corridors.

Among the outer-city growth poles increasingly associated with concentrations of specialized activities, airport cores are most widespread. Every major metropolis today possesses a thriving suburban airport–freeway complex consisting of shopping centers, industrial parks, office campuses, hotels, and residential towers. These complexes command enormous prestige value and often radiate outward for miles along main airport approach routes. The area around O'Hare International Airport just outside Chicago is the quintessential example, with local businesses only too eager to identify with the glamorous jet-age image of "the world's busiest airport" (Berry and Cohen, 1973, pp. 446–447). Such nodes are often the leading metropolitan employment center after the CBD; not surprisingly, over one-third of suburban Chicago's office space has been attracted to O'Hare's vicinity, and at least 75 percent of the 25,000+ employees at the vast Centex Industrial Park in nearby Elk Grove Village reverse-commute from the central city's blue-collar neighborhoods. Moreover, as a hotel–convention–entertainment center, the O'Hare area has become Chicago's "Second City," with nearly 50 hotels, over 7500 guest rooms, and a year-round occupancy rate above 90 percent. Huge airports also play a major role at the national level as U.S. economic and societal organization reach continental proportions. Social commentator Tom Wolfe, only partly in jest, has already pronounced O'Hare America's intellectual center, because at any one time more artists and intellectuals en route to public appearances can be found there awaiting connecting flights than anywhere else in the nation. In fact, such airports are even achieving global stature: the gateway function of Miami International, for instance, has attracted the Latin American division headquarters of Exxon, Goodyear, Dow Chemical, Texaco, and more than 50 other big multinational corporations to the nearby suburb of Coral Gables.

Nowhere is the growing importance of the suburban airport complex more evident than in northern Texas' Dallas–Fort Worth metropolis, where it has become the centerpiece of a regional "Metroplex" that includes 11 counties, 161 incorporated cities, and a rapidly growing population of over 3 million (*Fortune*, October 1976). The ultramodern Dallas–Fort Worth Airport, opened in 1974, is the largest and most efficient facility in the United States and when developed to full capacity will handle more daily traffic than New York City's three airports combined. Its suburban location midway between the two CBDs has already acquired a metropolitan-wide magnetism so powerful that even the mayor of Dallas has conceded that "the airport creates a commonality of interest, tending to melt away the importance of city limits" (*Fortune*, October 1976, p. 62). The suburbs of Arlington, Grand Prairie, and Irving that surround the airport (Figure 4.14) are enjoying an economic boom in an already burgeoning region which is virtually unparalleled anywhere in the country. Business activities of every sort continue to migrate into this prospering corner of the Sunbelt, lured by the area's prestige, growth mentality, newness of suburban facilities, recreational amenities, and relatively modest cost of living. American Airlines is but one of the many large companies that has relocated its home office to the Metroplex, which is already in the top 10 of corporate headquarters complexes and steadily moving up.

Whereas minicities are likeliest to develop around the most accessible suburban points where two freeways intersect, numerous multipurpose activity concentrations of smaller proportions appear at less superior locations on the highway network. These lesser multifunctional centers are often

Figure 4.14 An aerial view showing a portion of the rapidly growing suburban corridor that links the Dallas–Fort Worth Airport with Dallas itself (left horizon). Among the suburban facilities that line the John W. Carpenter Freeway looping to the right between our vantage point and the Dallas city line are the regional headquarters of Allstate Insurance, the University of Dallas campus, and Texas Stadium (home of the NFL's Dallas Cowboys). (Courtesy of Southland Real Estate Resources, Inc., developer of the 3500-acre Las Colinas planned community to occupy most of the open space in the lower half of the photograph.)

partially formed minicities in that one element, such as the regional mall or office complex, is missing; others may be incipient suburban cores whose activities have not yet attained a scale to qualify them for minicity status. Many will continue or resume their growth and become complete minicities, although the sharply rising costs of land at these high-access locations will almost surely dictate tighter activity clustering. Recognizing such heightening economic pressures, Douglass (1974) has predicted that minicities will evolve into high-rise "omnicenters" characterized by more intensified vertical uses of space, featuring multilevel complexes of mixed activities built over indoor parking facilities. These forces are also beginning to encourage the growth of minicities at points other than new freeway locations. We have already noted that both Stamford and White Plains in suburban New York's Fairfield–Westchester corporate business complex are old towns that are being totally revitalized as major retail–employment cores. Not every older suburb is a candidate for such a renaissance—both Stamford and White Plains are close to regional freeways—but where a burgeoning suburban economy, good accessibility, local political clout, and a lack of nearby competing activity centers coincide, the superimposing of minicities on preexisting settlements is a trend that can be expected to persist.

Before the appearance of minicities in the early 1970s, suburban economic activities were more geographically dispersed than they are today. Although centralization—increasingly reinforced by energy considerations—has now become a powerful force even in those classic "spread cities" of southern California and Long Island, the result has not always been the rise of compact nucleations. In many suburban rings, the activity concentration process has also occurred with respect to expressway corridors in which the components of a minicity are spread in linear fashion among closely spaced interchanges along several miles of superhighway. Baerwald (1978b) has defined this major variant of the minicity the *suburban freeway corridor* (SFC), and has documented its emergence along a 7-mile stretch of Interstate 494 in the southern Minneapolis suburbs of Bloomington, Edina, and Richfield near the Twin Cities' airport. This SFC contains a complete mix of metropolitan-scale entertainment, shopping, and business establishments; not only is it the second largest concentration of employment in the Minneapolis–St. Paul region, but also the area's "nighttime capital" and business meeting center that contains more hotel rooms than both CBDs combined. The linear pattern superseded the more common minicity nucleation here because there was no initial dominant regional shopping mall to focus growth at a single interchange. Since the other high-order uses did not particularly attract or repel each other, they were free to sort themselves out at adjacent interchanges within the coalescing development corridor, their specific locations a function of land availability, timing of building, and competitive economic position vis-à-vis other activities. Baerwald concludes that SFCs—and most other minicities as well, for that matter—are especially attracted to intersuburban circumferential freeway corridors, important broader arcs of new suburban nonresidential development that are now examined in detail.

Minicities, Beltways, and the Multinodal Metropolis

Although minicities function as the focal points and anchors of individual sectors of suburbia, at the metropolitan scale one observes that an increasingly unified system of minicities and lesser suburban activity concentrations now dominates the geographical structuring of the entire outer city. This multinodal system is shaped by the configuration of the interconnecting expressway network, primarily circumferential *beltways*, which have become the most prominent routes in the suburban freeway matrix because they directly link the booming sectors of the outer ring.

Circumferential superhighways were originally conceived as bypasses around major cities, but rapid development after World War II of the peripheries of these urban centers soon provided such arteries with a more important function: to serve the large new suburban population that had settled in its girdling corridor. The nation's first limited-access high-speed circumferential, Massachusetts Route 128, built around Boston in the late 1940s and early 1950s, was an initial response to the region's postwar suburbanization. Route 128 was constructed not to satisfy existing travel demands but rather to make the automobile the primary metropolitan transport mode to facilitate intersuburban trip making (Schaeffer and Sclar, 1975, pp. 90–91). This highly successful expressway shaped the population growth of Boston's suburbs in the fifties. Also known as "Electronics Highway"—a name not really deserved since that dispersing industry was only attracted to the highway's general vicinity (and increasingly to more glamorous Sunbelt locations, such as Silicon Valley and Texas' Metroplex in the 1980s—Route 128 appealed powerfully to many other employers and retailers who flocked to locate within the corridor.

The 1956 Federal Interstate Highway Act greatly accelerated the spread of the circumferential freeway. The intercity expressways mandated by this law required that central city bypass routes be built in most metropolitan areas, especially in the congested northeastern seaboard Megalopolis, where the original bypass links constructed around major cities (e.g., Baltimore's Harbor Tunnel Thruway) were often later extended into complete beltways. By the early seventies more than 80 beltways were in operation, and even in metropolises containing only partially circumferential freeways, the attractions of these corridors promoted considerable suburban economic growth. Although the peak access interchanges (where beltways and radial expressways converge) were likeliest to spawn complete minicities, highly visible corridor segments lying between exits were also prized for their free advertising potential and are usually lined solidly with eye-catching industrial parks, office buildings, and apartment complexes.

The growing locational pull of such high-status beltways as Atlanta's Perimeter, Houston's Loop, and Chicago's Tri-State Tollway dominates the post-1975 suburbanization of people and activities. Also affected are outer-city facilities which predated the construction of beltways: large retail and employment centers frequently induced planners to route new freeways near them; their operations increasingly focus on the new opportunities created by rapid growth within recently opened circumferential corridors; and their own physical expansion stimulated by this suburban development is likely to be oriented to the beltway and its concentrated minicities and SFCs. Hughes (1974, p. 4) captures exactly the flavor of this ongoing movement:

> Vast arcs of economic activity have sprouted along newly-completed circumferential roadways, which are dotted with the physical monu-

ments to the suburban success story. Regional shopping centers, office towers, and sprawling campus-style corporate headquarters represent the fullest flowering of the historic migration out of American cities. Huge numbers of Americans live, work, play, shop and dine within the physical confines of this freeway culture [as the suburbs emerge] as entities independent of the older central cities which they surround.

Thus, we are now witnessing the rise of a continuous unitary curvilinear outer city whose circumferential freeway spine functions as both lifeline and Main Street of suburbia and is increasingly the key to understanding its overall spatial organization. The consequences of this trend for total intrametropolitan travel flows can be observed in Figure 4.15. This 1980 traffic pattern forecast for the Baltimore region, based on a projection of early 1970s flow data, shows the dominance of circumferential automobile travel focused on various suburban activity cores, with only 7 percent of the traffic destined for the CBD (Ward and Paulhus, 1974, p. 25). The situation is much the same throughout metropolitan America. Greene (1978) and Gruenstein (1979) find, in a half-dozen large SMSAs studied, that up to

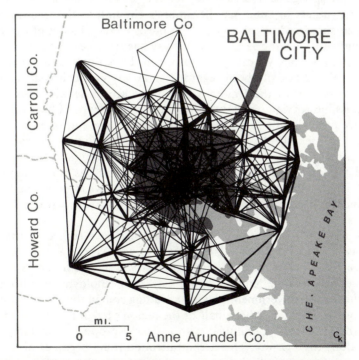

Figure 4.15 Forecasted 1980 travel desires among the internal districts of metropolitan Baltimore. (Source: Avery, 1972, p. 14. Reproduced by permission of the National Academy of Sciences.)

31 percent of total metropolitan employment is already clustered in a small number of suburban municipalities. And the U.S. Department of Labor has acknowledged since 1977 that the fastest creation of jobs in the nation is very likely taking place within the suburban beltway corridors of both large and small SMSAs in every region.

The travel flows predicted in Figure 4.15 may even be conservative given the continuing remarkable development along suburban Baltimore's Beltway. Known locally as the "Golden Horseshoe," this corridor is capturing much of the productive activity in the metropolis. Several important suburban facilities were already located close to its path (e.g., Bethlehem Steel's vast Sparrows Point complex, which employs more than 30,000 workers), and new employers continue to be attracted in rising numbers. The most spectacular acquisition of the seventies was the U.S. Social Security Administration (13,000+ employees), which relocated from the central city to its new headquarters office complex adjacent to the Beltway in the western suburb of Woodlawn. Moreover, the county seat of Towson, located at the apex of the Golden Horseshoe, has expanded into an impressive minicity that includes government and hospital complexes as well as two major college campuses (Goucher and Towson State).

The success of suburban Baltimore's circumferential freeway corridor has been surpassed in the adjoining suburbs of the District of Columbia to the southwest, where the Capital Beltway has truly become Main Street for all of metropolitan Washington. Although the nation's capital and its suburbs have traditionally been regarded as an atypical urban area with little to teach the rest of the United States, there are those who insist that it is now possible to view the District region as a metropolis "where the problems are basically the same as those in most others, but often more clearly defined" (Grier, 1971, p. 45). Because the Washington metropolis grew more rapidly in the 1960s than any of the other largest SMSAs, was one of the first to complete its suburban beltway and has since become a national leader among postindustrial complexes, what is happening there may indeed be indicative of trends emerging in urban America during the eighties.

Since 1960, over 1 million new residents have settled in the Capital Beltway corridor. A dozen regional malls as well as several other major suburban activity nuclei have sprung up at nearly every one of the 38 exits along the freeway's 66-mile length (Figure 4.4). New employment is burgeoning, with the federal government playing a leading role in the economic development of the corridor. About half of the region's federal jobs have dispersed from the District of Columbia, with a sizable proportion of them now located along the Beltway. This decentralization trend began prior to the construction of the superhighway, and many government facilities situated in or near the circumferential corridor enjoyed enhanced accessibility and rapid expansion with the arrival of the expressway. Among the myriad large headquarters and branch offices of federal agencies which are found in this suburban corridor are HEW's Public Health Service, Commerce's Bureau of the Census, Defense's Department of the Navy, The National Agricultural Research Center, The Central Intelligence Agency, The Atomic Energy Commission, and The National Bureau of Standards. The last two facilities are located a short distance beyond the girdling corridor but draw most of their works forces via the Beltway, and all except the Census Bureau grew to their present major size in the suburbs following the introduction of this ring freeway.

Private business activity is also growing swiftly in the flourishing Beltway corridor (see Table 4.2) as the postindustrial national economy matures and companies increasingly cluster around information-rich Washington. Corporate headquarters activity had been minimal through the mid-seventies, but times are changing and more recent developments may be harbingers of things to come in the near future (DeWitt, 1978). Since 1976 such firms as Time–Life Books, Marriott, AAA, and VISA have arrived in the D.C. suburbs, and Mobil Oil's 1980 opening of its U.S. divisional headquarters at Falls Church, near Tyson's Corner, Virginia, is viewed by some as a prelude to moving down the rest of its corporate operations from Manhattan. Besides the area's natural amenities and best-educated labor pool in the country, pleased executives cite suburban Washington's transportation and unparalleled communication advantages for contact with agencies of the federal government. Indeed, the growing involvement of that government in business affairs has lured in so many trade associations that the Washington region surpassed New York City in the mid-1970s as the premier location for these activities. Moreover, such glamorous new industries as energy are increasingly attracted, not only to be near—and influence—regulators, but also to more aggressively compete for federal research monies (Figure 4.16). The intensifying linkage between the private and public sectors shown in the map is embodied, too, in the current explosion of small consulting firms: in fact, the local Washington media often complain about "Beltway bandits," a post-Watergate expression for hustling government executives who take early retirements in order to set up lucrative consultantship businesses serving their former agencies.

Perhaps the most far-reaching impact of the Capital Beltway and its sister circumferential freeways is the suburban economic self-sufficiency they foster by connecting minicities together. With these multifunctional cores offering the full array of urban goods and services and with driving times such that half the beltway can be traversed in less time than it takes to travel from any point on it into the CBD, a steadily increasing majority of suburban people and businesses are finding that contact with the nearby central city is no longer necessary. This brings us full circle back to the polycentric Urban Realms model introduced in the opening chapter (Figure 1.3), a construct that has been derived step by step here in Chapter 4. To be

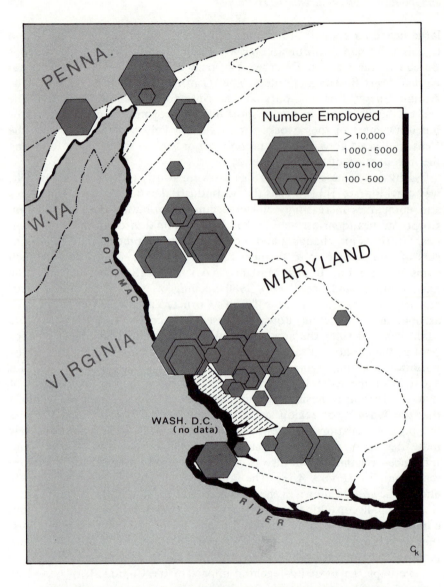

Figure 4.16 Research, development, and scientific activities in Maryland, 1972. The huge activity complex ringing the District of Columbia dominates the map. The cartographic projection used is centered on the state's population centroid. (Source: Derek Thompson, Joseph W. Wiedel and Associates, *An Economic and Social Atlas of Maryland*, College Park: University of Maryland, Department of Geography, and the Maryland Department of Economic and Community Development, 1974, p. 86; adaptation prepared by permission of the Chancellor of the University of Maryland.)

sure, this model was only intended as a broad organizational framework to accommodate intrametroplitan spatial changes which began to occur in the mid-1960s. However, the preponderance of recent empirical evidence gathered by Greene (1980), Hirsch (1977), Schneider and Noguchi (1977), Gottdiener (1977), and other researchers demonstrates both the continuing validity of the construct as well as its potential for upgrading into a much-needed theoretical structural model of the transformed metropolis. The elements for such formal model-building involve Vance's Realms notion, the noneconomic forces shaping the location of urban activities, minicity and SFC formation, and the influence of circumferential freeways. But any blending of these variables must also recognize the tightening energy supply situation of the late twentieth century, an increasingly discussed suburban issue that we shall take up next.

Energy and the New Urban Form: Will the Suburbs Survive the Energy Crisis?

The increasing cost and scarcity of energy, abetted by the supply interruption "crises" of 1974 and 1979, prompts unrelenting speculation about suburban collapse, widespread return to the central cities and mass transit, and profound changes in automobile-based American lifestyles (Reinhold, 1979). Let us immediately respond to these doomsayers and put any doubts to rest right here at the outset of our discussion: this recentralization scenario is based on a misreading of the forces currently shaping urban spatial structure—often deliberately by emotional critics of suburbanization—and there is no chance of such metropolitan implosion in the foreseeable future. A critical mass of higher-order economic activities has, almost certainly, irreversibly suburbanized since the 1960s, and the national commitment and investment vis-à-vis the outer city's new business complexes is so enormous that energy prices will never even approach the costs of relocating those facilities. This is the metropolitan reality of the 1980s, and the starting point for any serious discussion of energy and urban form.

Within the transformed metropolis it is clear that minicities are going to play a pivotal role, because if urban contraction does occur it will be with reference to them and not the central city's CBD. A far likelier scenario is that gasoline prices and availability will simply curtail further urban expansion, thus assuring that existing suburban cores may well avoid having their dominance challenged by newer exurban centers that would presumably arise along an advancing metropolitan frontier. In and of themselves, minicities are already helping to meet the societal goal of reduced energy use by offering a powerful centralized alternative to the suburban-wide dispersion of nonresidential activities. It is also worth noting that nearly all of these cores were developed by private-sector resources and arose without the intervention of public policymakers and planners. Geographical efficiency, as we saw repeatedly in Chapter 2, simply made good business sense as metropolitan structure once again readapts to an apparently changing mobility framework.

Intuitively, of course, one sees the multinodal metropolis as much more energy-efficient than a single-centered urban region, because the average distance to the nearest high-order activity core will be significantly lower for the total residential population (see Figure 1.2). This perception is confirmed by the measures made in recent studies of transportation researchers, who conclude that in a polycentric metropolis individual trip lengths may be up to 30 percent shorter and use 57 percent less gasoline (Ramsey, 1978; Greene, 1977, p. 2). Their most detailed investigations have dealt with the suburban journey to work, and their findings contradict many popular beliefs about contemporary commuting behavior. Although it is true that the automobile has engendered the spreading of the labor force and employers through much of the outer city, the opportunity of access to the best-perceived communities in the dispersed residential mosaic afforded by a suburban workplace has not been abused. Hartshorn (1978) thus finds that in Atlanta's outer ring, work trips are not randomly oriented but are highly organized into regular flows which focus on new suburban employment cores; he also notes that such compact energy-efficient laborsheds are being observed in several metropolitan areas. This finding that a reasonable accordance between the location of suburban home and work still exists is further borne out in the latest national commuting data for 1975 (U.S. Bureau of the Census, 1979). The average work-trip distance for people living and working in suburbia is only 8 miles (80 miles per week), as opposed to 12 miles for the decreasing number of suburbs-to-CBD commuters, again underscoring the efficiency of the multicentered metropolis. Mean travel times (21 to 22 minutes) are virtually identical for commuting in central cities and suburbs despite longer distances in the latter, but for those who both reside and hold jobs in the outer city the work trip drops to 17 minutes, which averages out to a very respectable 28+ mph for peak-hour driving. Moreover, these present energy efficiencies are believed to be capable of considerable improvement. Vance (1976, p. 40), for one, predicts that workers can and will move closer to their workplaces as travel costs multiply, a desirable reduction in the total urban journey to work that can much more easily be achieved by the continued use of cars than by a shift to mass transit.

That continued emphasis will undoubtedly be challenged by planners and urbanologists, most of whom have vigorously waged a "war" against the automobile for decades. Bruce-Briggs (1977), however, presents a persuasive counterargument by demonstrating the unfairness of these attacks. Automobiles won out over all competing forms of transportation because they constitute the superior movement system by offering unparalleled convenience, speed, and flexibility for point-to-point travel. Suburbanization is seen as one of the auto's chief benefits, because it made a better-quality life possible for tens of millions, an advantage that overwhelmingly outweighs the costs cited by critics. These polemics aside, Americans are not about to abandon their commitments to cars and suburbs as the price of gasoline rises. People proved during the Depression of the 1930s that they were willing to make great financial sacrifices to keep their cars, and in western Europe today an automobile culture flourishes as fuel prices soar to triple U.S. levels. Despite its substantial recent increases, American gasoline prices (which constitute only a tiny percentage of the total cost of operating a car) are still fairly inexpensive. Even at 70 cents per gallon in the mid-1970s gasoline remained relatively cheaper as a proportion of median family income than in 1960 (Bruce-Briggs, 1974); the 1979 increase to above $1 a gallon has changed that very little, and it is hardly reasonable to expect people to alter their lifestyles to save $5 per week! Reducing the supply of gasoline will probably have a more pronounced effect but is not expected to produce basic suburban changes. In the event of further supply interruptions there will again be inconvenience but still sufficient fuel available to permit essential driving for commuting, shopping, and family business purposes. According to a survey by the U.S. Department of Transportation in the late 1970s, those essential trips amount to only 58 percent of total automobile usage, so that there is wide latitude for gasoline conservation. The remaining 42 percent largely involves driving for social and recreational purposes, and it is here that cutbacks are rather easily made; this happened during the mid-1979 fuel shortage, with long-distance vacation trips the major casualty. Thus, the dominance of the automobile will persist and perhaps even intensify, a trend that will be supported by federal government policies (Holsendolph, 1979). Programs encouraging the "reinvention" of the auto will be emphasized so as to quickly produce a new generation of smaller, more-fuel-efficient vehicles. The suburban majority in the House of Representatives, certain to be increased markedly after the 1981 reapportionment, also guarantees that considerable future expenditures will be made on improving worn-out metropolitan roadways. On the other hand, new mass transit programs are not likely to be heavily stressed in the 1980s, because they are increasingly unable to respond to urban travel needs.

Mass transit has been a declining mode of suburban transportation since the 1920s, and the recent emergence of the multinodal metropolis has rendered its CBD-oriented network almost totally irrelevant to the travel needs of the outer city. Curiously, the obsolete central-city-as-hub pattern was stubbornly adhered to in the new subway systems planned in the 1970s (for Washington, Atlanta, Denver, Miami, Baltimore, and Buffalo), despite mounting evidence (e.g., Schneider and Noguchi, 1977) that direct circumferential links among suburban activity centers would be far more successful in the outer ring. However, even these routes would be limited in their overall effectiveness because fixed transit lines can only serve corridors in which travel demands are heavily concentrated, while the overwhelming number of suburban trip origins and destinations are so widely dispersed that only the automobile will work. Nowhere is this better demonstrated than in the case of metropolitan San Francisco's Bay Area Rapid Transit (BART) system, an ultramodern CBD-focused rail network that was unfortunately built in the sixties and early seventies at precisely the time that the urban region was turning inside out. Webber (1976) also cites additional reasons for BART's failure, lessons that he urges other metropolises to heed in their own transport planning: the system had no effect in shaping regional structure, especially in suburbia; commuters rank speed well below door-to-door, transfer-free convenience; a majority of riders were those who formerly used buses within BART's corridors, whereas the number of car drivers attracted were too few to reduce highway traffic congestion; many of those suburbanites seduced away from their autos chose to ride express buses directly to the CBD rather than transfer to BART, despite a general dislike for bus commuting; and most distressing of all, the area's poor paid for BART through taxes while its mostly affluent outer-suburban riders enjoyed the subsidized train fares. Vance (1976, pp. 40–42, 46–48), arguing for nonintervention and letting auto users make their own adjustments to fuel scarcity, not only concurs in these findings but warns further that new transit systems are energy-*gluttonous* both to construct and in the longer-distance travel they obviously encourage. Such thinking is finally beginning to take hold at the federal level, and the outlook for future suburban transit now appears to involve far less grandiose plans and a shift from rail to modest bus schemes.

All current signs indicate that the suburbs will not only survive the energy crisis but continue to prosper and grow even more dominant economically. Energy's main structural impact is likeliest to be slackened outward metropolitan expansion accompanied by a more intensive use of space within the built-up suburban ring. The ongoing nucleation trend vis-à-vis activity centers can be expected to continue strongly, perhaps even resulting in the spread of high-rise minicities. Residentially, higher densities are anticipated as multiple dwellings become more widely accepted, particularly in the inner suburbs and rail corridors, where the aging housing stock is increasingly in need of replacement. Beyond these superficial changes, the suburban status quo will almost surely persist because there is so much room for conservation and accommodation to the changed energy situation. Since vast private and public resources underpin much of suburban society, new energy-saving solutions in everyday life will proliferate fastest there—especially more-fuel-efficient houses and cars. That clout also extends to the broader political scene at both the state and national level, and could well translate into additional government aid if suburban constituents are threatened by an unexpected worsening of energy conditions.

Summary

This chapter has surveyed the ongoing irreversible suburbanization of a critical mass of economic activity and the resulting transformation of intraurban spatial structure. A layer-by-layer integration of retailing, manufacturing, and office–industry employment revealed that all three are responding to new locational forces that are producing an interconnected multinodal metropolis increasingly dominated by suburban minicities and related concentrations of highest-order business activities. Prestigious superregional shopping malls paved the way for this ultimate deconcentration of the American city, providing both activity and social focal points for the previously centerless suburban ring. Manufacturers and then office companies, no longer bound to the central city and increasingly guided by noneconomic location factors, were quickly attracted in steadily rising numbers to the vicinities of these high-status retail nodes. By 1980, these multifunctional cores were achieving equality with the CBD as downtown lost the final traces of its former metropolitan centrality advantage. In one urban region after another, the essence of the contemporary metropolis was becoming so embodied in its vast beltway-linked, curvilinear outer city that even the looming energy shortage could not threaten suburban dominance.

This turning inside out of the metropolis is accompanied by its splitting asunder, as the trends discussed here in Chapter 4 amount to nothing less than the arrival of the economic and cultural independence of suburbia from the central city that spawned it. The shattering of intrametropolitan interdependency in the 1970s, of course, marks a momentous watershed in U.S. urban history. As the suburbs achieve freedom from reliance on the nearby central city, they increasingly depend on other places, many of them distant, to which they are directly connected by a growing complex of highway, airplane, cable, computer, and even satellite networks (Birch, 1975, p. 31). More research is urgently needed on this fascinating reorientation as suburbia swiftly forges its own separate links to the national and international economies. There is also a pressing need to better understand the internal geography of the outer city's economy, especially whether or not the independent suburban realms described in Chapter 1 are persisting as newly completed beltways facilitate the circumferential coalescence of outer-ring-activity interactions.

Perhaps the most immediate and significant impact of this new independence of the outer city is the rapidly growing suburban avoidance of central cities. Several press reports (Rosenthal, 1974; U.S.N.W.R., 1972, and Karasik, 1973) reveal a widening suburbanite perception of the central city as an increasingly irrelevant place, corroborated decisively in *The New York Times* poll discussed in Chapter 1. This is quite understandable, because everything the suburban resident requires now lies within easy automobile reach in the outer city. When a rare good or service is not available, a close suburban substitute is usually accepted in place of the undesirably perceived trip to the CBD; not surprisingly, most suburbanites interviewed either could not remember their last visit downtown or recalled only a single trip there in connection with a special occasion. Scholarly investigations of this form of geographical avoidance behavior are badly needed. In fact, in the entire pre-1980 social science literature on suburbia only one published research report directly addressed this question: Zikmund's (1971) brief and now-dated study of the frequency of downtown use by affluent and well-educated residents of one of Philadelphia's wealthiest suburban Main Line townships. He found that even in this hardly typical outer-city municipality, with its excellent commuter rail connection and strong traditional working, shopping, and cultural ties to Center City Philadelphia, trends similar to those now reported in the popular media were observed. Suburbanites, particularly middle-class families, increasingly have no use for the central city, and what contact does occur is directly related to daily commuting to the CBD (which has been declining steadily since 1960).

Detachment from the central city can also be interpreted according to the demographic composition of today's suburban population. The postwar generation is to a large degree suburban-born, without firsthand experience in true city living. Moreover, and more important, the lion's share of recent migration to the suburbs has come not from the adjacent central city but from largely suburban sources in other metropolises (Birch, 1975). Thus,

> Most new suburbanites have no ties whatsoever to the old [central] city. It is not the hub of their cultural, economic, material, or social lives; it is not their previous home; it is *nothing* to them— just another place (not even a relatively large place) in their sprawling metropolitan home territory. What impact do arguments of moral responsibility or abstract dependency have for these people? Virtually none (Zikmund, 1975, p. 43).

Given this attitude on the part of residents and producers in the ever more functionally independent outer city of the 1980s, what is to become of the central city? Very clearly, the intraurban deconcentration of its most vital population groups and economic activities cannot persist for much longer before we become a nation without important large cities (see Patterson, 1976). Although many urban planners and other proponents of city living insist that central cities can recover their leadership, trends shaping the metropolitan reality in the closing decades of this century would dictate otherwise. The big city is not about to die because large numbers of people will continue to prefer to live and work there, and the CBD will continue to service the innermost urban realm. Yet, as an activity center that is increasingly coequal with the burgeoning suburban minicities that now surround the old metropolitan core, downtown's *raison d'être* as regional economic focus is disappearing. Although little can be done to reverse that structural transformation, economic problems might be ameliorated through enlightened policymaking which recognizes (1) the sharply reduced role of large cities in today's suburban-dominated multicentered metropolis, and (2) that existing CBD activities remain located there by choice and not necessity. Although vital central cities are no longer essential to the nation's economic well-being, perhaps a time will come again when they will have a leading role to play in urban America. For the foreseeable future, however, Irving Kristol's (1974, p. 282) pronouncement is worth keeping in mind:

> . . . we can say with fair certainty that we are moving toward an urban civilization without great cities—and that this movement is so without precedent that prophecies of doom or hopes of utopia are both premature.

SUGGESTED READINGS

BERRY, BRIAN J. L., AND YEHOSHUA S. COHEN. "Decentralization of Commerce and Industry: The Restructuring of Metropolitan America," in Louis H. Masotti and Jeffrey K. Hadden, eds., *The Urbanization of the Suburbs* (Beverly Hills: Sage Publications, Urban Affairs Annual Reviews, Vol. 7, 1973), pp. 431–455.

BIRCH, DAVID L. "From Suburb to Urban Place," *The Annals of the American Academy of Political and Social Science*, 422 (1975), 25–35.

BRECKENFELD, GURNEY. "'Downtown' Has Fled to the Suburbs," *Fortune*, October 1972, 80–87, 156, 158, 162.

BRUCE-BRIGGS, BARRY. *The War against the Automobile* (New York: E. P. Dutton & Company, Inc., 1977).

GOTTDIENER, MARK. *Planned Sprawl: Private and Public Interests in Suburbia* (Beverly Hills: Sage Publications, Sage Library of Social Research, Vol. 38, 1977).

HARTSHORN, TRUMAN A. "Industrial/Office Parks: A New Look for the City," *Journal of Geography*, 72 (1973), 33–45.

HIRSCH, WERNER Z. "The Coming Age of the Polynucleated Metropolis," in Herrington J. Bryce, ed., *Small Cities in Transition: The Dynamics of Growth and and Decline* (Cambridge, MA: Ballinger Publishing Co., 1977), pp. 267–281.

KOWINSKI, WILLIAM S. "The Malling of America," *New Times Magazine*, May 1, 1978, 30–55.

MANNERS, GERALD. "The Office in Metropolis: An Opportunity for Shaping Metropolitan America," *Economic Geography*, 50 (1974), 93–110.

MULLER, PETER O. "The Suburbanization of Corporate Headquarters: What Are the Trends and Consequences?" *Vital Issues* (Washington, CT: Center for Information on America, April, 1978).

QUANTE, WOLFGANG. *The Exodus of Corporate Headquarters from New York City* (New York: Praeger Publishers, Inc., 1976).

STANBACK, THOMAS M., AND RICHARD KNIGHT. *Suburbanization and the City* (Montclair, NJ: Allanheld, Osmun & Co., 1976).

References

ABLER, RONALD F. *Employment Shifts and Transportation Policy: Changes in the Locations of Corporate Headquarters in Pennsylvania, 1950-1970* (University Park, PA: Pennsylvania Transportation Institute, Pennsylvania State University, 1974).

ADAMS, JOHN S. "Residential Structure of Midwestern Cities," *Annals of the Association of American Geographers*, 60 (1970), 37–62.

ANAS, ALEX, AND LEON N. MOSES. "Transportation and Land Use in the Mature Metropolis," in Charles L. Leven, ed., *The Mature Metropolis* (Lexington, MA: Lexington Books, 1978), pp. 149–168.

ANASTASIA, G. "Mt. Laurel: Responsibility vs. Reality—'Moral Victory' Won't Build Homes," *The Philadelphia Inquirer*, October 12, 1975, 1-B, 4-B.

ARMSTRONG, REGINA B. (WITH BORIS PUSHKAREV, ED.). *The Office Industry: Patterns of Growth and Location* (Cambridge, MA: The MIT Press, 1972).

ARNOLD, JOSEPH L. *The New Deal in the Suburbs: A History of the Greenbelt Town Program, 1935-1954* (Columbus: Ohio State University Press, 1971).

ASHTON, PATRICK J. "The Political Economy of Suburban Development," in William K. Tabb and Larry Sawers, eds., *Marxism and the Metropolis: New Perspectives in Urban Political Economy* (New York: Oxford University Press, 1978), pp. 64–89.

AVERY, WILLIAM H. "Practical Requirements for Advanced Public Transportation Systems," *Highway Research Record*, 397 (1972), 12–25.

BABCOCK, RICHARD F. "Exclusionary Zoning: A Code Phrase for a Notable Legal Struggle," in Louis H. Masotti and Jeffrey K. Hadden, eds., *The Urbanization of the Suburbs* (Beverly Hills: Sage Publications, Urban Affairs Annual Reviews, Vol. 7, 1973), pp. 313–328.

BAERWALD, THOMAS J. "Locational Constraints on Large Suburban Residential Builders," paper presented at the annual meeting of The Association of American Geographers (1978a).

BAERWALD, THOMAS J. "The Emergence of a New 'Downtown'," *Geographical Review*, 68, 308–318 (1978b).

BAKER, EARL M., GUEST ED. "The Suburban Reshaping of American Politics," *Publius*, 5 (Winter, 1975), 1–144.

BALTZELL, E. DIGBY. *Philadelphia Gentlemen: The Making of a National Upper Class* (Chicago: Quadrangle Books, 1958).

BANHAM, REYNER. *Los Angeles: The Architecture of Four Ecologies* (New York: Penguin Books, 1971).

BARRATT, ROBERT N. *Exodus from New York City: An Investigation and Analysis of the Relocation of Corporate Headquarters out of New York City* (Clifton, NJ: Louis Schlesinger Company, 1977).

BEDERMAN, SANFORD H., AND JOHN S. ADAMS. "Job Accessibility and Underemployment," *Annals of the Association of American Geographers*, 64 (1974), 378–386.

BENSMAN, JOSEPH, AND ARTHUR VIDICH. "The New Class System and Its Life Styles," in Saul D. Feldman and Gerald W. Thielbar, eds., *Life Styles: Diversity in American Society* (Boston: Little, Brown and Company, 2nd rev. ed., 1975), pp. 129–143.

BERENS, RAYMOND A. "Danes to Build Princeton Center," *Philadelphia Bulletin*, November 26, 1978, F1, F2.

BERGER, BENNETT M. *Working Class Suburb: A Study of Auto Workers in Suburbia* (Berkeley: University of California Press, 1960).

BERGER, BENNETT M. "Suburbs, Subcultures, and Styles of Life," in Bennett M. Berger, *Looking for America: Essays on Youth, Suburbia, and Other American Obsessions* (Englewood Cliffs, NJ: Prentice-Hall, Inc., 1971), pp. 165–187.

BERGMAN, EDWARD M. *Eliminating Exclusionary Zoning: Reconciling Workplace and Residence in Suburban Areas* (Cambridge, MA: Ballinger Publishing Company, 1974).

BERRY, BRIAN J. L. "Contemporary Urbanization Processes," in Frank E. Horton, ed., *Geographical Perspectives and Urban Problems* (Washington, DC: National Academy of Sciences, 1973a), pp. 94–107.

BERRY, BRIAN J. L. *The Human Consequences of Urbanisation* (New York: St. Martin's Press, 1973b).

BERRY, BRIAN J. L. "The Decline of the Aging Metropolis: Cultural Bases and Social Process," in George Sternlieb and James W. Hughes, eds., *Post-industrial America: Metropolitan Decline & Inter-regional Job Shifts* (New Brunswick, NJ: Center for Urban Policy Research, Rutgers University, 1975a), pp. 175–185; final comment, pp. 266–267.

BERRY, BRIAN J. L. "Short-Term Housing Cycles in a Dualistic Metropolis," in Gary Gappert and Harold M. Rose, eds., *The Social Economy of Cities* (Beverly Hills: Sage Publications, Urban Affairs Annual Reviews, Vol. 9, 1975b), pp. 165–182.

BERRY, BRIAN J. L. *Conceptual Lags in Retail Development Policy or Can the Carter White House Save the C.B.D.?* (Cambridge, MA: Harvard University, Department of City and Regional Planning, Policy Note P79-3, December 1979).

BERRY, BRIAN J. L., AND YEHOSHUA S. COHEN. "Decentralization of Commerce and Industry," in Louis H. Masotti and Jeffrey K. Hadden, eds., *The Urbanization of the Suburbs* (Beverly Hills: Sage Publications, Urban Affairs Annual Reviews, Vol. 7, 1973), pp. 431–455.

BERRY, BRIAN J. L., AND DONALD C. DAHMANN. *Population Redistribution in the United States in the 1970s* (Washington, DC: National Academy of Sciences, 1977).

BERRY, BRIAN J. L., AND JOHN D. KASARDA. *Contemporary Urban Ecology* (New York: Macmillan Publishing Co., Inc., 1977).

BERRY, BRIAN J. L., CAROLE A. GOODWIN, ROBERT W. LAKE, AND KATHERINE B. SMITH. "Attitudes toward Integration: The Role of Status in Community Response to Racial Change," in Barry Schwartz, ed., *The Changing Face of the Suburbs* (Chicago: University of Chicago Press, 1976), pp. 221–264.

BIES, SUSAN S. "The Suburbanization of Banking Services," paper presented at the Regional Science Association Meeting, 1974.

BIRCH, DAVID L. "From Suburb to Urban Place," *The Annals of the American Academy of Political and Social Science*, 422 (1975), 25–35.

BIRMINGHAM, STEPHEN. *The Golden Dream: Suburbia in the 1970s* (New York: Harper & Row, Publishers, 1978).

BITTAN, DAVID. "Levitt or Leave It," *Philadelphia Magazine*, September, 1972, 79–85, 190–195.

BLUMBERG, LEONARD, AND MICHAEL LALLI. "Little Ghettoes: A Study of Negroes in the Suburbs," *Phylon*, 27 (1966), 117–131.

BOURNE, LARRY S. *Perspectives on the Inner City: Its Changing Character, Reasons for Decline and Revival* (Toronto: University of Toronto, Centre for Urban and Community Studies, Research Paper No. 94, February, 1978).

BRECKENFELD, GURNEY. "'Downtown' Has Fled to the Suburbs," *Fortune*, October, 1972, 80–87, 156, 158, 162.

BRECKENFELD, GURNEY. "Is the One-Family House Becoming a Fossil? Far from It," *Fortune*, April, 1976, 84–89, 164–165.

BROWNELL, BLAINE A. "A Symbol of Modernity: Attitudes toward the Automobile in Southern Cities in the 1920s," *American Quarterly*, 24 (March, 1972), 42–43.

BRUCE-BRIGGS, BARRY. "Gasoline Prices and the Suburban Way of Life," *The Public Interest*, 37 (Fall, 1974), 131–136.

BRUCE-BRIGGS, BARRY. *The War against the Automobile* (New York: E. P. Dutton & Company, Inc., 1977).

BUDER, STANLEY. *Pullman: An Experiment in Industrial Order and Community Planning, 1880–1930* (New York: Oxford University Press, 1967).

BUDER, STANLEY. "The Future of the American Suburbs," in Philip C. Dolce, ed., *Suburbia: The American Dream and Dilemma* (Garden City, NY: Anchor Press/Doubleday, 1976), pp. 193–216.

BURNS, ELIZABETH K. "The Enduring Affluent Suburb," *Landscape*, 24 (1980), 33–41.

Business Week. "More than a Suburb, Less than a City," September 5, 1977a, 76–77.

Business Week. "New York's Loss is Fairfield County's Gain," April 25, 1977b, 121–122.

CALDWELL, EARL. "The Problems of a Black Suburb," in Louis H. Masotti and Jeffrey K. Hadden, eds., *Suburbia in Transition* (New York: New Viewpoints, for *The New York Times*, 1974), pp. 78–81.

CALDWELL, WILLIAM A., ED. *How to Save Urban America: Key Issues Confronting Cities and Suburbs* (New York: Signet Books, 1973).

CASSIDY, ROBERT. "Moving to the Suburbs," *The New Republic*, January 22, 1972, 20–23.

CHOW, WILLARD TIM. "Minorities in the Suburbs: The Promise of Growth," in Leo E. Zonn, ed., *Minority Populations and the American City: A Geographic Approach* (Silver Spring, MD: Victor H. Winston & Sons, 1980).

CHRISTIAN, CHARLES M. "Emerging Patterns of Industrial Activity within Large Metropolitan Areas and Their Impact on the Central City Work Force," in Gary Gappert and Harold M. Rose, eds., *The Social Economy of Cities* (Beverly Hills: Sage Publications, Urban Affairs Annual Reviews, Vol. 9, 1975), pp. 213–246.

CHUDACOFF, HOWARD P. *The Evolution of American Urban Society* (Englewood Cliffs, NJ: Prentice-Hall, Inc., 1975). Second edition publ. 1980.

City, Magazine of Urban Life and Environment. "The Suburbs: Frontier of the 70s," January–February, 1971.

CLARK, SAMUEL D. *The Suburban Society* (Toronto: University of Toronto Press, 1966).

CLARK, THOMAS A. *Blacks in Suburbs: A National Perspective* (New Brunswick, NJ: Center for Urban Policy Research, Rutgers University, 1979).

CLAWSON, MARION. *Suburban Land Conversion in the United States* (Baltimore: Johns Hopkins University Press, 1971).

CLAY, GRADY. *Close-up: How to Read the American City* (New York: Praeger Publishers, 1973; also published in paperback by University of Chicago Press, 1980).

CLAY, PHILLIP L. "The Future of Suburban Cities and Their Black Populations," in Herrington J. Bryce, ed., *Small Cities in Transition: The Dynamics of Growth and Decline* (Cambridge, MA: Ballinger Publishing Company, 1977), pp. 301–312.

COLBY, CHARLES C. "Centrifugal and Centripetal Forces in Urban Geography," *Annals of the Association of American Geographers*, 23 (1933), 1–20.

COLEMAN, RICHARD P. "Patterns in Housing Market Goals by Socio-economic Class and Life Stages," in David L. Birch et al., eds., *America's Housing Needs: 1970 to 1980* (Cambridge, MA: Joint Center for Urban Studies of MIT and Harvard University, 1973), pp. 5-6-5-43.

COLLURA, JOHN, AND JAMES J. SCHUSTER. *Accessibility of Low Income Residential Areas in Philadelphia to Regional Industrial Parks* (Villanova, PA: Institute for Transportation Studies, Villanova University, 1971).

COLMAN, WILLIAM G. *Cities, Suburbs, and States: Governing and Financing Urban America* (New York: The Free Press, 1975).

CONNOLLY, HAROLD X. "Black Movement into the Suburbs: Suburbs Doubling Their Black Populations during the 1960s," *Urban Affairs Quarterly*, 9 (1973), 91–111.

COTTINGHAM, PHOEBE H. "Black Income and Metropolitan Residential Dispersion," *Urban Affairs Quarterly*, 10 (1975), 273–296.

COX, KEVIN R. *Conflict, Power and Politics in the City: A Geographic View* (New York: McGraw-Hill Book Company, 1973).

CREWDSON, JOHN M. "Houston Has Misgivings over Problems of Growth," *The New York Times*, August 13, 1979, A14.

CUTLER, IRVING. *Chicago: Metropolis of the Mid-continent* (Chicago: The Geographic Society of Chicago, 1973).

CYBRIWSKY, ROMAN A. "Revitalization of Downtown-Area Neighborhoods in the 1970s," in Stanley D. Brunn and James O. Wheeler, eds., *The American Metropolitan System: Present and Future* (Silver Spring, MD: Victor H. Winston & Sons, 1980), Chap. 2.

DANIELS, PETER W. "New Offices in the Suburbs," in James H. Johnson, ed., *Suburban Growth: Geographical Processes at the Edge of the Western City* (London: John Wiley & Sons Ltd., 1974), pp. 177–200.

DANIELSON, MICHAEL N. "Differentiation, Segregation, and Political Fragmentation in the American Metropolis," in A. E. Keir Nash, ed., *Governance and Population: The Governmental Implications of Population Change* (Washington, DC: Commission on Population Growth and the American Future, Research Reports, Vol. 4, 1972), pp. 143–176.

DANIELSON, MICHAEL N. *The Politics of Exclusion* (New York: Columbia University Press, 1976).

DARDEN, JOE T. "Blacks in the Suburbs: Their Number Is Rising, but Patterns of Segregation Persist," *Vital Issues* (Washington, CT: Center for Information on America, December, 1977).

DARNTON, JOHN. "The Service Industries Follow the Corporations," in Louis H. Masotti and Jeffrey K. Hadden, eds., *Suburbia in Transition* (New York: New Viewpoints, for *The New York Times*, 1974), pp. 90–94.

DAVIDOFF, LINDA, PAUL DAVIDOFF, AND NEIL N. GOLD. "The Suburbs Have to Open Their Gates," in Louis H. Masotti and Jeffrey K. Hadden, eds., *Suburbia in Transition* (New York: New Viewpoints, for *The New York Times*, 1974), pp. 134–150.

DAVIDOFF, PAUL, AND MARY E. BROOKS. "Zoning Out the Poor," in Philip C. Dolce, ed., *Suburbia: The American Dream and Dilemma* (Garden City, NY: Anchor Press/Doubleday, 1976), pp. 135–166.

DAWSON, JOHN A. "The Suburbanization of Retail Activity," in James H. Johnson, ed., *Suburban Growth: Geographical Processes at the Edge of the Western City* (London: John Wiley & Sons, Ltd., 1974), pp. 155–175.

DELANEY, PAUL. "Negroes Find Few Tangible Gains," in Louis H. Masotti and Jeffrey K. Hadden, eds., *Suburbia in Transition* (New York: New Viewpoints, for *The New York Times*, 1974a), pp. 278–282.

DELANEY, PAUL. "Dayton Suburbs Tackle Problems of 'Fair Share' Housing," *The New York Times*, November 17, 1974b, 67.

DEVISÉ, PIERRE. "The Suburbanization of Jobs and Minority Employment," *Economic Geography*, 52 (1976), 348–362.

DEWITT, KAREN. "More Business and Other Groups Find Washington Is Place to Be," *The New York Times*, February 6, 1978, D1, D3.

DINGEMANS, DENNIS J. "The Urbanization of Suburbia: The Renaissance of the Row House," *Landscape*, 20 (October, 1975), 20–31.

DINGEMANS, DENNIS J. "Rapid Transit and Suburban Residential Land Use," *Traffic Quarterly*, 32 (1978), 289–306.

DOBRINER, WILLIAM M., ED. *The Suburban Community* (New York: G. P. Putnam's Sons, 1958).

DOBRINER, WILLIAM M. *Class in Suburbia* (Englewood Cliffs, NJ: Prentice-Hall, Inc., 1963).

DOLCE, PHILIP C., ED. *Suburbia: The American Dream and Dilemma* (Garden City, NY: Anchor Press/Doubleday, 1976).

DONALDSON, SCOTT. *The Suburban Myth* (New York: Columbia University Press, 1969).

DOUGLASS, HARLAN P. *The Suburban Trend* (New York: Arno Press reprint of the 1925 original, 1970).

DOUGLASS, LATHROP. "Tomorrow: Omnicenters on the Landscape?" *Harvard Business Review*, March–April, 1974, 8, 12.

DOWNES, BRYAN T., AND JOHN N. COLLINS. "Community Stabilization in the Inner Suburbs," *Urban Analysis*, 4 (1977), 135–159.

DOWNS, ANTHONY. *Opening Up the Suburbs: An Urban Strategy for America* (New Haven: Yale University Press, 1973).

DOWNS, ANTHONY. "Squeezing Spread City," *The New York Times* Magazine, March 17, 1974, 38–40, 42, 44, 46–47.

DOWNS, ANTHONY. "The Future of Large, Older American Cities to the Year 2000," in John J. Mulhern, ed., *The Future of American Cities* (Philadelphia: Federal Reserve Bank of Philadelphia, 1976), pp. 9–19.

DRENNAN, MATTHEW, AND ROBERT COHEN. *The Corporate Headquarters Complex in New York City* (New York: Conservation of Human Resources Project, Columbia University, December, 1977).

DUNCAN, JAMES S. "Landscape Taste as a Symbol of Group Identity: A Westchester County Village," *Geographical Review*, 63 (1973), 334–355.

EDEL, MATTHEW, JOHN R. HARRIS, AND JEROME ROTHENBERG. "Urban Concentration and Deconcentration," in Amos H. Hawley and Vincent P. Rock, eds., *Metropolitan America in Contemporary Perspective* (New York: Halsted Press, 1975), pp. 123–156.

ELAZAR, DANIEL J. "Are We a Nation of Cities?" in Charles M. Haar, ed., *The End of Innocence: A Suburban Reader* (Glenview, IL: Scott, Foresman and Company, 1972), pp. 8–13.

ELAZAR, DANIEL J. "Suburbanization: Reviving the Town on the Metropolitan Frontier," *Publius*, 5 (Winter, 1975), 53–80.

EPSTEIN, BART J. "The Trading Function," in Jean Gottmann and Robert A. Harper, eds., *Metropolis on the Move: Geographers Look at Urban Sprawl* (New York: John Wiley & Sons, Inc., 1967), pp. 93–101.

Equal Opportunity in Suburbia (Washington, DC: The United States Commission on Civil Rights, July, 1974).

ERICKSEN, EUGENE P., AND WILLIAM L. YANCEY. "Work and Residence in Industrial Philadelphia," *Journal of Urban History*, 5 (1979), 147–182.

ERICKSON, RODNEY A. "Spatial Dynamics of Employment Growth and Structure among Suburban Communities," forthcoming.

ERNST, ROBERT T. "Growth, Development, and Isolation of an All-Black City: Kinloch, Missouri," in Robert T. Ernst and Lawrence Hugg, eds., *Black America: Geographic Perspectives* (Garden City, NY: Anchor Press/Doubleday, 1976), pp. 368–388.

FAGIN, HENRY. "Problems of Planning in the Suburbs," in William M. Dobriner, ed., *The Suburban Community* (New York: G. P. Putnam's Sons, 1958), pp. 362–371.

FARLEY, REYNOLDS. "Suburban Persistence," *American Sociological Review*, 29 (1964), 38–47.

FARLEY, REYNOLDS. "The Changing Distribution of Negroes within Metropolitan Areas: The Emergence of Black Suburbs," *American Journal of Sociology*, 75 (1970), 512–529.

FARLEY, REYNOLDS, HOWARD SCHUMAN, SUZANNE BIANCHI, DIANE COLASANTO, AND SHIRLEY HATCHETT. "Chocolate City, Vanilla Suburbs: Will the Trend toward Racially Separate Communities Continue?" *Social Science Research*, 7 (1978), 319–344.

FARRELL, WILLIAM E. "Suburb Weighs Curb on Blacks in Bid to Spur Racial Integration," *The New York Times*, February 10, 1974, 46.

FARRELL, WILLIAM E. "Impact of Court's Ruling on Low-Income Housing Is Seen Far Off," *The New York Times*, April 26, 1976, 42.

FAVA, SYLVIA F. "The Pop Sociology of Suburbs and New Towns," *American Studies*, 14 (1973), 121–133.

FAVA, SYLVIA F. "Beyond Suburbia," *Annals of the American Academy of Political and Social Science*, 422 (1975), 10–24.

FELDMAN, SAUL D., AND GERALD W. THIELBAR, EDS., *Life Styles: Diversity in American Society* (Boston: Little, Brown and Company, 2nd rev. ed., 1975).

FELLOWS, LAWRENCE. "Hartford Battles Suburbs for Federal Aid," *The New York Times*, November 17, 1975, 33, 51.

FELLOWS, LAWRENCE. "Hartford Blocks Aid for Suburbs," *The New York Times*, January 29, 1976, 1, 58.

FERON, JAMES, RICHARD L. MADDEN, AND ROBERT REINHOLD. Findings and Analysis of *The New York Times* Suburban Poll, *The New York Times*, November 13, 1978, B1, B4; November 14, 1978, B3; November 15, 1978, B4; November 16, 1978, B4.

FISCHER, CLAUDE S. "The Suburban Experience," in *The Urban Experience* (New York: Harcourt Brace Jovanovich, Inc., 1976), pp. 204–233.

FLINK, JAMES J. *America Adopts the Automobile: 1895–1910* (Cambridge, MA: The MIT Press, 1970).

FLINK, JAMES J. *The Car Culture* (Cambridge, MA: The MIT Press, 1975).

FOLEY, DONALD L. "Institutional and Contextual Factors Affecting the Housing Choice of Minority Residents," in Stephen Gale and Eric G. Moore, eds., *The Manipulated City: Perspectives on Spatial Structure and Social Issues in Urban America* (Chicago: Maaroufa Press, Inc., 1975), pp. 168–181.

FORD, LARRY, AND ERNST GRIFFIN. "The Ghettoization of Paradise," *Geographical Review*, 69 (1979), 140–158.

Fortune. "Dallas/Fort Worth—The Southwest Metroplex (Advertising Supplement)," October, 1976, 51–81.

Fortune. "A Park That Reversed a Brain Drain," June, 1977, 148–153.

FOSBURG, LACEY. "Coast City Upheld on Broad Growth Curbs," *The New York Times*, August 17, 1975.

FRIED, JOSEPH P. *Housing Crisis U.S.A.* (Baltimore: Penguin Books, 1972).

FRIEDEN, BERNARD J. "Blacks in Suburbia: The Myth of Better Opportunities," in Lowdon Wingo, series ed., *Minority Perspectives* (Baltimore: Johns Hopkins University Press, for Resources for the Future, Inc., The Governance of Metropolitan Regions No. 2, 1972), pp. 31–49.

FRIEDEN, BERNARD J., ARTHUR P. SOLOMON, DAVID L. BIRCH, AND JOHN PITKIN. *The Nation's Housing: 1975 to 1985* (Cambridge, MA: Joint Center for Urban Studies of MIT and Harvard University, 1977).

GALLION, ARTHUR B., AND SIMON EISNER. *The Urban Pattern: City Planning and Design* (New York: D. Van Nostrand Company, 3rd rev. ed., 1975).

GANNON, COLLIN A., AND MICHAEL J. DEAR. "Rapid Transit and Office Development," *Traffic Quarterly*, 29 (1975), 223–242.

GANS, HERBERT J. "Urbanism and Suburbanism as Ways of Life: A Re-evaluation of Definitions," in Arnold Rose, ed., *Human Behavior and Social Processes* (Boston: Houghton Mifflin Company, 1962), pp. 625–648.

GANS, HERBERT J. *The Levittowners: Ways of Life and Politics in a New Suburban Community* (New York: Vintage Books, 1967).

GANS, HERBERT J. "The White Exodus to Suburbia Steps Up," in Louis H. Masotti and Jeffrey K. Hadden, eds., *Suburbia in Transition* (New York: New Viewpoints, for *The New York Times*, 1974), pp. 46–61.

GANS, HERBERT J. "Why Exurbanites Won't Reurbanize Themselves," *The New York Times*, February 12, 1977, 21.

GLANTZ, FREDERIC B., AND NANCY J. DELANEY. "Changes in Nonwhite Residential Patterns in Large Metropolitan Areas, 1960 and 1970," *New England Economic Review*, Federal Reserve Bank of Boston, March–April, 1973, 2–13.

GLENN, NORVAL D. "Suburbanization in the United States since World War II," in Louis H. Masotti and Jeffrey K. Hadden, eds., *The Urbanization of the Suburbs*

(Beverly Hills: Sage Publications, Urban Affairs Annual Reviews, Vol. 7, 1973), pp. 51–78.

GOHEEN, PETER G. "Interpreting the American City: Some Historical Perspectives," *Geographical Review*, 64 (1974), 362–384.

GOLD, NEIL N. "The Mismatch of Jobs and Low-Income People in Metropolitan Areas and its Implications for the Central City Poor," in Sara M. Mazie, ed., *Population, Distribution, and Policy* (Washington, DC: Commission on Population Growth and the American Future, Research Reports, Vol. 5, 1972), pp. 441–486.

GOLDBERGER, PAUL. "New Buildings Squeezing into a Crowded Midtown," *The New York Times*, December 11, 1978, B1, B19.

GOLDFIELD, DAVID R. "The Limits of Suburban Growth: The Washington, D.C. SMSA," *Urban Affairs Quarterly*, 12 (1976), 83–102. Additional commentaries by Joseph Zikmund and Jeffrey K. Hadden, with a rejoinder by David R. Goldfield, 103–116.

GOTTDIENER, MARK. *Planned Sprawl: Private and Public Interests in Suburbia* (Beverly Hills: Sage Publications, Sage Library of Social Research, Vol. 38, 1977).

GREENE, DAVID L. "Multinucleation in Urban Spatial Structure," unpublished Ph.D. dissertation, Department of Geography and Environmental Engineering, Johns Hopkins University, 1977.

GREENE, DAVID L. "Urban Subcenters: Recent Trends in Urban Spatial Structure," *Growth and Change*, 11 (1980), 29–40.

GRIER, GEORGE. "Washington: A Beltway is 'Creating New Patterns Which Increase the Independence of the Suburbs from Their Parent,'" *City, Magazine of Urban Life and Environment*, January–February, 1971, 45–49.

GRIER, EUNICE, AND GEORGE GRIER. *Black Suburbanization at the Mid-1970's* (Washington: The Washington Center for Metropolitan Studies, 1978).

GRUEN, NINA J., AND CLAUDE GRUEN. *Low and Moderate Income Housing in the Suburbs: An Analysis for the Dayton, Ohio Region* (New York: Praeger Publishers, Inc., 1972).

GRUEN, VICTOR. *Centers for the Urban Environment* (New York: Van Nostrand Reinhold Company, 1973).

GRUENSTEIN, JOHN. "A New Job Map for the Philadelphia Region," *Business Review*, Federal Reserve Bank of Philadelphia, January–February, 1979, 13–22.

GUEST, AVERY M. "Population Suburbanization in American Metropolitan Areas, 1940–1970," *Geographical Analysis*, 7 (1975), 267–283.

GUEST, AVERY M. "Nighttime and Daytime Populations of Large American Suburbs," *Urban Affairs Quarterly*, 12 (1976), 57–82.

GUEST, AVERY M. "Residential Segregation in Urban Areas," in Kent P. Schwirian, ed., *Contemporary Topics in Urban Sociology* (Morristown, NJ: General Learning Press, 1977), pp. 268–336.

GUEST, AVERY M. "Suburban Social Status: Persistence or Evolution?" *American Sociological Review*, 43 (1978), 251–264.

GUTERBOCK, THOMAS M. "The Push Hypothesis: Minority Presence, Crime, and Urban Deconcentration," in Barry Schwartz, ed., *The Changing Face of the Suburbs* (Chicago: University of Chicago Press, 1976), pp. 137–161.

HAAR, CHARLES M., ED. *The End of Innocence: A Suburban Reader* (Glenview, IL: Scott, Foresman and Company, 1972).

HAAR, CHARLES M., ED. *Suburban Problems: The President's Task Force, Final Report* (Cambridge, MA: Ballinger Publishing Company, 1974).

HAAR, CHARLES M., AND D. S. IATRIDIS. *Housing the Poor in Suburbia: Public Policy at the Grass Roots* (Cambridge, MA: Ballinger Publishing Company, 1974).

HADDEN, JEFFREY K., AND JOSEF J. BARTON. "An Image That Will Not Die: Thoughts on the History of Anti-urban Ideology," in Louis H. Masotti and Jeffrey K. Hadden, eds., *The Urbanization of the Suburbs* (Beverly Hills: Sage Publications, Urban Affairs Annual Reviews, Vol. 7, 1973), pp. 79–119.

HAGGETT, PETER. *Locational Analysis in Human Geography* (New York: St. Martin's Press, 1965).

HAHN, HARLAN. "Ethnic Minorities: Politics and the Family in Suburbia," in Louis H. Masotti and Jeffrey K. Hadden, eds., *The Urbanization of the Suburbs* (Beverly Hills: Sage Publications, Urban Affairs Annual Reviews, Vol. 7, 1973), pp. 185–209.

HALL, MILLICENT. "The Park at the End of the Trolley," *Landscape*, 22 (Autumn, 1977), 11–18.

HALL, PETER. "The Urban Culture and the Suburban Culture," in R. Eells and C. Walton, eds., *Man in the City of the Future: A Symposium of Urban Philosophers* (London: Collier-Macmillan Ltd., 1968), pp. 99–145.

HAMER, ANDREW M. *Industrial Exodus from the Central City: Public Policy and the Comparative Costs of Location* (Lexington, MA: D. C. Heath and Company, 1973).

HAMER, ANDREW M., GUEST ED. "Perspectives on Urban Atlanta," *Atlanta Economic Review*, 28 (January–February, 1978), 3–62.

HAMILTON, D. L., AND G. D. BISHOP. "Attitudinal and Behavioral Effects of Initial Integration of White Suburban Neighborhoods," *Journal of Social Issues*, 32 (1976), 47–67.

HARDWICK, WALTER G. "Vancouver: The Emergence of a 'Core-Ring' Urban Pattern," in R. Louis Gentilcore, ed., *Geographical Approaches to Canadian Problems* (Scarborough, Ontario: Prentice-Hall of Canada Ltd., 1971), pp. 112–118.

HARKNESS, RICHARD C. "Communication Innovations, Urban Form and Travel Demand: Some Hypotheses and a Bibliography," *Transportation*, 2 (1973), 153–193.

HARRIS, NEIL. "Spaced-out at the Shopping Center," *The New Republic*, December 13, 1975, 23–26.

HARRISON, BENNETT. *Urban Economic Development: Suburbanization, Minority Opportunity and the Condition of the Central City* (Washington, DC: Urban Institute, 1974).

HART, JOHN FRASER. *The Look of the Land* (Englewood Cliffs, NJ: Prentice-Hall, Inc., 1975).

HARTSHORN, TRUMAN A. "Industrial/Office Parks: A New Look for the City," *Journal of Geography*, 72 (1973), 33–45.

HARTSHORN, TRUMAN A. "Getting around Atlanta: New Approaches," *Atlanta Economic Review*, 28 (January–February, 1978), 43–51.

HARTSHORN, TRUMAN A. *Interpreting the City: An Introduction to Urban Geography* (New York: John Wiley & Sons, Inc., 1980).

HARTSHORN, TRUMAN A., SANFORD BEDERMAN, SID DAVIS, G. E. ALAN DEVER, AND RICHARD PILLSBURY. *Atlanta: Metropolis in Georgia* (Cambridge, MA: Ballinger Publishing Company, 1976).

HARVEY, DAVID. *Society, the City and the Space-Economy of Urbanism* (Washington, DC: Association of American Geographers, Commission on College Geography, Resource Paper No. 18, 1972).

HAWLEY, AMOS H., AND VINCENT P. ROCK, EDS. *Metropolitan America in Contemporary Perspective* (New York: Halsted Press, 1975).

HAWLEY, AMOS H., ET AL., for the National Research Council. *Toward an Understanding of Metropolitan America* (San Francisco: Canfield Press/Harper & Row, Publishers, 1975).

HIRSCH, WERNER Z. "The Coming Age of the Polynucleated Metropolis," in Herrington J. Bryce, ed., *Small Cities in Transition: The Dynamics of Growth and Decline* (Cambridge, MA: Ballinger Publishing Company, 1977), pp. 267–281.

HOLLIE, PAMELA G. "Glittering Stores for Sheiks, Stars," *The New York Times*, December 14, 1978, D1, D5.

HOLSENDOLPH, ERNEST. "U.S. Planners Expect Auto's Role to Be Unaffected by Gas Scarcity," *The New York Times*, June 18, 1979, A1, B8.

HOLT, GLEN E. "The Changing Perception of Urban Pathology: An Essay on the Development of Mass Transit in the United States," in Kenneth T. Jackson and Stanley K. Schultz, eds., *Cities in American History* (New York: Alfred A. Knopf, Inc., 1972), pp. 324–343.

HORVATH, RONALD J. "Machine Space," *Geographical Review*, 64 (1974), 167–188.

HUGHES, JAMES W., ED. *Suburbanization Dynamics and the Future of the City* (New Brunswick, NJ: Center for Urban Policy Research, Rutgers University, 1974).

HUGHES, JAMES W. "Dilemmas of Suburbanization and Growth Controls," *Annals of the American Academy of Political and Social Science*, 422 (1975), 61–76.

HUGHES, JAMES W., AND FRANKLIN J. JAMES. "Suburbanization Dynamics and the Transportation Dilemma," in James W. Hughes, ed., *Suburbanization Dynamics and the Future of the City* (New Brunswick, NJ: Center for Urban Policy Research, Rutgers University, 1974), pp. 19–42.

HUME, PAUL. "Acres for the Arts: Wolf Trap Farm Park," *Opera News*, June, 1974, 22–25.

JACKSON, KENNETH T. "Metropolitan Government versus Suburban Autonomy: Politics on the Crabgrass Frontier," in Kenneth T. Jackson and Stanley K. Schultz, eds., *Cities in American History* (New York: Alfred A. Knopf, Inc., 1972), pp. 442–462.

JACKSON, KENNETH T. "The Crabgrass Frontier: 150 Years of Suburban Growth in America," in Raymond A. Mohl and James F. Richardson, eds., *The Urban Experience: Themes in American History* (Belmont, CA: Wadsworth Publishing Company, Inc., 1973), pp. 196–221.

JACKSON, KENNETH T. "Urban Deconcentration in the Nineteenth Century: A Statistical Inquiry," in Leo F. Schnore, ed., *The New Urban History: Quantitative Explorations by American Historians* (Princeton: Princeton University Press, 1975), pp. 110–142.

JACKSON, KENNETH T. "The Effect of Suburbanization on the Cities," in Philip C. Dolce, ed., *Suburbia: The American Dream and Dilemma* (Garden City, NY: Anchor Press/Doubleday, 1976), pp. 89–110.

JAMES, FRANKLIN J., JR., AND JAMES W. HUGHES. "The Process of Employment Location Change: An Empirical Analysis," *Land Economics*, 49 (1973), 404–413.

JENSEN, HOLGER. "Defeat for Builders: California Cities Can Limit Growth," *Sacramento Bee*, March 7, 1976.

JOHNSON, JAMES H., ED. *Suburban Growth: Geographical Processes at the Edge of the Western City* (London: John Wiley & Sons Ltd., 1974).

KAIN, JOHN F. "The Distribution and Movement of Jobs and Industry," in James Q. Wilson, ed., *The Metropolitan Enigma: Inquiries into the Nature and Dimensions of America's "Urban Crisis"* (Cambridge, MA: Harvard University Press, 1968), pp. 1–43.

KAPLAN, SAMUEL. *The Dream Deferred: People, Politics, and Planning in Suburbia* (New York: The Seabury Press, 1976a); paperback edition published by Vintage Books, 1977).

KAPLAN, SAMUEL. "THEM—Blacks in Suburbia," *New York Affairs*, 3 (Winter, 1976b), 20–41.

KARASIK, ELLEN. "Philadelphia No Longer Is 'Hub of World' to Suburbanites: Bedroom Communities Grow to Mini-cities," *Philadelphia Inquirer*, February 9, 1973, 1A, 8A.

KASARDA, JOHN D. "The Impact of Suburban Population Growth on Central City Service Functions," *American Journal of Sociology*, 77 (1972), 1111-1124.

KASARDA, JOHN D. "The Changing Occupational Structure of the American Metropolis: Apropos the Urban Problem," in Barry Schwartz, ed., *The Changing Face of the Suburbs* (Chicago: University of Chicago Press, 1976), pp. 113-136.

KASARDA, JOHN D. "Urbanization, Community, and the Metropolitan Problem," in David Street and Associates, *Handbook of Contemporary Urban Life: An Examination of Urbanization, Social Organization, and Metropolitan Politics* (San Francisco: Jossey-Bass, Inc., Publishers, 1978), pp. 27-57.

KASARDA, JOHN D., AND GEORGE V. REDFEARN. "Differential Patterns of City and Suburban Growth in the United States," *Journal of Urban History*, 2 (1975), 43-66.

KERSTEN, EARL W., JR., AND D. REID ROSS. "Clayton: A New Metropolitan Focus in the St. Louis Area," *Annals of the Association of American Geographers*, 58 (1968), 637-649.

KIHSS, PETER. "Migration From the Metropolitan Area Viewed by Planning Group as Threat," *The New York Times*, January 30, 1975.

KING, SETH S. "Suburban 'Downtowns': The Shopping Centers," in Louis H. Masotti and Jeffrey K. Hadden, eds., *Suburbia in Transition* (New York: New Viewpoints, for *The New York Times*, 1974), pp. 101-104.

KOWINSKI, WILLIAM S. "The Malling of America," *New Times Magazine*, May 1, 1978, 30-55.

KRAMER, JOHN. "The Other Mayor Lee," *Focus/Midwest*, 5 (1967). Reprinted in Kramer, 1972, pp. 185-200.

KRAMER, JOHN, ED. *North American Suburbs: Politics, Diversity, and Change* (Berkeley: The Glendessary Press, Inc., 1972).

KRIM, ARTHUR J., ET AL. *Northwest Cambridge: Survey of Architectural History in Cambridge, Report Five* (Cambridge, MA: The MIT Press, for the Cambridge Historical Commission, 1977).

KRISTOL, IRVING. "America's Future Urbanization," in James W. Hughes, ed., *Suburbanization Dynamics and the Future of the City* (New Brunswick, NJ: Center for Urban Policy Research, Rutgers University, 1974), pp. 271-282.

KRON, JOAN. "An Infiltrator's Guide to the Main Line," *Philadelphia Magazine*, June, 1973, 114-117, 168-171.

LAKE, ROBERT W. "Racial Transition and Black Homeownership in American Suburbs," *The Annals of the American Academy of Political and Social Science*, 441 (1979), 142–156.

LAKE, ROBERT W. *Race and Housing in the Suburbs* (New Brunswick, NJ: Center for Urban Policy Research, Rutgers University, 1980).

LAKE, ROBERT W., AND SUSAN CARIS CUTTER. "A Typology of Black Suburbanization in New Jersey since 1970," *Geographical Review*, 70 (April, 1980), 167–181.

LESSARD, SUZANNAH. "The Suburban Landscape: Oyster Bay, Long Island," *The New Yorker*, October 11, 1976, 44–79.

LEVEN, CHARLES L., ED. *The Mature Metropolis* (Lexington, MA: Lexington Books, 1978).

LIEBERSON, STANLEY. "Suburbs and Ethnic Residential Patterns," *American Journal of Sociology*, 67 (1962), 673–681.

LINDSEY, ROBERT. "Experts Say Housing Programs Fail to Open Suburbs to the Poor," *The New York Times*, November 11, 1975.

LINDSEY, ROBERT. "Baseball Victory Is No Joke to Anaheim," *The New York Times*, September 29, 1979, 6.

LINEBERRY, ROBERT L. "Suburbia and the Metropolitan Turf," *Annals of the American Academy of Political and Social Science*, 422 (1975), 1–9.

LONGBRAKE, DAVID B., AND WOODROW W. NICHOLS, JR. *Miami: Sunshine and Shadows* (Cambridge, MA: Ballinger Publishing Company, 1976).

MCKAY, ROBERTA V. "Commuting Patterns for Inner-city Residents," *Monthly Labor Review*, November, 1973, 43–48.

MCQUISTON, JOHN T. "L. I. Industry Heads for 2d Record Year," *The New York Times*, April 29, 1979, 44.

MADDEN, RICHARD L. "Firms Branch to Serve Connecticut Business Giants," *The New York Times*, March 21, 1978, 37.

MALLACH, STANLEY. "The Origins of the Decline of Urban Mass Transportation in the United Staes," *Urbanism Past and Present*, 8 (Summer, 1979), 1–17.

MANNERS, GERALD. "The Office in Metropolis: An Opportunity for Shaping Metropolitan America," *Economic Geography*, 50 (1974), 93–110.

MASOTTI, LOUIS H., GUEST ED. "The Suburban Seventies," *Annals of the American Academy of Political and Social Science*, 422 (1975), vii–151.

MASOTTI, LOUIS H., AND DEBORAH ELLIS DENNIS, COMPILERS. *Suburbs, Suburbia, and Suburbanization: A Bibliography* (Monticello, IL: Council of Planning Librarians, 2nd rev. ed., Exchange Bibliography Nos. 524–525, 1974).

MASOTTI, LOUIS H., AND JEFFREY K. HADDEN, EDS. *The Urbanization of the Suburbs* (Beverly Hills: Sage Publications, Urban Affairs Annual Reviews, Vol. 7, 1973).

MASOTTI, LOUIS H., AND JEFFREY K. HADDEN, EDS. *Suburbia in Transition* (New York: New Viewpoints, for *The New York Times*, 1974).

MASTERS, STANLEY H. *Black–White Income Differentials: Empirical Studies and Policy Implications* (New York: Academic Press, Inc., Research on Poverty Monograph Series, 1975).

MAYER, HAROLD M. "Centex Industrial Park: An Organized Industrial District," in Richard S. Thoman and Donald J. Patton, eds., *Focus on Geographic Activity: A Collection of Original Studies* (New York: McGraw-Hill Book Company, 1964), pp. 135–145.

MEINIG, DONALD W. "Symbolic Landscapes: Some Idealizations of American Communities," in Donald W. Meinig, ed., *The Interpretation of Ordinary Landscapes: Geographical Essays* (New York: Oxford University Press, 1979), pp. 164–192.

MEYER, HERBERT E. "Why Corporations Are on the Move," *Fortune*, May, 1976, 252–258, 262, 266, 270, 272.

MICHELSON, WILLIAM H. *Man and His Urban Environment: A Sociological Approach* (Reading, MA: Addison-Wesley Publishing Company, Inc., 2nd ed. rev., 1976).

MILLER, HERMAN P., AND STUART GARFINKLE. *Philadelphia's Inner City: An Analysis of the 1970 Census Employment Survey* (Philadelphia: U.S. Bureau of Labor Statistics, Mideast Region, Report No. 6, March, 1973).

MILLER, ROGER P. *Household Activity Patterns in the Emerging Nineteenth-Century Suburb* (Philadelphia: University of Pennsylvania, Philadelphia Social History Project, 1978).

MILLISON, MARTIN B. *Teenage Behavior in Shopping Centers* (New York: International Council of Shopping Centers, 1976).

MILLS, EDWIN S. "Urban Density Functions," *Urban Studies*, 7 (1970), 5–20.

MORRIS, JACK H. "'Meet Me at the Mall'—Big Shopping Centers Are Becoming the Focus of Life in the Suburbs," *Wall Street Journal*, February 20, 1969, 1, 9.

MULLER, PETER O. "Social Transportation Geography," in Christopher Board, Richard J. Chorley, Peter Haggett, and David R. Stoddart, eds., *Progress in Geography: International Reviews of Current Research, Volume 8* (New York: St. Martin's Press, 1975), pp. 208–230.

MULLER, PETER O. *The Outer City: Geographical Consequences of the Urbanization of the Suburbs* (Washington, DC: Association of American Geographers, Resource Papers for College Geography, No. 75-2, 1976).

MULLER, PETER O. "The Evolution of American Suburbs: A Geographical Interpretation," *Urbanism Past and Present*, 4 (Summer, 1977), 1–10.

MULLER, PETER O. "The Suburbanization of Corporate Headquarters: What Are the Trends and Consequences?" *Vital Issues* (Washington, CT: Center for Information on America, April, 1978).

MULLER, PETER O. "Suburbanization in the 1970s: Interpreting Population, Socioeconomic, and Employment Trends," in Stanley D. Brunn and James O. Wheeler, eds., *The American Metropolitan System: Present and Future* (Silver Spring, MD: Victor H. Winston & Sons, Scripta Series in Geography, 1980), pp. 39–51.

MURPHY, THOMAS P., AND JOHN REHFUSS. *Urban Politics in the Suburban Era* (Homewood, IL: The Dorsey Press, 1976).

NARVAEZ, ALFONSO A. "Jersey Says It's Getting 5 More Wall St. Firms," *The New York Times*, February 5, 1976.

NELSON, KATHRYN P. *Recent Suburbanization of Blacks: How Much, Who, and Where* (Washington, DC: U.S. Department of Housing and Urban Development, Office of Economic Affairs of the Office of Policy Development and Research, HUD-PDR-378, February, 1979).

NEUTZE, MAX. *The Suburban Apartment Boom: Case Study of a Land Use Problem* (Baltimore: Johns Hopkins Press, for Resources for the Future, Inc., 1968).

Newsday. "The Real Suburbia," *LI Magazine*, April 29, 1973, 7–29.

Newsweek. "The Battle of the Suburbs," November 15, 1971, 61–64, 69–70.

Newsweek. "Runaways of Fairfield County," August 16, 1976, 64–66.

New York Times. "San Diego Attracts Electronics Plants," March 28, 1979, D1, D13.

NIEDZIELSKI, RUDI. "Touching Down in O.C.: The Rams Aren't Here for Mickey Mouse Reasons," *New Worlds Magazine*, October/November, 1979, 26–32.

NORWOOD, L. K., AND ERNEST A. T. BARTH. "Urban Desegregation: Negro Pioneers and Their White Neighbors," in Charles M. Haar, ed., *The End of Innocence: A Suburban Reader* (Glenview, IL: Scott, Foresman and Company, 1972), pp. 118–123.

O'DONNELL, FRANKLIN, AND JOHN GREGORY. "The Irrepressible Orange: If the Rams Are Coming Can Statehood Be Far Behind?," *New Worlds Magazine*, October/November, 1979, 18–25.

OSER, ALAN S. "Supreme Court Ruling in Chicago Case Is Likely to Have Only a Limited Effect," *The New York Times*, April 22, 1976.

OUTTZ, JANICE H. "Area Real Estate Advertising Practices Improving but Some 'Questionable' Wordings Remain," *Metropolitan Bulletin: Agenda for the 70s*, Washington D.C. Center for Metropolitan Studies, August, 1974, 4.

OWENS, BILL. *Suburbia* (San Francisco: Straight Arrow Books, 1973).

OWENS, BILL. *Our Kind of People: American Groups and Rituals* (San Francisco: Straight Arrow Books, 1975).

PACK, HOWARD, AND JANET R. PACK. "Metropolitan Fragmentation and Suburban Homogeneity," *Urban Studies*, 14 (1977), 191–201.

PACKARD, VANCE. *A Nation of Strangers* (New York: David McKay Co., Inc., 1972).

PALEN, J. JOHN. "Life-Styles: The Suburbs," *The Urban World* (New York: Mc-Graw-Hill Book Company, 1975), pp. 147–175.

PALMER, MARTHA E., AND MARJORIE N. RUSH. "Houston," in John S. Adams, ed., *Contemporary Metropolitan America*, Vol. 4: *Twentieth Century Cities* (Cambridge, MA: Ballinger Publishing Company, 1976), pp. 109–149.

PATTERSON, JACK. "The Prospect of a Nation with No Important Cities, *Business Week*, February 2, 1976, 66, 69.

PENDLETON, WILLIAM W. "Blacks in Suburbs," in Louis H. Masotti and Jeffrey K. Hadden, eds., *The Urbanization of the Suburbs* (Beverly Hills: Sage Publications, Urban Affairs Annual Reviews, Vol. 7, 1973), pp. 171–184.

PERLOFF, HARVEY S. "The Central City in the Postindustrial Age," in Charles L. Leven, ed., *The Mature Metropolis* (Lexington, MA: Lexington Books, 1978), pp. 109–129.

PHALON, RICHARD. "Will Jersey City Replace Wall St.?" *The New York Times*, October 12, 1975, Section 3, 1, 4.

PHILLIPS, KEVIN. "The Balkanization of America," *Harper's*, May, 1978, 37–47.

PLATT, RUTHERFORD H. *Land Use Control: Interface of Law and Geography* (Washington, DC: Association of American Geographers, Resource Papers for College Geography, No. 75-1, 1976).

POPENOE, DAVID. *The Suburban Environment: Sweden and the United States* (Chicago: University of Chicago Press, 1977).

QUANTE, WOLFGANG. *The Exodus of Corporate Headquarters from New York City* (New York: Praeger Publishers, Inc., 1976).

RABIN, YALE. "Highways As a Barrier to Equal Access," *Annals of the American Academy of Political and Social Science*, 407 (1973), 63–77.

RABINOVITZ, FRANCINE F., AND WILLIAM J. SIEMBIEDA. *Minorities in the Suburbs: The Los Angeles Experience* (Lexington, MA: Lexington Books, 1977).

RAE, JOHN B. *The American Automobile: A Brief History* (Chicago: University of Chicago Press, 1965).

RAE, JOHN B. *The Road and the Car in American Life* (Cambridge, MA: The MIT Press, 1971).

RAINWATER, LEE. "Fear and the House-as-Haven in the Lower Class," *Journal of the American Institute of Planners*, 32 (1966), 23–30.

RAINWATER, LEE. "Post-1984 America," in Helen I. Safa and Gloria Levitas, eds., *Social Problems in Corporate America* (New York: Harper & Row, Publishers, 1975), pp. 371–378.

RAMSEY, BRUCE. "Activity Centers: It's a Nice Idea, but Will It Work?" *Seattle Journal-American*, February 11, 1978, B7.

REES, JOHN. "Manufacturing Headquarters in a Post-industrial Urban Context," *Economic Geography*, 54 (1978), 337–354.

REINHOLD, ROBERT. "U.S.-backed Chicago Test Offers Suburban Life to Ghetto Blacks," *The New York Times*, May 22, 1978, A1, A18.

REINHOLD, ROBERT. "Scholars Take Optimistic View of Energy Problems," *The New York Times*, July 5, 1979, B7.

REYNOLDS, DAVID R. "Progress toward Achieving Efficient and Responsive Spatial-Political Systems in Urban America," in John S. Adams, ed., *Urban Policy-making and Metropolitan Dynamics: A Comparative Geographical Analysis* (Cambridge, MA: Ballinger Publishing Company, 1976), pp. 463–537.

ROBERTSON, WYNDHAM. "The Greening of the Irvine Co.," *Fortune*, December, 1976, 84–96.

ROMANOS, MICHAEL C. "Energy Price Effects on Metropolitan Spatial Structure and Form," *Environment and Planning A*, 10 (1978), 93–104.

ROOF, WADE CLARK, GUEST ED. "Race and Residence in American Cities," *Annals of the American Academy of Political and Social Science*, 441 (1979), vii–196.

ROSE, HAROLD M. *Social Processes in the City: Race and Urban Residential Choice* (Washington, DC: Association of American Geographers, Commission on College Geography, Resource Paper No. 6, 1969).

ROSE, HAROLD M. "The All-Black Town: Suburban Prototype or Rural Slum?" in Harlan Hahn, ed., *People and Politics in Urban Society* (Beverly Hills: Sage Publications, Urban Affairs Annual Reviews, Vol. 6, 1972), pp. 397–431.

ROSE, HAROLD M. *Black Suburbanization: Access to Improved Quality of Life or Maintenance of the Status Quo?* (Cambridge, MA: Ballinger Publishing Company, 1976).

ROSE, JEROME, AND ROBERT E. ROTHMAN, EDS. *After Mount Laurel: The New Suburban Zoning* (New Brunswick, NJ: Center for Urban Policy Research, Rutgers University, 1977).

ROSENTHAL, JACK. "Toward Suburban Independence," in Louis H. Masotti and Jeffrey K. Hadden, eds., *Suburbia in Transition* (New York: New Viewpoints, for *The New York Times*, 1974), pp. 295–302.

RUBINOWITZ, LEONARD S. *Low-Income Housing: Suburban Strategies* (Cambridge, MA: Ballinger Publishing Company, 1974).

SALPUKAS, AGIS. "Wall Street Blues," *The New York Times* Magazine, December 18, 1977, 43–44, 98–107.

SARGENT, CHARLES S. "Land Speculation and Urban Morphology," in John S. Adams, ed., *Urban Policymaking and Metropolitan Dynamics: A Comparative Geographical Analysis* (Cambridge, MA: Ballinger Publishing Company, 1976), pp. 21–57.

SARGENT, CHARLES S., ED. *Urban Dynamics: The Wall Street Journal Views the Changing Face of America's Cities* (Princeton: Dow Jones Books, 1977).

SCHAEFFER, K. H., AND ELLIOT SCLAR. *Access for All: Transportation and Urban Growth* (Baltimore: Penguin Books, 1975).

SCHMITT, PETER J. *Back to Nature: The Arcadian Myth in Urban America* (New York: Oxford University Press, 1969).

SCHNALL, RABBI DAVID J. *Ethnicity and Suburban Local Politics* (New York: Praeger Publishers, 1975).

SCHNEIDER, JERRY B., AND TOMOKI NOGUCHI. *Transit's Role in the Creation of the Polycentric City: An Initial Assessment*, University of Washington Urban Transportation Program Research Report No. 77-6 (Springfield, VA: National Technical Information Service, PB 275-043/AS, 1977).

SCHNORE, LEO F. *Class and Race in Cities and Suburbs* (Chicago: Rand McNally, for Markham Publishing Co., 1972).

SCHNORE, LEO F., CAROLYN D. ANDRÉ, AND HARRY SHARP. "Black Suburbanization, 1930–1970," in Barry Schwartz, ed., *The Changing Face of the Suburbs* (Chicago: University of Chicago Press, 1976), pp. 69–94.

SCHUYTEN, PETER J. "Xerox Is Entering Telecommunications: Will Challenge A.T.&T., I.B.M.," *The New York Times*, November 17, 1978, D1, D15.

SCHWARTZ, BARRY. "Images of Suburbia: Some Revisionist Commentary and Conclusions," in Barry Schwartz, ed., *The Changing Face of the Suburbs* (Chicago: University of Chicago Press, 1976), pp. 325–340.

SCHWARTZ, BARRY, ED. *The Changing Face of the Suburbs* (Chicago: University of Chicago Press, 1976).

SCHWARTZ, JOEL. "The Evolution of the Suburbs," in Philip C. Dolce, ed., *Suburbia: The American Dream and Dilemma* (Garden City, NY: Anchor Press/Doubleday, 1976), pp. 1–36.

SCHWARTZ, JOEL, AND DANIEL PROSSER, EDS. *Cities of the Garden State: Essays in the Urban and Suburban History of New Jersey* (Dubuque, IA: Kendall/Hunt Publishing Company, 1977).

SCOTT, THOMAS M. "Implications of Suburbanization for Metropolitan Political Organization," *Annals of the American Academy of Political and Social Science*, 422 (1975), 36–44.

SEVERO, RICHARD. "For Middle-Class Puerto Ricans, The Bias Problem Hasn't Ended," *The New York Times*, November 23, 1977, 1, 36.

SHAFER, THOMAS W. *Urban Growth and Economics* (Reston, VA: Reston Publishing Company, Inc., 1977).

SHOUMATOFF, ALEX. *Westchester: Portrait of a County* (New York: Coward, McCann & Geoghegan, 1979).

SIEMBIEDA, WILLIAM J. "Suburbanization of Ethnics of Color," *Annals of the American Academy of Political and Social Science*, 422 (1975), 118–128.

SINGLETON, GREGORY H. "The Genesis of Suburbia: A Complex of Historical Trends," in Louis H. Masotti and Jeffrey K. Hadden, eds., *The Urbanization of the Suburbs* (Beverly Hills: Sage Publications, Urban Affairs Annual Reviews, Vol. 7, 1973), pp. 29–50.

SLOANE, LEONARD. "Wall Street Could Be Anywhere, U.S.A.," *The New York Times*, February 5, 1978a, Section 4, 6.

SLOANE, LEONARD. "Electronic Trading Gains Favor: Intermarket Volume Grows," *The New York Times*, November 27, 1978b, D1, D4.

SMITS, EDWARD J. *Nassau: Suburbia, U.S.A.* (Garden City, NY: Doubleday, for Friends of the Nassau County Museum, 1974).

SOBIN, DENNIS P. *The Future of the American Suburbs: Survival or Extinction?* (Port Washington, NY: Kennikat Press, 1971).

SOLOMON, ARTHUR P., ED. *The Prospective City: Economic, Population, Energy, and Environmental Developments Shaping Our Cities and Suburbs* (Cambridge, MA: The MIT Press, 1980).

SOMMER, JOHN W. "Fat City and Hedenopolis: The American Urban Future?" in Ronald Abler, Donald G. Janelle, Allen K. Philbrick, and John W. Sommer, eds., *Human Geography in a Shrinking World* (North Scituate, MA: Duxbury Press, 1975), pp. 132–148.

STAHURA, JOHN M. "The Evolution of Suburban Functional Roles," *Pacific Sociological Review*, 21 (1978), 423–439.

STAHURA, JOHN M. "Structural Determinants of Suburban Socioeconomic Compositions," *Sociology and Social Research*, 63 (1979), 328–345.

STANBACK, THOMAS M., AND RICHARD KNIGHT. *Suburbanization and the City* (Montclair, NJ: Allanheld, Osmun & Co., 1976).

STERBA, JAMES P. "How New York Almost Lost the Amex," *The New York Times*, November 27, 1978, B1, B10.

STERNE, MICHAEL. "Union Carbide, 3,500 on Staff, to Quit City," *The New York Times*, March 20, 1976, 1, 31.

STERNE, MICHAEL. "Corporate Moves: New York Region Holds Its Own," *The New York Times*, August 14, 1977, 1–NJ, 6–NJ, 7–NJ.

STERNLIEB, GEORGE. "The City as Sandbox," *Public Interest*, 25 (1971), 14–21.

STERNLIEB, GEORGE. "Death of the American Dream House," *Society*, February, 1972, 39–42.

STERNLIEB, GEORGE, AND W. PATRICK BEATON. *The Zone of Emergence: A Case Study of an Older Suburb* (New Brunswick, NJ: Transaction Books, 1972).

STERNLIEB, GEORGE, AND JAMES W. HUGHES, EDS. *Post-industrial America: Metropolitan Decline & Inter-regional Job Shifts* (New Brunswick, NJ: Center for Urban Policy Research, Rutgers University, 1975).

STERNLIEB, GEORGE, AND JAMES W. HUGHES. "New Regional and Metropolitan Realities of America," *Journal of the American Institute of Planners*, 43 (1977), 227–241.

STERNLIEB, GEORGE, AND JAMES W. HUGHES. *Current Population Trends in America* (New Brunswick, NJ: Center for Urban Policy Research, Rutgers University, 1978).

STERNLIEB, GEORGE, AND JAMES W. HUGHES. "Back to the Central City: Myths and Realities," *Traffic Quarterly*, 33 (1979), 617–636.

STERNLIEB, GEORGE, AND ROBERT W. LAKE. "Aging Suburbs and Black Homeownership," *Annals of the American Academy of Political and Social Science*, 422 (1975), 105–117.

STERNLIEB, GEORGE, ROBERT BURCHELL, AND LYNNE SAGALYN. *The Affluent Suburb: Housing Needs and Attitudes* (New Brunswick, NJ: Transaction Books, 1971).

STEVENS, WILLIAM K. "Suburb Is Fighting Annexation by Houston," *The New York Times*, March 18, 1978, 8.

STEVENS, WILLIAM K. "Minorities' Influence Will Rise Next Week in Houston's Election," *The New York Times*, November 1, 1979, A1, B24.

STILL, BAYRD. *Urban America: A History With Documents* (Boston: Little, Brown and Company, 1974).

STRUYK, RAYMOND J., AND FRANKLIN J. JAMES. *Intrametropolitan Industrial Location: The Pattern and Process of Change* (Lexington, MA: Lexington Books, 1975).

STUTZ, FREDERICK P. *Social Aspects of Interaction and Transportation* (Washington, DC: Association of American Geographers, Resource Papers for College Geography, No. 76-2, 1977).

SUTTLES, GERALD D. *The Social Construction of Communities* (Chicago: University of Chicago Press, 1972).

SUTTLES, GERALD D. "Community Design: The Search for Participation in a Metropolitan Society," in Amos H. Hawley and Vincent P. Rock, eds., *Metropolitan America in Contemporary Perspective* (New York: Halsted Press, 1975), pp. 235–297.

TAEUBER, KARL E. "Racial Segregation: The Persisting Dilemma," *Annals of the American Academy of Political and Social Science*, 422 (1975), 87–96.

TARR, JOEL A. "From City to Suburb: The 'Moral' Influence of Transportation Technology," in Alexander B. Callow, Jr., ed., *American Urban History: An Interpretive Reader with Commentaries* (New York: Oxford University Press, 2nd ed. rev., 1973), pp. 202–212.

TAYLOR, GEORGE ROGERS. "Building an Intra-urban Transportation System," in Allen M. Wakstein, ed., *The Urbanization of America: An Historical Anthology* (Boston: Houghton Mifflin Company, 1970), pp. 128–150.

TAYLOR, GRAHAM R. *Satellite Cities: A Study of Industrial Suburbs* (New York: Arno Press reprint of the 1915 original work, 1970).

TAYLOR, ROBERT W. *Suburbanization of the Elderly: A Case Study of Clifton, New Jersey* (Upper Montclair, NJ: Montclair State College, Department of Geography and Urban Studies, July, 1976).

TEAFORD, JON C. *City and Suburb: The Political Fragmentation of Metropolitan America, 1850–1970* (Baltimore: Johns Hopkins University Press, 1979).

THORNS, DAVID C. *Suburbia* (London: MacGibbon and Kee, Ltd., 1972).

Time. "Hidden Side of Inflation," November 4, 1974, 102.

Time. "Housing: It's Outasight—Sales Surge, But Prices Endanger a Durable Dream," September 12, 1977, 50–57.

Time. "Luring Blacks, Keeping Whites—A Tale of Two Suburbs: Signs of Failure and Success," October 31, 1977, 16, 21.

Time. "The Immobile Society: Is America Settling Down in Middle Age?" November 28, 1977, 107–108.

Time. "Down Silicon Valley," February 20, 1978, 51.

Time. "The Tight U.S. Apartment Squeeze: Rents Soar as Construction Cannot Meet Demand," May 1, 1978, 43.

Time. "Mobile Society Puts Down Roots: Young Executives—and Their Families—Resist the Nomadic Life," June 12, 1978, 73–74.

Time. "Bedroom to Board Room: Headquarters—and Headaches—in Suburbia," August 28, 1978, 54–55.

TOBIN, GARY A. "Suburbanization and the Development of Motor Transportation: Transportation Technology and the Suburbanization Process," in Barry Schwartz, ed., *The Changing Face of the Suburbs* (Chicago: University of Chicago Press, 1976), pp. 95–111.

TOMASSON, ROBERT E. "Colleges Take Aim on Fairfield Market," *The New York Times*, September 11, 1977, Sec. 12, 17.

TOMASSON, ROBERT E. "Fairfield Finding Jobs in Factories Becoming Scarce: Corporation Headquarters Replacing Old Plants," *The New York Times*, December 28, 1978, B1, B6.

TRILLIN, CALVIN. "U.S. Journal: Mount Laurel, N.J.—Some Thoughts on Where Lines Are Drawn," *The New Yorker*, February 2, 1976, 69–74.

TUAN, YI-FU. *Topophilia: A Study of Environmental Perception, Attitudes, and Values* (Englewood Cliffs, NJ: Prentice-Hall, Inc., 1974).

ULLMANN, JOHN E., ED. *The Suburban Economic Network: Economic Activity, Resource Use, and the Great Sprawl* (New York: Praeger Publishers, 1977).

U.S. BUREAU OF THE CENSUS. "Social and Economic Characteristics of the Metropolitan and Nonmetropolitan Population: 1974 and 1970," *Current Population Reports*, Series P-23, No. 55, September, 1975.

U.S. BUREAU OF THE CENSUS. "Social and Economic Characteristics of the Metropolitan and Nonmetropolitan Population: 1977 and 1970," *Current Population Reports*, Series P-23, No. 75, November, 1978.

U.S. BUREAU OF THE CENSUS. "The Journey to Work in the United States: 1975," *Current Population Reports*, Series P-23, No. 99, July, 1979.

U.S. News and World Report. "Are Big Cities Worth Saving?—Interview With George S. Sternlieb," July 26, 1971, 42–46, 49.

U.S. News and World Report. "New Role of the Suburbs," August 7, 1972, 52–56.

U.S. News and World Report. "How Shopping Malls Are Changing Life in U.S.," June 18, 1973, 43–46.

U.S. News and World Report. "Shopping Centers of the Future: Smaller, More Fun," September 30, 1974, 67–68.

U.S. News and World Report. "'We're on Our Way to a Racial Showdown'—Interview With Roy Wilkins, Executive Director, NAACP," February 2, 1976, 74–75.

VANCE, JAMES E., JR. "Emerging Patterns of Commercial Structure in American Cities," in Knut Norborg, ed., *Proceedings of the I.G.U. Symposium in Urban Geography, Lund 1960* (Lund, Sweden: Royal University of Lund, Studies in Geography, Series B, No. 24, 1962), pp. 485–518.

VANCE, JAMES E., JR. *Geography and Urban Evolution in the San Francisco Bay Area* (Berkeley: University of California, Berkeley, Institute of Governmental Studies. 1964).

VANCE, JAMES E., JR. "California and the Search for the Ideal," *Annals of the Association of American Geographers*, 62 (1972), 185–210.

VANCE, JAMES E., JR. "The American City: Workshop for a National Culture," in John S. Adams, ed., *Contemporary Metropolitan America*, Vol. 1: *Cities of the Nation's Historic Metropolitan Core* (Cambridge, MA: Ballinger Publishing Company, 1976), pp. 1–49.

VANCE, JAMES E., JR. *This Scene of Man: The Role and Structure of the City in the Geography of Western Civilization* (New York: Harper's College Press, 1977).

VASILIADIS, C. G. "The Arts and the Suburbs," in Philip C. Dolce, ed., *Suburbia: The American Dream and Dilemma* (Garden City, NY: Anchor Press/Doubleday, 1976), pp. 111–134.

WALKER, RICHARD A. "The Transformation of Urban Structure in the Nineteenth Century and the Beginnings of Suburbanization," in Kevin R. Cox, ed., *Urbanization and Conflict in Market Societies* (Chicago: Maaroufa Press, 1978), pp. 165–212.

WALLACE, WILLIAM N. "The Suburbanization of Professional Sports," in Louis H. Masotti and Jeffrey K. Hadden, eds., *Suburbia in Transition* (New York: New Viewpoints, for *The New York Times*, 1974), pp. 109–110.

WALTER, BENJAMIN, AND FREDERICK M. WIRT. "Social and Political Dimensions of American Suburbs," in Brian J. L. Berry and Katherine B. Smith, eds., *City Classification Handbook: Methods and Applications* (New York: John Wiley & Sons, Inc., 1972), pp. 97–123.

WARD, DAVID. "A Comparative Historical Geography of Streetcar Suburbs in Boston, Massachusetts and Leeds, England: 1850–1920," *Annals of the Association of American Geographers*, 54 (1964), 477–489.

WARD, DAVID. *Cities and Immigrants: A Geography of Change in Nineteenth Century America* (New York: Oxford University Press, 1971).

WARD, JERRY D., AND NORMAN G. PAULHUS, JR. *Suburbanization and Its Implications for Urban Transportation Systems* (Washington, DC: U.S. Department of Transportation, Office of R.&D. Policy, 1974).

WARNER, EDWIN. "Suburbia's Gift to the Cities," *Horizon Magazine*, September, 1977, 14–25.

WARNER, SAM BASS, JR. *Streetcar Suburbs: The Process of Growth in Boston, 1870–1900* (Cambridge, MA: Harvard University and The MIT Press, 1962; paperback edition published by Atheneum Publishers, 1974).

WARNER, SAM BASS, JR. *The Urban Wilderness: A History of the American City* (New York: Harper & Row, Publishers, 1972).

WEBBER, MELVIN M. "Order in Diversity: Community without Propinquity," in Lowdon Wingo, ed., *Cities and Space* (Baltimore: Johns Hopkins University Press, 1963), pp. 23–54.

WEBBER, MELVIN M. "The Post-city Age," *Daedalus*, 97 (1968), 1091–1110.

WEBBER, MELVIN M. "The BART Experience—What Have We Learned?" *Public Interest*, Fall, 1976, 79–108.

WEBER, ADNA F. *The Growth of Cities in the Nineteenth Century: A Study in Statistics* (Ithaca, NY: Cornell University Press reprint of the original 1899 work, 1963).

WESTCOTT, RICHARD N. "Jobs Make the Neighborhood," *Temple University Alumni Review*, Fall, 1977, 10–14; see also Eugene P. Ericksen and William L. Yancey, "Work and Residence in Industrial Philadelphia," *Journal of Urban History*, 5 (1979), 147–182.

WHITE, MORTON, AND LUCIA WHITE. *The Intellectual versus the City: From Thomas Jefferson to Frank Lloyd Wright* (Cambridge, MA: Harvard University and The MIT Press, 1962; paperback edition with new Foreword published by Oxford University Press, 1977).

WICKER, TOM. "A Prophecy Fulfilled," *The New York Times*, July 17, 1977, Sec. 4, 21.

WILLIAMS, LENA. "Helena Rubenstein Moves; The Beauty Part Is That It's Back to City," *The New York Times*, February 25, 1978, 25.

WILLIAMS, ROGER M. "The Assault on Fortress Suburbia: How Long Can the Poor Be Kept Out?" *Saturday Review*, February 18, 1978, 17–24.

WILLIE, CHARLES V. "Life Styles of Black Families: Variations by Social Class," in Saul D. Feldman and Gerald W. Thielbar, eds., *Life Styles: Diversity in American Society* (Boston: Little, Brown and Company, 2nd rev. ed., 1975), pp. 406–417.

WILSON, WILLIAM H. *Coming of Age: Urban America, 1915–1945* (New York: John Wiley & Sons, Inc., 1974).

WINDSOR, DUANE. *Fiscal Zoning in Suburban Communities* (Lexington, MA: Lexington Books, 1979).

WIRT, FREDERICK M., BENJAMIN WALTER, FRANCINE F. RABINOVITZ, AND DEBORAH R. HENSLER. *On the City's Rim: Politics and Policy in Suburbia* (Lexington, MA: D. C. Heath and Company, 1972).

WOOD, PETER A. "Urban Manufacturing: A View from the Fringe," in James H. Johnson, ed., *Suburban Growth: Geographical Processes at the Edge of the Western City* (London: John Wiley & Sons Ltd., 1974), pp. 129–154.

WRIGHT, ALEXANDER S., III. "The Office Market: Central Atlanta vs. Suburbs," *Atlanta Economic Review*, 28 (January–February, 1978), 34–36.

YEATES, MAURICE H., AND BARRY J. GARNER. *The North American City* (New York: Harper & Row, Publishers, 3rd rev. ed., 1980).

ZELINSKY, WILBUR. *The Cultural Geography of the United States* (Englewood Cliffs, NJ: Prentice-Hall, Inc., 1973).

ZELINSKY, WILBUR. "Personality and Self-discovery: The Future Social Geography of the United States," in Ronald Abler, Donald G. Janelle, Allen K. Philbrick, and John W. Sommer, eds., *Human Geography in a Shrinking World* (North Scituate, MA: Duxbury Press, 1975), pp. 108–121.

ZIKMUND, JOSEPH, II. "Do Suburbanites Use the Central City?" *Journal of the American Institute of Planners*, 37 (1971), 192–195.

ZIKMUND, JOSEPH, II. "Sources of the Suburban Population: 1955–1960 and 1965–1970," *Publius*, 5 (Winter, 1975), 27–44.

ZIKMUND, JOSEPH, II, AND DEBORAH ELLIS DENNIS, EDS. *Suburbia: A Guide to Information Sources* (Detroit: Gale Research Company, 1979).

ZIMMER, BASIL G. "The Urban Centrifugal Drift," in Amos H. Hawley and Vincent P. Rock, eds., *Metropolitan America in Contemporary Perspective* (New York: Halsted Press, 1975), pp. 23–91.

ZSCHOCK, DIETER K., ED. *Economic Aspects of Suburban Growth: Studies of the Nassau-Suffolk Planning Region* (Stony Brook, NY: Economic Research Bureau, SUNY at Stony Brook, 1969).

Geographical Index

Subject Index